HARVEST OF
MESSERSCHMITTS

HARVEST OF MESSERSCHMITTS

The Chronicle of a Village at War ~ 1940

DENNIS KNIGHT

Based on the diary of
Mary Smith of Elham

FREDERICK WARNE

Published by Frederick Warne (Publishers) Ltd 1981
© Text and artwork Dennis Knight 1981
© Diary entries Mary Smith 1981

Front endpaper : A Messerschmitt Bf 109E (Robert Hunt Library)
Back endpaper : Supermarine Spitfires of 610 Sqdn. on patrol duty (Imperial War Museum)

ISBN 0 7232 2772 1

Filmset and printed in Great Britain by BAS Printers Limited, Over Wallop, Hampshire

Contents

Acknowledgements

To Mary Smith I shall for ever be grateful because through her little diary the pulse of life started beating again when trying to relive the story of 1940, via rather bland historical records.

The preparation of this book started several years ago and its accuracy would never have been possible if it had not been for the enthusiasm and co-operation of so many people, too numerous to list. Many flit in and out of the narrative and range from domestic servants to Air Chief Marshals. I can only hope I have done justice to them and the year. The story is theirs, they made it and Churchill gave it a name—'Their Finest Hour'.

To pinpoint the locations of many incidents that were not properly recorded in contemporary documents, I must mention the unstinting help of aviation historians and enthusiasts with whom I have enjoyed some stimulating detective work, trying to separate truth from folk-lore and conjecture. I list them in alphabetical order: Alan Brown, David Buchanan, Peter Cornwell, Peter Foote, James Howard, Roy Humphreys, Simon Parry and Jerry Williams.

The railway buffs also rallied to my aid and, without Michael Forwood's permission to quote from his book *The Elham Valley Railway* and detailed information from Leslie Seppings, I would not have been able to narrate some fascinating anecdotes about this extinct railway line.

Lastly, and certainly not least, I am indebted to Lewis Angel, who generously allowed me to draw on material contained in his unpublished manuscript, which describes so vividly his experiences as Quartermaster of a regiment in Elham valley.

Glossary and Abbreviations

In the interests of brevity, simple abbreviations have been used for some ranks, units and weapons, and the list below will explain most of those that appear in the chronicle, together with some service nomenclature.

AA	Anti-aircraft	Lt.	Lieutenant; Leutnant
AC2	Aircraftsman class 2	Lt. Comdr.	Lieutenant Commander
Angels	Unit of height (1,000 ft)	Me 109	Messerschmitt Bf 109
ARP	Air Raid Precautions (Civil Defence)	Me 110	Messerschmitt Bf 110
		MO	Medical Officer
Bandits	German raiders	Obfw.	Oberfeldwebel
Bofors	40 mm light AA gun	Oberst	German Colonel
Bty.	Battery	Oblt.	Oberleutnant
C-in-C	Commander-in-Chief	P/O	Pilot Officer
CO	Commanding Officer	QM	Quartermaster
Erks	Aircraftsmen	RA	Royal Artillery
F/Lt.	Flight Lieutenant	2 i/c	Second in Command
F/O	Flying Officer	Sgt.	Sergeant
F/Sgt.	Flight Sergeant	S/Ldr.	Squadron Leader
Fw.	Feldwebel	Snappers	High-flying German fighters
Gefr.	Gefreiter		
Hptm.	Hauptmann	Sqdn.	Squadron
JG	Jagdgeschwader (Luftwaffe fighter wing of 9 Staffeln)	Staffel	Squadron
		Sub. Lt.	Sub-Lieutenant
		Uffz.	Unteroffizier
LAC	Leading Aircraftsman	Wg. Cdr.	Wing Commander

Introduction

In this chronicle of the year 1940, the strands of history have been woven together to present a detailed account of the events that occurred—on the ground and in the air—over a very beautiful part of England, and in particular over and around the Kent village of Elham.

During this year, Mary Smith, the school teacher daughter of the village postmaster, kept a small diary. In it she recorded both the major news headlines and the simple domestic occurrences that affected her and her family in Elham. It is these short notes (printed in heavy type) that form the framework on which this book is based. Using Mary's diary—plus contemporary newspaper accounts and the combat reports of both British and German pilots—it has been possible to give a blow-by-blow record of the epic air battle and at the same time place it in the wider context of the theatre of war in Europe.

The village of Elham lies in the Nailbourne valley, near where the eastern end of the North Downs reaches the sea. The pleasant High Street opens out to set off the beauty of a row of houses with overhanging half-timbered upper storeys supporting heavy eaves. Just off the High Street to the east is a quiet little Market Square, which with its red brick and white-windowed houses and the stout grey tower of the church rising over the roofs, has all the dignity of a cathedral close in miniature. At that time the village boasted a population of 1,200.

1940 was an extraordinary year for the British because it started in the period of the so-called 'Phoney War' when Britain and France were facing Germany across clearly-defined borders, having hardly fired a shot during the four months they had been at war. During that period, Mary Smith made only sparse notes in her diary. The year also started with some of the coldest weather ever recorded in Britain and at times Elham valley was cut off by deep snow drifts and the nearby military aerodrome of Hawkinge lay under a thick carpet of snow. With the spring came the shattering German 'Blitzkrieg' attacks against France, Holland and Belgium and Mary started recording the day-by-day events soon after the BEF (British Expeditionary Force) were rescued from the beaches of Dunkirk. Without allies, and singularly little in the way of weapons, the British withdrew into their island and the pastoral valley of Elham was suddenly in the front line.

Nothing can offer a better example of both the reality and unreality of war quite so clearly as the juxtaposition of Mary's terse entries with the intense drama that was being acted out that year in the skies over the peaceful fields and villages of southern England.

Those on the ground were totally unaware that the noise and furious action going on all round them would later become famous as the Battle of Britain, and indeed would be considered in the future to have constituted one of the most decisive events in world history. Equally, those thrown so desperately into combat, so bravely facing almost insuperable odds, could be forgiven for being unaware that beneath them as they roared through the skies, the ordinary people were quietly going on with their daily lives almost as if nothing was happening.

Elham's 'Harvest of Messerschmitts' was indeed prodigious: there was a compound in the village where crashed Messerschmitts were dumped after they had been gleaned from fields around south-eastern England. However, from a glance at the map on page 156 showing the places where aircraft crashed, there appears to be a disproportionate number of RAF planes which came down compared to German aircraft. There are two reasons for this. Firstly, crippled British planes often crashed when attempting to reach Hawkinge to make an emergency landing. Secondly, the pilots of the crack Jagdgeschwader 51 were based just across the Channel and, as a recreational sport, their aces frequently came over to make lightning hit-and-run attacks on patrolling British fighters.

It is hoped that this book has succeeded in conveying the atmosphere of those memorable times and that it will be regarded as a memorial to all those on both sides who took part in the battle, whether tacitly, unwittingly, or in combat.

Harvest of Messerschmitts

1st January

The beauty of Elham valley was hard to discern on that New Year's Day, especially when the weather deteriorated and a blanket of freezing fog formed over the hills. Hawkinge Aerodrome Operational Record Book reported: *After a covering of snow the previous day, it dawned fine but turned to fog later. The Commanding Officer, S/Ldr. A. Ferris visited (inspected) the AMES [secret radar station] at Rye.*

Hawkinge at that time was the base of No 3 Recruit Training Pool, where raw conscripted airmen were given six weeks' basic training. It was also the home of No 3 Fighter Sqdn., which had arrived there just before Christmas. To the north-east was Manston, another important airfield, and at 8.15 a.m. they sent up a section of three Hawker Hurricanes to intercept an unidentified aircraft, which proved to be a French plane escorting ships in the Channel. A similar incident took place in the afternoon.

The village of Elham nestles comfortably in the chalk Downs behind Folkestone, its name being an Anglo-Saxon word meaning 'a place with a heathen temple'. As the crow flies, it is about five miles from the seaport, but the road journey is considerably longer. There are two routes. One is the tortuous climb up the winding lane over Standard Hill to Acrise and then onto the high road to Hawkinge village. Hawkinge, with its aerodrome, is perched on the hilltops with a view out across the Channel, where on a clear day the coast of France is plainly visible. From Hawkinge the road winds down past the hump of Sugar Loaf Hill and drops away to the seafront of Folkestone. The alternative route is to travel south on the road that runs through Elham valley and proceed slightly uphill to Lyminge, a pleasant but not altogether pretty village, and then to Etchinghill to pass through the natural gap in the rolling Downs. On the right is Tolsford Hill, from where there is a breathtaking view of the weird flat landscape of Romney Marsh, stretching out to Dungeness and away to Rye and Fairlight to the west. Just below the Downs the London–Dover road is joined.

In 1940, Elham boasted a railway station and a little single-track line that threaded its way up the valley, crossing and recrossing the Nailbourne stream, which runs north to join the River Stour. At Barham, situated at the north end of the valley, the railway parted company with the stream and ran ahead through an orchard-studded landscape to the city of Canterbury. But the delightfully eccentric railway had been on the decline since the First World War; in fact, since the introduction of a regular motor-bus service running through the valley.

That evening the Elham Parish Council met in the ex-Services hall with Edward Smith, the Postmaster, as Chairman. It was desperately cold and after reading the minutes of the previous meeting, they went through matters swiftly, only lingering when they came to their pride and joy—the new King George playing field, which had been created as a patriotic gesture to commemorate the recent coronation.

2nd January

It was a cold cloudless day. Hurricane fighters flew Channel patrols from Hawkinge and an air raid practice was arranged for the following day, in co-operation with the local authorities. Fortunately, the visit of an Air Vice Marshal was postponed and there was a little light relief when Dr Tinsey (an autogyro expert) visited the station with a wingless flying machine. At Manston there was an unfortunate tragedy at 3.20 p.m. when P/O T. S. Lewis, a fighter pilot with 79 Sqdn., took AC2 S. H. Smith up for air experience in a two-seater Magister. Whilst attempting a roll, the plane stayed upside down and flew into the ground.

3rd January

Hawkinge aerodrome reported: *Full air raid defence practice at 11.00 hours, including the use of siren.*

On the north side of Church Square, opposite the church with its silver-grey spire, is 'King-post', a house then being used as the village post office. The brick-built Georgian façade concealed a much older, timber-framed building with some massive joists and a crown-post. Every morning, except for Sundays, Edward Smith the Postmaster rose at 5 a.m. to receive the letters and parcels when they arrived from Canterbury in the red Royal Mail van. He always shaved—except for his full moustache—carefully brushed his hair, and was always properly dressed, wearing a starched white collar attached to his striped viyella shirt with studs and a neat tie.

The fire was lit and he had made a pot of tea. Upstairs there were his wife Mary Ellen ('Nellie') and his two unmarried daughters, both in their thirties. His wife had come down from Nottingham over 40 years ago and had taught at the village infant school before Edward married her in 1901. As Chairman of Elham Parish Council he took a consumate interest in all his responsibilities.

4th January

In the still pre-dawn dew, coal fire smoke started rising from chimneys along Elham valley. Those working on the land had animals to look after and most folk started their work at 8 a.m., many having to walk or bicycle for many miles.

Two men were up even before Edward Smith. They were Horace Cook and his son Horace Henry, who had the baker's shop in Church Square. They had been working since about 3.30 a.m. The ovens were all going, the dough had been mixed and, after a lull, waiting for it to rise, there had been the knocking-back and filling of baking tins. Crusty loaves, cottage loaves, some whirls, a few rolls; the process went on into the morning as they varied the mixes to make light buns called 'huffkins' and cakes. It was hard physical work; not so much a living, more a way of life.

Horace junior was a skilled woodcraftsman and would have preferred to be working in the furniture business, but with the recession he had been obliged to join his father in the bakery. From mid-morning he got out the heavy tradesman's bicycle and pedalled off on his delivery rounds with the big basket full of warm bread. A previous owner of the bakery business was Walter 'Justice' Hawkins, who lived at 'Old Mill' and now had time for his work with the Parish Council. Or at least that had been the case until he became Elham's Head ARP Warden.

Just before Christmas the parish magazine had contained the following hints about ARP:

1 Mr Hawkins is chief Air Raid Warden for this district, and the headquarters are the Fellowship Hall.
2 Be polite to your Air Raid Warden and make a friend of him. His is a trying job, and he is anxious to help you. He has no doubt called at your house to see about your gas mask. Remember that he has voluntarily given up a great deal of his spare time to make things safer for you.
3 Very carefully screen all your lights after sunset.
4 Make sure that your gas mask is in good condition, fits you, and is always handy.
5 The sign that a hostile air raid is approaching is a siren sounded in short blasts or rising and falling in tone. The 'raiders passed' signal is a long steady note on the siren.
6 DON'T throw water on an incendiary bomb. Smother it in sand or earth and convey it out of danger.
7 Make up your mind beforehand what is the best thing to do in the case of an air raid. If you are out of doors, you are safer lying down than standing up.

Although winter had set in, this last hint caused ribald comments from some of the young men of the village.

5th January

At about 7.30 a.m., when the postmen were all making their deliveries, the Postmaster would go into his spacious living-room at King-post where there was the sound of sizzling bacon from the stove. The *Daily Telegraph* would arrive and Edward Smith would sit down to a good breakfast with Nellie and his two daughters.

Mary was the elder, having been born on 3rd October 1904 in No 2 Southdown Cottage in the Row, whereas Margaret was born five years later when the family had moved into King-post. Both girls were nurtured carefully by Mr and Mrs Smith, who insisted that they applied themselves assiduously to their school work, that being their only path to advancement and independence in life. Mary's basic education came from her parents and the village school, but she also attended a quaint private school in Church Square owned and staffed by the six maiden daughters of Henry Rigden. The climax of this primary education, grooming and encouragement was the supreme test of Mary's childhood: the Grammar School entrance exam. When the all important day arrived, she was taken into Canterbury to sit the written exam for entrance into the Simon Langton Girls' School. But she failed.

Fortunately the adjudicators recognized a bright child with an obvious flair for prose, but little or no aptitude for mathematics. They wanted to know more about Mary Smith and, after an anxious delay, the school agreed to accept her. Her parents would have to

(Above) Mary Smith; (right) Margaret Smith; (far right) Edward Smith, Elham's Postmaster and Chairman of the Parish Council

pay travelling expenses—something they were only too willing to do. Sister Margaret followed her into the same school but, unlike Mary, she had no problems in coping with the concept of abstract mathematics and, as a result, was destined to help in the post office.

It was the dawning of the age of freethinking women and Mary proved a competent scholar and an enlightened young woman. She charted her own course by going to University College and Goldsmiths' College, London, where she lived away from the sheltered life in Elham. She read English and Latin, emerging with an honours degree and the University Diploma in Education. At the outbreak of the war, Mary was teaching at a private school in Folkestone, but this closed down.

6th January

Archibald MacGregor and Kathleen Noel Patterson were married at Elham by the Reverend R. H. Isaac Williams. The bride was the Vicar's sister-in-law and the four Williams' daughters acted as bridesmaids, each wearing a long crimson velvet dress and holding a posy of cream roses with tartan streamers. It was bitterly cold and when the children posed for photographs outside the church, they clamped their jaws to stop their teeth chattering and their bare arms were covered in goose-pimples. Afterwards the reception was held at the vicarage, where champagne corks popped with great gusto.

7–8th January

The severe frost continued. Elham is an immensely ancient settlement and Roman coins are still found in the cottage gardens. It is not known when the pagan temple was replaced by a Christian shrine, but a legend tells of St Augustine and his retinue of monks coming into the valley in AD 597, during a dreadful drought that destroyed the crops and killed the livestock. The worshippers of the heathen gods Odin and Thor, accused the Christians of causing the famine by displeasing the rulers in Valhalla and this prompted a contest. St Augustine prayed for rain, but instead the Nailbourne stream sprang out of the ground and sent its clear waters trickling down the valley, whilst the pagan gods darkened the sky, shook the heavens and cracked the land open to swallow up the waters. Thereafter the Nailbourne has been a mysterious, shy and fickle stream, only rising every few years and associated with supernatural happenings.

The autumn of 1939 had been the wettest on record and the Nailbourne in full spate had transformed the whole valley into a chain of shallow lakes from Lyminge to Barham. Some folk in the valley were very superstitious about the Nailbourne and they reasoned amongst themselves that this flooding must be an omen.

9th January. Another Finnish victory acclaimed.

This was the first entry in Mary Smith's diary.

10th January

The Anglican vicar, Reverend Isaac Williams, expressed his views about the war in a letter appearing in the parish magazine.

> We have now been at war for two months, and perhaps we have wondered at times why the RAF has not dropped bombs upon military objectives in Germany, instead of showering propaganda leaflets far and wide throughout the country. Perhaps the fear of reprisals may have had something to do with it, but I do not think that this is the real reason, for it would not have been impossible to have come to terms with Russia and utterly to have strangled and over-run Germany, as Poland was subdued. . . . No doubt all nations have been partly responsible for this state of things, but the result is that no nation in Europe, whether great or small, is safe from aggression. Germany has revolted against all accepted decencies of international conduct and defied all the other members of the European family. She must at all cost then—for her own sake, no less than for others—be brought to a better frame of mind. She must be forced, even by war if need be, to respect good faith, the liberties of others and the decencies of national and international life. Then, without bitterness, she must be readmitted into the family circle. Hence all this pathetic appeal to the German people by aeroplane propaganda. It is as though we were saying: 'Put your house in order, and come back within the family circle of European nations and live peaceably with us all as good neighbours.'

Reverend Williams was still considered new to the village, having arrived with his large family in 1935, following the death of his predecessor—who had reigned there for 35 years. It had been, and still was, very High Church and the pomp and protocol were strictly observed. In fact, when the Vicar first came to the village, he wore full-length robes and a bereta, and there were some in the village, especially the Methodists, who thought he conducted Roman Catholic liturgies. But with the war things became more relaxed and there was some breaking down of sacred, secular and social barriers.

The Church of St Mary's the Virgin in Elham is a typical architectural progression, being a Norman structure that had been expanded in later years by the addition of aisles and then the piercing of the walls to make graceful arches. The original thirteenth-century tower was virtually rebuilt in Tudor times and the broad buttressed structure is surmounted with a slender lead-covered spire. It is a fine, well-kept church that through the years has been beautified with the blandishments of well-meaning patrons.

11th January. Attempted raids.

Hawkinge reported: *Weather—cold and fine—patrols carried out over Channel No. 3 Sqdn. Practice General Alarm carried out on the Station—considered satisfactory.*

The beautification of Elham Church had progressed considerably during the incumbency of the previous vicar, paralleled by some astonishing improvements and additions to the vicarage. Many were the architectural whims which obviously gave enjoyment to the architect, the Vicar and the craftsmen who lingered in the village to complete these delightful tasks. The whole edifice was reminiscent of a Mediterranean villa, and the arched gateway with gabled dovecot was a work of sheer inspiration.

12th January

Thirty-six degrees of frost had been recorded. Robert Kennelly, a strange hatchet-faced bachelor and keen naturalist who had come to lodge in the village, noted in his journal of the Elham countryside: *During the great black frost the moon was copper coloured, like a dirty orange, and gave a dim and weird light. The contours of the hills and woods were clearly defined, but one appeared to be looking at them through sunglasses. Everything was in perfect focus, but the negative appeared terribly under-exposed. Sound appeared to be smothered and the Angelus was barely perceptible, neither the striking of the hours throughout the night. The strokes could just be heard and that's all. . . .*

13th January

At 2.50 p.m. Manston sent 6 Hurricanes of 79 Sqdn. to patrol Hawkinge. The pilots were F/O Mitchell, P/Os Morris (South African), Parker, Hulse and Clift, and Sgt. Spencer. Looking down over the valley and coastline from 8,000 ft, nothing could be seen because of the carpet of freezing fog. Before landing, they flew over to France and observed a leave-boat and a low-flying RAF Anson.

14th January. Week-end threat to Holland and Belgium.

Local people said 'It were too cold to snow.'

15th January

Hawkinge reported: *Weather fine—turning to snow late in the day. Air Ministry Auditors reported to carry out half-year Audit of Station. Air Raid yellow warning soon after breakfast for four minutes.* A blizzard raged over eastern Kent that night.

Spitfires of 609 Sqdn. at 'readiness' in the snow

16th January. Three British submarines lost.

Hawkinge reported: *Snow—61 recruits posted to Station for disciplinary training. Lt. Comdr. R. T. H. Coach, H. M. S. Esk visited Station. Lt. E. Esmond Jones of 1st Queen's Westminsters KRRC of Reinden House visited Station concerning arrangements for assistance to be rendered in the event of a ground attack on the Aerodrome. 3 Blenheims of 500 Sqdn. forced landed in snow storm. Two landed on the airfield and one ended up in a field undamaged at Swingfield, about 5 miles away.*

At Manston snow was falling heavily and 79 Fighter Sqdn. was crippled by sickness amongst the pilots. F/Lt. C. L. C. Roberts and F/Lt. R. S. J. Edwards had influenza, P/Os E. J. Morris,* D. G. Clift and R. Herrick had German measles, and F/Sgt. F. S. Brown was down with tonsilitis.

17th January. Deep snow.

The snow was about eighteen inches deep on level ground, but when driven by the wind, the drifts were ten feet or more. Manston aerodrome was unusable.

Arthur Wootten, the Elham garage proprietor, was finding things very trying. Petrol was rationed and cars were not being manufactured. Even the few people who had cars were unable to use them because of the snow. He'd never known it so bad. The buses had stopped running and the tradesmen were not delivering. He lived in Hythe with his wife and twin daughters and drove to his business every day in his Morris Oxford. He had purchased the blacksmith's forge in the High Street and in 1936 had built a proper showroom and workshop to the designs made by John Conrad, the architect son of

---

*'Teddy' Morris, one of two South African brothers flying with the RAF, was *hors de combat* with meningitis following this illness and was not to rejoin his squadron until the summer. He is celebrated for his first combat report which stated: 'One Heinkel bomber destroyed by collision.'

17

Dump of wrecked Messerschmitts

Kennels
E.K.H

Old Manor House

Abbots' Fireside

New Inn

Rose & Crown

To Lyminge

School

Bakery

Yard

Cricket Field

To Canterbury

Wesleyan Church

Office (King-post)

King's Arms

The village of Elham in 1940

To Railway Station

Joseph Conrad. There was a mock-Tudor gable with a few heraldic roses embedded in the cementwork, and the brick arch to the workshop had a Gothic flavour. The building had domestic accommodation above and this was to prove a shrewd step in view of what lay ahead.

18th January

The three forced-landed Blenheims managed to get off the ground from Hawkinge to return to their parent station.

For Lieutenant R. L. Angel, MM,† Quartermaster of the London Rifle Brigade, it was the most hectic period of his life. He was a Lloyd's claims settler who had been a Territorial Army enthusiast since the early twenties. His regiment, like many others in the 1st London Division, comprised of TA volunteers, mostly drawn from particular City institutions and largely made up of Lloyd's professional men and clerks who knew, liked and trusted each other. However, the situation was a QM's nightmare, because there were various companies and platoons scattered all the way up Elham valley with troops quartered for the most part in large requisitioned houses with plumbing and cesspits quite unequal to the logistics involved. The QM's days were spent visiting billets, making lists of requirements and jobs to be done, whilst paperwork went on until late every night.

HQ was in Beachborough Park in the foothills of the Downs and Lewis Angel with the Padre, Hugh Gough,* and the Adjutant, Edwin Hedley, were billeted in a delightful little house called Temple Cottage, which had Gothic windows and an extraordinary white belfry that looked like something from a chess-board. The officers were well off for fuel, but there were nights when they thought they were going to perish. The extremely cold weather caused an acute shortage of fuel in the men's billets and stern measures had to be taken, such as only allowing them to burn fallen wood. If the officers hadn't kept a firm grip on the situation, the soldiers would have felled the magnificent parkland trees around the houses. Doors, chairs, even wooden scrubbing brushes were inclined to disappear and they all had to be accounted for. Several billets were cut off by snowdrifts and the men collected rations on home-made sledges.

19th January

The Reverend Williams got around his parish riding one of his children's ponies. He was a beaming man in full flower, and all was perfect in his life except for one great unhappiness. His only son, then two years old, had been born with an incurable spinal defect and was to die before the war was over. He believed his pastoral responsibilities extended to setting an example in ARP matters and Elham's new doctor, Conrad Hunter-Smith, was amazed to see the Vicar going about on horseback or in a huge Austin saloon, with a red gas-mask case strapped to him at all times.

†Lewis Angel served with the Civil Service Rifles in 1918 and was awarded the Military Medal for bravery at the age of 18.

*Subsequently became Primate of all Australia.

Herbert Wilcox, Headmaster of Elham village school, looked around at the handful of red-cheeked children who had managed to get there. He couldn't see out of the windows for ice, the pipes were frozen, the lavatories wouldn't work and there wasn't any water. He decided to close the school.

20–24th January

The snow and freezing conditions continued. At Hawkinge aerodrome the station was brought to a standstill. The 121 luckless recruits, who had arrived on the 19th, were herded about over the crunching snow by crisp NCOs. When they were released from seemingly endless drill and physical training exercises, they clustered around their cast-iron barrack hut stoves, shovelling in the small ration of spitting coke.

'King-post' in use as Elham post office

Because of the weather, the mail at Elham was very late some mornings—but it always got through from Canterbury.

25–26th January
After a thaw, driving sleet turned to snow and Hawkinge village and the aerodrome were snowbound and cut off. Buses stopped running and the road to Folkestone was impassable.

27–29th January
Dr Conrad Hunter-Smith, a dapper full-faced man with his hair parted in the middle, had recently taken over a practice that covered a wide rural district. He was having a frightful time in the bad weather and couldn't reach some of his patients. After taking morning surgery in his house in the southern outskirts of Elham, the young doctor, accoutred with long scarf and wellingtons, would trudge off with his bag on his rounds. His visiting lists were made out the previous night, but his plans kept going awry. In fact, to get to Acrise and his out-station surgery in Hawkinge, he had to drive over via Folkestone. To make matters worse, he couldn't get anti-freeze for his car and he had to drain the cooling system every night and refill it in the morning.

30th January
Another 70 shivering, stamping recruits arrived at Hawkinge for disciplinary training. Quartermaster Lt. Angel travelled as best he could between the scattered units of the London Rifle Brigade, which had two companies at Horton Park, near Lympne aerodrome, which was also snowbound. Another company was at Lyminge and a training company of conscripts was in the requisitioned Wampach Hotel at Folkestone. The cold weather was causing havoc amongst the animal population and QM Angel saw starving sheep and dead rabbits all over the place. In their frantic efforts to keep alive, animals had gnawed the bark from trees and stripped the hedges of twigs.

31st January
An order was sent to Hawkinge from Group HQ: *Station ordered to clear landing lanes through the snow on the airfield—the clearance work to start immediately.*

1–2nd February
A dense fog covered the Downs, but the thaw had started. A snow plough arrived at Hawkinge aerodrome to augment the pathetic achievements of relays of airmen with shovels. A landing lane was just about clear late on the 2nd.

3–5th February
This was a period of coping and clearing up for both civilians and servicemen. QM Angel noted that the Engineer Platoon couldn't cope with the burst water pipes that sent water cascading through the troops' billets.

22

6th February

Mr J. D. Busteed of the Aeronautical Inspection Department reported from HQ Fighter Command for inspection of explosives at Hawkinge.

In freezing fog, the funeral of F/Lt. C. H. Leggott, of RAF Church Fenton, took place at Hawkinge, the pilot being buried with a regulation service in the local cemetery. This was to become a very familiar routine in the months ahead.

7th February

Hawkinge reported: *Information received. The posting of Training Command recruits to Hawkinge for disciplinary training is to stop. From this day the Station is transferred to FIGHTER COMMAND. S/Ldr. Skelton visited the Station to make arrangements for bringing No 16 Sqdn., with Lysanders, to Hawkinge.*

The fog lifted and the frost returned.

8–11th February

The shouting, posturing drill instructors were sent to Morecambe to torment the recruits there. Although Hawkinge was now a fighter station, No 3 Sqdn., which was based there with Hurricanes, left on the 10th for Kenley.

Dr Conrad Hunter-Smith at Elham in 1940

12th February

Snow began to fall again and a road party of the Lysander Sqdn. arrived at Hawkinge from Old Sarum. Manston was closed because of snow.

13th February

Main party No 16 Sqdn. arrived by rail, having been collected from Folkestone in a snow storm. Hawkinge reported that the Pilotless Aircraft Unit at Henlow would soon be arriving with their radio-controlled Tiger Moth biplanes, known as 'Queen Bees' and used for target practice by anti-aircraft gunners.

14–15th February

It was very cold and the ground was covered with snow.

16th February

On a bright but bitterly cold afternoon the sky filled with noise as 18 Lysanders arrived, the high-winged monoplanes looking just like insects as they circled over the Downs. The news was received from Manston that one of their Hurricanes (L1699), flown by P/O Tarlington, was missing. It had been patrolling over a train ferry off Reculver, when it crashed into the sea and disappeared.

17th February. Rescue of 200 prisoners from Altmark by HMS Cossack.

In this incident, Winston Churchill, then First Lord of the Admiralty, gave orders for the Royal Navy to enter Norwegian waters to rescue some British seamen held captive on the German supply ship *Altmark*. The news of this cheered the British immensely and Mary Smith made a rare entry in her diary at this period.

18th February

Another blizzard cut Elham off from the outside world, but somehow the Royal Mail van got up Derringstone Hill and along the valley. Another onerous duty for the Elham post office was having to man the telephone switchboard for 24 hours a day to put through any trunk calls. The switchboard, in its tall wooden cabinet, stood in the front room at King-post, and all the family were trained to use it. Very few people in the district were on the telephone and not many of them made long-distance calls in the dead of night, but occasionally someone had to pull on a dressing-gown and pad downstairs to attend to an urgent call.

Today was the birthday of farmer Herbie Palmer, who lived in a bungalow overlooking the mist-covered valley. He and his brothers owned North Elham Farm, but their father, old George Palmer, although in his eighties, was still giving the orders. Old George, with his hob-nailed boots and rough tweeds, seemed as wide as he was tall and his sapphire blue eyes twinkled out of a completely circular face. He was a bit obstinate, but liked by everybody and had only just come off the Parish Council. There had been Palmers farming around Elham for generations and lots of people were distantly related to them. Old George's father had gone into the next world with some panache, when he broke his neck trying to enter the 'Black Duck' inn on horseback.

19th February

The freezing fog was accompanied by rain and snow. Thirteen RAF trailer lorries arrived at Hawkinge with the crated aircraft of the Pilotless Aircraft Unit.

20th February. Fuss over the Altmark.

This incident had caused a flurry in diplomatic circles because Britain had violated Norwegian territorial waters to rescue the seamen.

22–23rd February

There were so many sick airmen at Hawkinge that the MO had to insist on being allocated extra accommodation.

24th February

79 Sqdn. sent a lone Hurricane to climb four miles up above Canterbury to investigate an unidentified plane, which was lost to view when it flew north. Fighter pilots were always hopeful of finding a raider and it had been in the previous November that F/O Jimmy Davies, who came from New Jersey, USA, and F/Sgt. Brown, both of 79 Sqdn., had been sent to look for an unidentified plane above Hawkinge and found a Dornier 'Flying Pencil'. They attacked quickly, but the raider was lost in cloud out to sea and Davies could only claim to have damaged it. However, there was jubilation when the destroyer, HMS *Boreas*, cruising off Dover, found wreckage from a Dornier floating in the sea.

25–27th February

It continued cold, but temperatures rose above freezing during the day. The thaw sent

Steam locomotive coming out of Barham station on the Elham valley line (Michael Forwood)

torrents of icy water pouring down from the hills and, to add to the misery, low-lying roads and cottages were flooded.

The Elham valley railway line did not become single track until drastic economy cuts were introduced by Southern Railway in 1931. The little stations, which had been staffed by eight men, were from then on manned by only two porter-signalmen who ran the stations single-handed, dividing the day into an early and a late shift. Elham was an exception because they had 'Sunny' Caple, stationmaster for Elham, Lyminge, Barham and Bishopsbourne, in fact all the stations in the valley. He would come out of his cottage every day and cycle off to visit all his stations. Some said they had seen the ubiquitous stationmaster on the platform of one stop and when the little train chugged into the next, he was there also.

The most comfortable billet for troops in Elham valley was that of Lieutenant Colonel Tommy Fairfax Ross, CO of the London Rifle Brigade, who had retired from the regular Army and gone into the insurance world. He and his second-in-command, Major Kenneth Hicks, were offered quarters in Sibdon Park at Lyminge, where the owner, Mrs Leach, included full use of the reception rooms, dining room silver and her domestic staff, which they accepted with alacrity.

28th February

Cruising up and down the Channel with the Royal Navy destroyers and gun boats was the *Campeador*, an indeterminate vessel on the establishment of the Portsmouth Patrol as an armed yacht. The *Campeador* patrolled the Channel continuously like the Flying Dutchman and spent 84 days at sea in the bitter weather and only 15 in harbour. Her crew was remarkable. Her captain, called Davey, was a retired commander and ex-master of foxhounds in his sixties and his three sub-lieutenants RNVR were even more extraordinary. One was a shipowner and well-known private yachtsman aged 59; another was a 58-year-old docks manager; and the third was a retired surgeon rear-admiral called Muir, author of a celebrated book entitled *Messing About in Boats*. Muir told Admiral Sir William James, the C-in-C Portsmouth, that he had knocked a few years off his true age as he thought he might not be accepted for active service at 71!

The C-in-C was rather amused to have these colourful gentlemen in his command and when Captain Davey actually wrote to him submitting recommendations for the sub-lieutenants to be promoted, the Admiral was so astonished on reading their histories, that he sent a copy to Winston Churchill. The document was returned with a scrawled note: 'Promote them. Age will be served.'

1st March

This was the first of twelve fine days. Orders were received that No 416 (Army Co-operation) Flight was to be formed at Hawkinge.

2nd March

At 7.10 a.m. a high-flying aircraft was seen over Dover making vapour trails at 25,000 ft plus. Three Hurricanes, led by F/O Davies, took off from Manston and climbed hard, but the unidentified plane passed away out to sea too high for them to intercept.

3rd March

This Sunday the suffragan Bishop of Dover conducted a confirmation service at Elham, when nine candidates from Lyminge and six from Elham were confirmed.

On this perfect cloudless day, F/Lt. S. P. Slocum, of the Photographic Development Unit, was flying above Gravesend in one of the new Lockheed Hudsons recently obtained from America. There were four aboard, including J. A. M. 'Tony' Reid, a fair-haired, fresh-faced young man from Newcastle who, as an ex-British Airways Pilot, had more experience than most regular RAF pilots. Coupled with this, he had survived being shot down by a British eight-gun fighter. This incident had occurred just before Christmas when several Handley Page Hampdens, returning in formation, were mistaken for German bombers off the coast of Scotland and attacked by 'The City of Glasgow' Spitfire Squadron. Two Hampdens went down and Tony Reid was rescued from the freezing North Sea. Aircraft recognition standards should have been better, but the slender Hampdens with their twin-rudders did look rather like Dorniers.

On this day there should have been no such error. The Hudson, although also having twin-rudders, could easily be distinguished by a fat oval fuselage. As fate would have it, however, a section of Hurricanes was homing on the Hudson, south of Gravesend, and

A radiant Queen Elizabeth chats with P/O Tony Reid at an investiture. Bomber pilot Reid was shot down twice by over-eager British fighter pilots in the first few months of the war. The pilot in the centre is P/O Desmond Sheen from Sydney, Australia, who so nearly lost his life over Elham in September 1940. The third officer is F/Lt. Eric Le Mesurier, a very skilled Spitfire reconnaissance pilot who was killed later in the war. (Dennis Knight)

they failed to distinguish the fat oval fuselage. The riddled Hudson burst into flames and fell at Meopham. Only Tony Reid escaped, but not until he had been exposed to a blow-torch of heat as he struggled to get out of the doomed machine. After protracted surgery, he made a remarkable recovery to receive a commission and the DFM.

4th March

The demolition of some old cottages on the south side of Church Square started again with the better weather. It was a pity they had to go, but they were delapidated and restricted the road coming into the square. At the Elham Parish Council meeting that evening, a letter was read out from Mr Constant, who offered to pay for shrubs to fill in the unsightly gap that would be left when demolition was completed. Martin Constant was genial and immensely wealthy and, like the vicar and doctor, he was also fairly new to the village but, unlike them, he had no immediate role to play in its parochial establishment.

5th March

With the better weather, the village shopkeepers perked up, but old Tom Goatman, delivering morning papers on foot, looked as miserable as ever. He and his wife kept the newsagent/tobacconists and they had a workshop where Tom did bicycle repairs.

The main shop in Elham—their advert in the local press read 'the largest and most up-to-date stores in the Elham Valley'—was Hubble & Son in the High Street, which was a general grocery store and haberdashers. Ken Hubble, bespectacled, pipe-smoking and slight of build, was a respected vice-chairman of the Parish Council, but in recent months he had been seen more and more wearing the uniform of a Navy League Lieutenant, having taken on the job of running the Elham Valley Sea Cadet Corps. His cadets were to be seen up and down the valley, waving flags about as they signalled frantically to each other. In fact, Ken Hubble worked them up to such a state of proficiency that they won the two national challenge cups for signalling, Ken receiving the awards from the hands of HRH the Duke of Kent.

At the north end of the village Ted Newing ran a sweet shop which also sold vegetables. He found it awkward wrapping things up because of an arm crippled during the First World War. The butcher's and slaughterhouse were next to the imposing but sombre façade of the Methodist church, which dominates the High Street and where the elders still spoke to people using Old Testament quotations. Frederick Smith had the shoemaker's, but he had been discovered by the Army quartermasters and found himself inundated with work and a contract to 'cobble all day and cobble all night' as truckloads of heavy black boots came and went.

6th March

The radar early-warning system and fighter control was constantly being tested at this time and Hurricanes intercepted four Dutch airliners and an Anson just off the coast.

7–8th March

These were fine cloudless days.

9th March

More Lysander aircraft arrived to equip 416 Flight, which was being formed at Hawkinge. F/O Davies and F/O 'Jumbo' Gracie patrolled above Hawkinge and escorted a convoy off Folkestone.

10th March

About a quarter of the revenue raised by the Elham Parochial Church Council was sent for the use of various missions throughout the world and included the support of Peter Mazhkata, an African boy at St Augustine's Mission, Penhalonga, Southern Rhodesia. The parishioners read in their magazine: *Peter Mazhkata . . . is growing up apace, and a new photograph of him will be found on the notice-board in the Church. He looks a happy, healthy and strong little fellow, and seems altogether most attractive.*

11th March

During a training exercise between fighters and Lysanders from Hawkinge, there was an accident which caused a Hurricane to spin into the ground, killing the pilot.

12th March

Heavy rain from the south-west swept in late in day.

13th March. Russo-Finnish treaty signed. Hostilities cease 11 a.m.

During the night the wind veered to north and the barometer fell to 29.

14th March. Snow blizzard.

The blizzard, driven by gale-force winds, lasted for five hours and Elham was again cut off.

Shepherd George Austin was a middle-aged bachelor who knew his job well and, with the possible exception of Bill Booth and old George Palmer, there was no one in the valley who knew more about sheep. Sheep farming was a tradition as much as an economic necessity in this part of England, and at North Elham Farm the Palmers had some 500 ewes up on the sloping pastures and the lambs had started to drop. It was an anxious labour-intensive period, calling for a 24-hour vigil that would go on until the end of April. Little lambing pens used to shelter ewes during delivery were dotted around the hills, these having been built during any spare hours over the winter. The customary bitterly cold wind from the north-east had suddenly cut across a sheep pasture from an unexpected direction and diligent shepherds and farm hands were having to trudge through the driving snow and sleet to reorientate the pens.

15–19th March

The weather continued inclement. At night the blackout regulations had to be enforced and PC Robert Hampshire would cycle slowly and sedately around the village with gas-mask and steel helmet strapped across one shoulder. Any offending chink of light would mean the householder received a rap on the door and instructions to do something about it at once. Generally the civilians were extraordinarily careful and, contrary to what was expected, it was the military who were lax and there were constant complaints about lights being seen from their billets.

20th March

Warmer weather began to arrive. At Hawkinge two RAF staff officers arrived to inspect the provisions made for the defence of the aerodrome and the AMES (radar stations) at Dover and Rye. S/Ldr. D. J. Earyes, who had been struggling for days with 13 officers and 202 other ranks to form 416 Lysander Flight, was told the unit was to be disbanded.

21st March

The first day of spring—fine but cloudy and the sap was beginning to rise. The people of Elham valley were incredibly hospitable to the troops and in the processes of courtship it wasn't long before local girls were forming what their parents liked to believe were going to be lasting and, even more important, contractual relationships.

22nd March
On this Good Friday, hot cross buns came from Horace Cook's ovens soon after dawn and Horace Henry, whistling a happy tune, was away with them on his rounds.

Organist and choirmaster at St Mary's, Bernard Taylor had been practising for this day for a long time. With the talents of some of the cultured and gentlemanly soldiers that came into the valley with the 1st London (TA) Division, the whole of the *St Matthew Passion* was sung by three voices, with choral reproaches. It was an inspired performance.

23rd March
The *St Matthew Passion* had been so successful that Bernard Taylor was offered an appointment at one of Canterbury's churches. Mr Wilcox agreed to take over as choirmaster and one of his teachers would become organist.

24th March. At home.
Like most of the civilian population, Mary Smith spent Easter Sunday with her family.

25–28th March
With the warmer weather came the unmistakable signs of spring. As the pale streaks of dawn appeared, the first birds started chirping in Elham. Within fifteen minutes every tree, hedge and bush was alive with bird song, until quite suddenly it tailed off and stopped as if terminated by some unseen conductor.

At the post office the three postmen arrived on their red bicycles to collect their mailbags, already sorted for delivery. The mail also had to be collected from all the district post-boxes twice a day and Edward Smith would seal it in regulation bags and see that it was dispatched to the central sorting office at Canterbury. Jack Barber was the youngest of the postmen and was in the ARP service, but his two colleagues had both been in the First World War. Arthur Arnold still had weak lungs from being gassed and Charles Lovell had been luckier than many, having been captured and taken to Germany as a prisoner of war. Postmaster and postmen all had such a sense of public duty that, if necessary, they would have protected the Royal Mail with their lives. However, because of the steep hills, the bicycles were pushed as often as they were ridden.

29th March
It was fine in the early morning, turning to rain later. A barrage balloon reported drifting eastwards towards Hawkinge was brought down at Rye by a fighter.

30th March
Four Gladiators of No 263 Sqdn. based at Filton landed at Hawkinge for refuelling. These obsolete biplane fighters still equipped a few RAF squadrons and some were actually in France, where they were likely to face the Luftwaffe's Messerschmitts.

Elham Parish Council. (Left-right standing) Lance Walker, Walter 'Justice' Hawkins (Head ARP warden), Major Crawford, Scot Whitehead, George Carswell, Thomas Thompson (Clerk of the Council). (Left-right sitting) Rex Ames, Harold Ames, Edward Smith (Chairman), Ken Hubble (Vice-Chairman), George Palmer. (Mary Smith)

1st April

No 16 Army Co-operation Sqdn. ordered to prepare to leave Hawkinge to join the BEF in France.

5–7th April

The weather was generally fine. The 416 Lysander Flight was disbanded over this period. Also arrangements were made for the Pilotless Aircraft Unit to carry out trials with their radio-controlled aircraft at Watchet in Somerset. During this time British Intelligence knew full well that the Germans were preparing to invade Norway.

8th April. Norwegian territorial waters mined in three places by Allies.

The Elham Parish Council met that evening and Edward Smith was again re-elected to serve as Chairman for the next year—a post he had held since 1934. The Chairman read out a letter from Ken Hubble, the retiring vice-chairman, who tendered his resignation because of the extra work involved as commanding officer of the local Sea Cadets. The Council regretted his decision and resolved to send him a letter of appreciation. The meeting proceeded and they discussed the difficulty they were having in getting someone to roll the recreation ground grass, despite the fact that they had offered a payment of ten shillings.

9th April. Germany invaded Norway and Denmark.

10th April. British Naval action against Norway.

This was the First Battle of Narvik when British and German destroyers clashed.

11th April. Churchill's statement on the naval war.

It was Churchill's statement in the House of Commons which ultimately contributed to Chamberlain's resignation.

12th April

The 1st London Division in Kent were instructed to form an Independent Infantry Company to fight the Germans in Norway, each regiment providing three officers and 39 other ranks. It was in fact the forerunner of the Commandos. Quartermaster Angel at Beechborough was given the job of kitting this new company out. Reading down the list of equipment they needed, he realized it would tax his resources to the full. Snow goggles didn't exist in any Army stores and some other items were also not obtainable anywhere. It was all very well someone in the War Office specifying two-man Alpine tents, but they weren't to be purchased anywhere and there was no time to have them made. Improvization was what was called for—one bell tent to eight men would have to suffice. The contingent, intended to be highly mobile, went on its way from New Romney bearing some ten tons of explosives, ammunition and tents, most of which were dumped on the quayside when they disembarked.

13th April. Christine helped me plant out sweet peas.

The Hawkinge Lysanders flew off to join the RAF units in France.

14th April. 7 German destroyers sunk at Narvik yesterday. Minefield extended to all German coasts.

Sunday. Mary's entry refers to the Second Battle of Narvik, in which eight German destroyers and a U-boat were sunk.

15th April. British Troops in Norway.

In Germany, 'Uncle Theo' Osterkamp celebrated his 48th birthday. He had been the most successful German Marine fighter pilot during the First World War, having scored 32 victories. After the war he continued military flying, volunteering for service with the Iron Division fighting Russian Bolsheviks in Finland and Lithuania. In 1933 he managed the German aerobatic team and later he joined the Luftwaffe, when it was still a clandestine organization.

In 1939 he had been ordered to form JG 51, a unit of nine *staffeln* (squadrons) equipped with Me 109s, which was now at combat readiness in Germany. Servicemen and civilians would peer curiously at his throat where he wore the Pour le Mérite, 'The Blue Max', awarded to him by Kaiser Wilhelm. His pilots, supremely confident with their Messerschmitts, were itching to meet French and British aircraft in combat.

16th April. French and Canadian troops in Norway.

Hawkinge received a signal stating that No 416 Lysander Flight, recently formed and disbanded, was to be reformed at Hawkinge forthwith.

17–18th April

Lambing still continued, but now the arable land had to be prepared for sowing. At North Elham Farm, the Palmers had two pairs of working horses, plus a single green Fordson tractor. This tractor, being a major piece of capital investment, represented high technology and it was the farmer's prerogative to use it himself. Rubber tyres were considered an unnecessary luxury and the big driving wheels were made of iron with steel spikes. The only concession to comfort was a spring supporting the steel seat-pan. These tractors with spiked wheels were not allowed on the roads, but since the Palmers' land was on either side of the Canterbury Road, there were occasions at dusk when lookouts would signal the absence of the constabulary and the Fordson would clatter into the road and dash into a field on the other side of the valley.

19th April. Men of HMS 'Hardy' in London.
There were 53 survivors from the destroyer *Hardy* lost at Narvik. They were addressed by Churchill on Horse Guards Parade. S/Ldr. Earyes again reported to Hawkinge aerodrome to reform 416 Lysander Flight. The officers and other ranks, having been dispersed, all had to be gathered up again.

20th April. Parcel from Mr Dryland.
It was Mr Dryland who had given Mary Smith her diary as a Christmas present.

Robert Kennelly noted the first cuckoo to be heard in Elham valley and the first swallows were seen the next day, but they didn't stay.

21–22nd April
Following news that British and French forces had been driven out of Norway by the Germans, the Vicar of Elham composed a letter which subsequently appeared in the parish magazine a good two weeks before Winston Churchill first started using similar phraseology, when he sought to rally the entire nation. In some passages the similarity of style was quite remarkable:

> . . . *In some ways, we are an easy-going people but all history goes to show that we are a bulldog race and that the British character shows to the best advantage in the face of national difficulty and danger. Let us not forget, then, that there are some 80 millions of people in Germany bent upon our destruction! We need stout hearts and indomitable wills. But we are united as never before, and at whatever the cost, we are determined to see this thing through—or perish in the attempt. No bombing nor lightning stroke of the enemy will shake us from our purpose. We are all in the 'front line', and by cheerfulness, hard work, and strict economy of money and materials, England expects each one of us to do our duty.*

23rd April. Duff Cooper spoke at Banquet
Alfred Duff Cooper, the former First Lord of the Admiralty, who had just returned from America, delivered a stirring speech on St George's Day.

24th April. Listened to Gigli.
This was a radio recital heard by Mary.

25–27th April
The news from Norway sounded gloomier, but the British people had no knowledge of the pathetically wasteful operations carried out by all three services. Wing Commander

W. L. Payne was posted to Hawkinge to take over from S/Ldr. Ferris by the 1st May.

28th April

This was Rogation Wednesday, and in Elham a few bewildered allotment holders were obliged to stop digging and take their hats off whilst the Vicar conducted a short service, blessing the crops. On the land the barley fields had been broken down to a fine tilth and seeded. Each grain was in the hands of God, the weather and the soil.

29–30th April

These were quiet days at Hawkinge, and the weather was generally fine. In the evenings a low mist formed in the meadows along the Nailbourne and, at daybreak, cattle appeared to be floating legless on the vapour and the sheep couldn't be seen at all.

1st May

'Henbury', the home of George Henry Parker, a Peckham building contractor, was situated along the ridge of hills to the east of Elham. He had come to the district quite a few years before the war and regarded this neo-Georgian structure as his country seat. On one flank the house had high crenellated walls linking outhouses, giving the impression that it formed part of a film set.

2nd May

Being Ascension Day, the children at the village school were given a half-day holiday, that is, all except the choir boys who were taken on a picnic by the Vicar and his family.

The Rose & Crown was the only hotel in the village, and before the war quite a number of Elham householders offered accommodation to visitors. One of these was Mrs Butcher of Orchard Cottage, who for several years had been visited by the Baronesse Van Heemstra, who would come over from Holland bringing a son and daughter. The children would stay for long periods and the local people got to know the strikingly attractive little girl with saucer eyes, called Audrey Ruston and known by the villagers as 'little Audrey'. She had been staying in Elham during the recent cold weather and attending the little private school run by the Misses Rigden. The family were in Arnhem and Mrs Butcher now received instructions to take Audrey to Gatwick Airport as she was to return to Holland in a Dutch plane. However, the plane skidded off the runway and got stuck in the Surrey clay and Audrey was brought back to Elham.

3rd May

Hawkinge reported: *Weather—overcast but dry. A. S. O. Baroness E. de Sercleas WAAF reported at Hawkinge and proceeded to AME Stations at Dover and Rye for WAAF administrative staff duties on behalf of 60 Group, returning the same day.* Having these WAAFs about was rather trying for station commanders because they had to be segregated, needed special lavatories and WAAF officers needed extra special lavatories.

In the immediate area at Dover, Rye, Fairlight and Dunkirk (near Canterbury) AMES (Air Ministry Experimental Stations) had been built, which were developing what later came to be known as 'radar'. The Dover stations were some of the first constructed and consisted of two sets of towers, normally three 350-foot steel aerial masts for transmissions and, at a short distance away, a cluster of four 250-foot wooden masts surmounted by receiver aerials. At ground level, there were buildings for a generator transmitter and receiver, separated so as to avoid interference.

The calibrated cathode ray tube was in a separate watch office where operators kept it under observation and diagnosed every blip and speck that flickered over the screen. Skilled operators could assess the height, range and estimated number of approaching aircraft and the officer, or an NCO on duty, would pick up a telephone and speak directly to 11 Group Filter Room, where WAAF plotters placed visual symbols on a map.

Sometimes these 'blips' were dismissed as friendly aircraft, others became X-plots (suspicious unidentified), whilst others were designated 'hostile'. As soon as the plot was identified as 'hostile' or 'suspected hostile', tellers lifted telephones and simultaneously HQ Fighter Command, Group Operations Room, Sector Operations Room and AA HQ received the information. These raids were allocated numbers and coloured arrows so that all controllers had the same immediate visual picture of the situation on big table-top maps.

Once the aircraft crossed over the coast, the Observer Corps assumed responsibility. The information from these comfortless little look-out posts was vital since it was more accurate than radar, in so much as they were able to gauge altitude better, indicate numbers and identify types of aircraft. However, at night or in overcast conditions their

(Far left) Cricketer Leslie Ames, born and brought up in Elham, was one of the finest wicketkeeper-batsmen of all times. (Left) Three-year-old Leslie Ames defending the wicket in the back garden of King-post

information was a lot less accurate. The whole system seemed to work in practice, but it had never been put to the test.

4–5th May
At Elham Mrs Butcher was told that another flight had been arranged to take Audrey Ruston back to Holland and she was put on a plane at Shoreham in Sussex. The next time the villagers would see 'little Audrey' would be on the cinema screen as Audrey Hepburn—the girl with the 'elfin look' who starred in some of the finest films of the fifties and sixties.

6th May
The Chairman of Elham Parish Council reported a grave matter that evening. Boys of the Sea Cadets had damaged the gate and fences of the new King George playing field. This act of vandalism had been perpetrated by the lads, who should have been in the charge of Ken Hubble. However, the Council received an assurance from Mr Hubble, as officer in charge, that he would speak to the culprits.

Quotations were obtained from Ames Bros. to repair the damage for the modest sum of £8 6s 0d. Harold Ames was stone deaf and had been a member of the Parish Council. He was the father of Leslie Ames, one of the most illustrious Kent and England cricketers, who was born and brought up in Elham. As a tiny tot Leslie had played cricket in the garden of King-post, defending a rudimentary wicket set up by Mary's father.

7th May
416 Lysander Flight was detached from Hawkinge to Exeter.

8th May. Vote of Censure.
The House of Commons had lost confidence in the Chamberlain government following the Norway débâcle.

9th May
The voices of cuckoos became monotonous from breakfast time as the birds started calling from every wood and copse across the Elham valley.

10th May. Germany invaded Belgium and Holland. Chamberlain resigned.
Hawkinge reported: *Weather fine—yellow alert. 0401 hours. Instructions received to cancel all leave. All those on leave recalled at once. No 25 Blenheim Sqdn. and 601 Hurricane Sqdn. arrived for operational duties. Emergency measures for airfield defence were put into operation and a platoon of the Queen's Westminsters KRRC took over guard duty of the W/T Station. Royal Artillery Officers moved in to site Bofors guns.*

The suddenness and extent of the German attack on the neutral countries took all by surprise. Dive-bombers, paratroops, gliders, Panzers and superbly trained assault infantry slashed into Holland and Belgium, whilst the Luftwaffe started the systematic bombing of French military airfields.

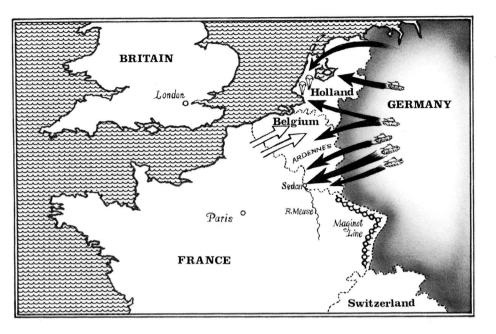

The German assault on Holland, Belgium and Luxemburg. British and French forces advance into Belgium to meet the attack

11th May

Chamberlain resigned as Prime Minister and within hours the King invited Winston Churchill to form a new coalition government. The British and French moved into Belgium to meet the German attack and RAF squadrons were engaged in confused and continuous fighting. 615 Sqdn. was in the process of converting from Gladiator biplanes to Hurricanes and some pilots with insufficient training elected to fly Gladiators against Messerschmitts. The battle situation on the ground was obscure, but the massive French Army and prepared defences were thought sufficient to contain the Germans.

12th May

This was Whit Sunday and Hawkinge was still at emergency stations. At 0720 hours military units in Elham valley were warned that enemy parachutists had landed in the district. Strong patrols were sent out but at 1000 hours there was a lot of whistle blowing and orders were received that it had been a false alarm.

During the afternoon armoured reconnaissance units of General Heinz Guderian's XIX Panzer Corps came out of the Ardennes, which had been considered impassable to tanks, and reached the River Meuse, taking Sedan. By evening German tanks were overlooking the Meuse all the way up to Dinant, but the bridges were blown and the French side bristled with artillery and anti-tank guns.

13th May. Queen Wilhelmina arrived in London.

The Dutch royal family had escaped to Britain. At Hawkinge machine gun posts were fully manned and senior NCOs were issued with revolvers.

From daybreak German tanks and motorized units massed at Sedan and just before noon a huge formation of Stuka dive-bombers appeared and started to pulverize the pill-boxes and gun emplacements on the French side of the Meuse. As wave after wave of bombers came down, any French fighters that tried to get at them were shot out of the sky by a host of circling Messerschmitts. At exactly 4.00 p.m., assault boats crossed the river and infantry stormed ashore to overcome the paralysed defences. By evening they had pushed through the town and engineers were assembling bridge sections for tanks to cross. At other points further north the French were fiercely repelling crossings, but near Dinant a junior Panzer general called Rommel had achieved a foothold on the other side and ferried a handful of light tanks across.

14th May. Holland surrendered late at night.

At Sedan German armour and motorized infantry had been crossing a single pontoon bridge throughout the night and had sufficient strength to hold their bridgehead against a French tank attack. By midday Guderians I and II Panzer Divisions were across and, with full fuel tanks, he led them off to motor through the soft rolling plains of France. At Dinant, Rommel completed bridging and by nightfall his armour was pouring over the river.

15th May. Dutch towns occupied by Germans.

The Commander of the French First Army in Belgium, with 22 divisions under his command, was greatly alarmed by the German breakthrough at Sedan to his south and decided summarily to withdraw to form another defence line 50 miles to the rear, but he omitted to inform his Belgian and British allies. All through the night the Panzers rumbled on and stupified French units were shattered when they discovered German tanks driving past their HQs.

At Elham it had been fine with a severe thunderstorm at night.

16th May

At dawn Lord Gort, commanding the BEF, learnt of the French withdrawal plan by accident. At 10 a.m., the stunned Belgians heard the news. As night fell, the Allies fell back in three stages and, to complicate matters, the French 7th Army on the left of the British and nearest the coast, was ordered to move south across the line of withdrawal of the British and Belgian forces. This caused such appalling confusion that various formations broke up and became lost. In the chaos that followed a German patrol actually captured General Giraud, Commander of the French 7th Army. To the south Guderian's tanks thrust deep into unprotected countryside. Everywhere enormous numbers of bewildered and demoralized French troops were beginning to give themselves up.

During the day, Anthony Eden broadcast to the men of Britain asking for volunteers to come forward to form the Local Defence Volunteers. After tea farmer Herbie Palmer drove his little Austin Seven down to Elham so as to volunteer for the emergency defence force. His brother Frank was in the ARP and brother Wallace was a special constable, and Herbie felt he must do something because the news over the radio was appalling.

Major Kingsley Dykes, OBE, MC, on the occasion of his marriage to the pretty nurse who finally restored him to health after being wounded for the third time during the First World War

About 20 local men turned up at the inaugural gathering, all curious to know what LDVs were supposed to do.

They congregated in what was an empty shop, two doors from the old post office; a policeman and some Army officials were there to record names. They were told to form themselves into a platoon and arm themselves at once to defend the Parish of Elham from invading Germans. Herbie looked around and saw his shepherd George Austin. He'd be useful as he'd been a regular in the Buffs. There was the huntsman 'Foxy' Sturmy, capable, reliable and an ex-sergeant in the First World War. There was Jessup, Thorpe, George Hogben, Goodearl, Harris, Swaffer, Fletcher, Boughton, and three formidable gentlemen from the parish, Messrs. Dykes, Constant and Parker.

Kingsley Dykes, OBE, MC, who lived at Ottinge Court, was a tall, well educated gentleman farmer who had been a major in the First World War. He had gone to Russia after the war to assist the White Russians fight the Bolsheviks and his brother was a General Staff officer. So it was a natural choice for him to be their Commander. However, there was George Henry Parker, the wealthy Peckham building contractor; he could virtually provide a platoon from his employees. Also there was their close friend

Martin Constant, the incumbent of Lower Court. In fact they had too many chiefs.

The matter was resolved for the time being. Major Kingsley Dykes would be Platoon Commander, George Henry Parker second-in-command, and 'Foxy' Sturmy would be the sergeant. Mr Constant would be another sergeant of what they'd call the 'Ottinge Section', the men being drawn mostly from his own staff at Lower Court. The three gentlemen were drinking chums at the Rose & Crown and they could sort out the finer points about rank at a later date.

Kingsley Dykes addressed his band of men, calling them 'gentlemen'. With his slight stutter, he thought it best to try and reassure them that the news from France might not be as bad as it seemed. They were asked to be in Elham Square the following night, armed with whatever weapons they could lay their hands on. When the meeting broke up, some went into the King's Arms, whilst others popped into the Rose & Crown or the New Inn, thereby presaging a custom that was to become well established.

17th May. Brussels captured.

No 17 Sqdn. arrived with their Hurricanes and ground crew at Hawkinge.

Colonel Charles de Gaulle, having been given permission to counter-attack with French armour, thrust three tank battalions at the Panzers near Montcornet. With air supremacy, the Germans radioed for dive-bombers, and Stukas came screaming down to help their companions on the ground. De Gaulle wrote: *All the afternoon the Stukas, swooping out of the sky and returning ceaselessly, attacked our tanks and lorries. We had nothing with which to reply. Finally, more and more German mechanized detachments arrived and started attacking us in the rear.* And whilst the Panzers scythed into France the vast, but largely obsolescent, Armée de l'Air flew with *élan* as they were systematically shot out of the sky or smashed on their airfields.

501 Sqdn. took their Hurricanes down to strafe a column of Panzer MK III tanks. Their eight machine-guns roared, sending streams of bullets at the tanks, the tracers dancing away in all directions as they glanced off the armour. It was all quite useless.

Herbie Palmer found himself standing in a line of men in Elham Square that evening wearing a trilby hat and trying to do some arms drill with his 12-bore shot-gun. In the pockets of his jacket he had about eight cartridges. Most of the men had shot-guns which ranged from trusty old hammer-guns to finely engraved sporting pieces, but there were some little .22 rifles. An army drill instructor was there and it was all rather embarrassing. Palmer's shepherd, who had been in the Buffs, seemed to know so much more about soldiering than the farmer. Quite a number of villagers gathered to watch and were greatly amused when, trying to slope-arms, the farmer clouted his head with his gun, knocking off his hat. Many of the new platoon popped into their pub before going home and it was arranged to have another muster on Sunday morning.

18th May

Hitler, as Supreme Commander of the German forces, decided to intervene. He had watched mesmerized by the astonishing progress of his tanks and now Reinhardt's Panzer Corps was racing after Guderian on a parallel course. They were stretching their lines of supply and could fall into a trap. Hitler wanted a halt to consolidate. Guderian argued passionately with his superior General Kleist, but was told to halt. He could only send reconnaissance units forward. The Panzer General climbed into one of the leading tanks and off they all went to resume their journey. He was on the Somme that night and would call this advance 'reconnaissance'.

19th May

Rommel's 7th Panzer Division and the 'Death's Head' SS Division reached Arras on the road to the Channel ports. They had wheeled inside Reinhardt's and Guderian's lines of advance that had now combined to form a 'Panzer corridor'. The BEF continued to make a fighting withdrawal, but were suffering considerable losses.

That night people abed in England knew nothing of all this and, although the news from France didn't sound encouraging, surely it was only a matter of time before the combined forces of France, Belgium and Britain would get the upper hand? They didn't know, for instance, that 53-year-old General Hastings Ismay had spent a considerable part of the night with Churchill deep down in the underground Cabinet War Room, and that the General was resolved to fly over the withdrawing British forces next morning and drop by parachute so as to ascertain the situation and rally the troops in the spirit of Maréchal Ney.

Ismay was dissuaded from the idea by his assistant, Colonel Leslie Hollis, who paced with him up and down Whitehall in the moonlight, putting forward reasoned arguments—the best of which was that they wouldn't know where the BEF was in the morning.

20th May

QM Angel climbed the conical hump of Summerhouse Hill, where his regiment kept an observation post and could see out to France. The spring was beautiful and Angel would never forget the image of Beachborough against a magnificent background of white chestnut trees.

Robert Kennelly, the local naturalist, was a prodigious walker and he became almost lyrical when he noted the extraordinary spring that followed one of the severest of winters: *Then the whole countryside burst into flower, primroses were exceptionally large, violets and wild hyacinths were a deep saxe blue, oxlips, buttercups, wood anemones and other flowers were in profusion, and the blackthorne resembled the snows of winter.*

In 1937, a Mr R. V. Kennelly, then living in Folkestone, wrote to the Elham Parish Council asking for permission to hold a public meeting under the auspices of the National Socialist Union, which was formerly known as the British Union of Fascists. Elham people are very tolerant and they instructed the Clerk of the Council to thank Mr Kennelly for his letter and tell him they had no objection to any public meeting being held, but the matter was for the police to decide. Subsequently the 'Blackshirts' held an assembly in Elham Square. From this time Mr Kennelly fades from this chronicle and it may be of significance that on 18th May 1940 Churchill urged immediate action to intern Communists and Fascists, a measure that was swiftly ratified by the Cabinet and put into action.

The 'Panzer corridor' reached Abbeville just after teatime, despite running short of fuel, which was partly overcome by using French supplies. Most units stopped, but Major Spitta, leading a forward battalion, checked his watch and the fuel situation and sped on. An hour later his vehicles topped some high ground, and there before them was the English Channel sparkling in the evening sun. Men and machines had been fighting and moving for ten whole days, but after a few gulps of the tangy sea air, the weary crews felt exalted. The British and a considerable part of the French Army—122 divisions in all—were trapped.

21st May. Germans captured Arras and Amiens—Folkestone warning at night.

There was bedlam at Hawkinge aerodrome with the coming and going of senior officers. Battle-weary RAF pilots brought a variety of aircraft back from France, whilst 605 Sqdn. came down from Scotland with their Hurricanes and announced that their ground personnel were following.

Secret orders were issued to the military at Elham that in the event of invasion, the road through the valley would only be used for military traffic. This also precluded pedestrians and refugees.

The overwhelming significance of their success was only just sinking in, and the German High Command was experiencing a period of indecision. Guderian chafed at the bit because he wanted to go straight for the Channel ports and cut off any British retreat or arrival of reinforcements.

At Arras the British 4th and 7th Royal Tank Regiments, supported by French Somua tanks, made a determined counter-attack and Rommel was surprized to find his Panzers couldn't knock out the heavily armoured Matilda tanks. So the resourceful General turned 88 mm anti-aircraft guns onto the British tanks and blew them to pieces.

By 21st May the 'Panzer Corridor' had reached the Channel coast encircling 122 British and French divisions

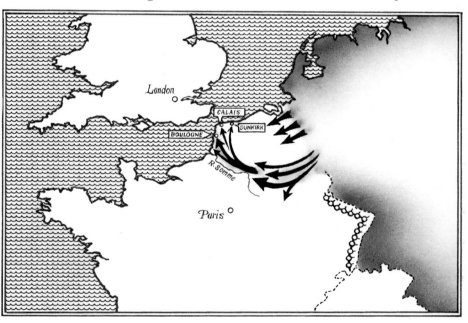

22nd May

The nucleus of the RAF Air Component HQ, still fighting in France, arrived at Hawkinge. It included Air Vice Marshal N. D. K. McEwan, CB, CMG, DSO, of 22 Group, and the New Zealander, Air Vice Marshal K. R. Park, MC, DFC, of 11 Group. The latter was to orchestrate the Battle of Britain in a few weeks' time.

The Army, called 'brown jobs' in a mildly derogatory way by the RAF, kept coming and going at Hawkinge—siting 3″ AA guns and Bofors guns and then taking them away again as orders were issued and countermanded.

The children from London and north Kent, who had been evacuated into Elham valley a few months earlier, were quickly labelled and hustled away with a lot of local children to the comparative safety of Wales.

Panzers moved on again with a three-pronged attack towards the three Channel ports of Boulogne, Calais and Dunkirk.

23rd May. Raid warning 'round about in evening.

The Inspector General of the RAF arrived at Hawkinge and preparations were made for what was to be a desperate gamble by all three Services.

The defenders of Boulogne fiercely resisted the Germans so waves of Stukas arrived and started hammering the beleaguered troops, sinking destroyers and transport ships.

24th May. Boulogne in Nazi hands. King spoke at 9.

Calais was sealed off and called to surrender. At Boulogne the medieval walls were blasted open at point-blank range and stormed using grenades and flame-throwers. Fierce hand-to-hand fighting followed.

QM Angel received orders to send his regiment's automatic weapons and anti-tank rifles to Folkestone immediately. The weapons that had been looked after with loving care were quickly assembled and rushed across the Channel to Calais. None of them was returned.

A party of 100 airmen arrived at Hawkinge to form a Maintenance, Refuelling and Re-arming Flight. They were to be ready as soon as possible to service fighter aircraft. At Bekesbourne, right up at the north end of the valley, some soldiers challenged another unidentified party of troops approaching and there was an exchange of small-arms fire, fortunately without casualties. When RHQ heard of the encounter, Capt. C. E. Mercer set out with 72 men to reinforce the Bekesbourne guard, who genuinely believed they had grappled with Germans. Their orders issued only a few days before were quite explicit: *In view of German action in Holland in landing troops in British uniform by parachute or troop-carrying aircraft, any men so dropped in this country will be treated as enemy and at once engaged by the nearest troops with all available weapons and with utmost ruthlessness. Speed is essence of problem.*

25th May

Boulogne surrendered; two generals and 5,000 British and French troops were captured. But Calais fought on, inflicting unacceptable casualties on the attackers. The

Germans, in squeezing the Allies back against the coast, were now having to enter low-lying terrain with dykes bordering the roads. It was unsuitable for tanks and Panzer commanders were ordered to halt and withdraw from Dunkirk until just out of artillery range. The Luftwaffe would deal with the beleagured army now. Similarly, if Calais didn't surrender, it too would be left to the Luftwaffe. Reichsmarshall Göring had assured Hitler that he could destroy the British if they didn't surrender.

The Vicar of Elham knew his duty. He got his wife and children away to Wales, along with Miss Deck their tutor. He would stay on 'alone', with young Enid the cook, Freda the parlourmaid, a gardener and two large ponies.

Vice Admiral Somerville arrived at Hawkinge and Colonel Huxtable of the Light AA Brigade turned up and decided to re-site all the guns—putting one outside the aerodrome. The alarm for 'enemy parachutists' was given and the station 'stood to' until dawn on the 26th.

26th May. Raid warning 12.50–2.10 a.m. Evacuation of E. and S.E. coast ordered.

This Sunday was a national day of prayer and at Elham a chain of worshippers was organized to pray continuously. It was cloudy, and the sound of distant gun fire was almost continuous from across the Channel. Calais was captured.

At 6.57 p.m. the Admiralty in London flashed the signal to Admiral Ramsay at Dover: 'Operation Dynamo to Commence'. This task was enormous, a race against time to save as many of the British Army as possible before they were killed or captured at Dunkirk.

27th May. King of Belgians gave up.

It was fine with patchy cloud. At Hawkinge Air Vice Marshal C. H. B. Blount arrived and immediately entered the square brick building with a glazed gallery, known as the Haskard Target Building, from where he conducted the RAF's operations providing aircover over Dunkirk.

At 12.30 p.m. King Leopold of the Belgians sent Field Marshal Lord Gort a message: *The army is very discouraged. It has been fighting continuously for four days under intensive bombardment and the moment is approaching when it will be unable to continue to fight. In these circumstances, the King will find himself forced to surrender to avoid a collapse.* A similar message was sent to the French during the afternoon. In the early hours of the following day the Belgians surrendered unconditionally, much to the indignation of the French, but just giving the 60th French Division time to join up with the BEF. At Lille a huge force of Allied troops was encircled with no hope of escape.

28th May. Raid warning in morning.

Hurricanes were repeatedly landing and taking off from Hawkinge. Some from 245 Sqdn. arrived from Scotland and relieved 605 Sqdn., which returned to Drem. Across the Channel there was an armada of ships of all sizes ploughing back and forth bringing the troops home, whilst the RAF's home-based fighters went into battle to try and stave off the German bombers.

The Spitfire was the RAF's newest and best fighter plane and Air Marshal Dowding, C-in-C Fighter Command, had jealously held them back in reserve. But he was now ordered to commit them to battle to reduce the pounding the Army and Navy were taking from the Luftwaffe. That night one or two German fighter aces—who'd been having things a bit too much their own way—went into their messes shaking their heads. The Messerschmitt 109 had met its match.

That evening a thick blanket of sea fog formed over the Channel.

Alice German, the Welsh school teacher living in Elham and often referred to in Mary Smith's diary as 'Ginger'

29th May

Alice 'Ginger' German, who is mentioned many times in Mary's diary, was a young school teacher living in the village. She had always found the people travelling on buses in Elham valley so very different to those in her native Wales. There wasn't the cheerful Welsh banter: the Kent people just didn't speak to each other unless they were acquainted. That morning she noticed a sudden change had come over them; they were raising their voices and talking to strangers, rejoicing in the thick morning mist that was rolling in from the Channel and helping get the men back from France. However, the fog cleared from the Channel late in the day and the Luftwaffe resumed bombing and strafing the crowded beaches and ships.

At Hawkinge 150 Royal Engineers arrived to provide gangs to repair the aerodrome if it should be bombed.

30th May

The day was overcast and misty as hundreds of little private boats arrived in the Channel to help rescue the BEF. They came from the Medway towns, East Anglia, the Thames and right along the south coast. Fishing boats, yachts and smart pleasure cruisers all converged on Dunkirk.

Marshal of the RAF, Viscount 'Boom' Trenchard ('Father' of the Royal Air Force), arrived at Hawkinge to see how the operation was going. 245 Sqdn. went up through the swirling mist with nine Hurricanes, supposedly to join up with other squadrons for a Dunkirk patrol, but visibility was so bad that they couldn't even keep formation. On their return six flew inland and found Kenley and the other three managed to get down in fields along the south coast.

31st May

By dawn, which was clear, S/Ldr. Whitley, the New Zealand CO of 245, had gathered most of his Hurricanes together again at Hawkinge. He took off on morning patrol over Dunkirk, leading F/Lt. Thomson, P/Os Yapp, Redman, Hill, Treanor, West and Howett, and Sgts. Tarrett and Banks. Ships were beavering away across the Channel, but there was no sign of enemy aircraft.

245 Sqdn. went over again in the afternoon and sighted some Me 109s that kept their distance. P/O McGlashan failed to return, having landed in France, and would have to try to get back the hard way. Some British pilots shot down around Dunkirk made their way back by sea in time to be back in action again the following day. But long lines of disgruntled soldiers, queuing under fire for hour after hour, didn't take kindly to these

bright faced young men being ushered past them to the front of the queue. In one incident a pilot was pushed off the causeway.

The 64th Field Regt. RA had just moved into Acrise Place, the once gracious home of the Papilon family, in the hills between Elham and Hawkinge. They should have had 24 field-guns, but were down to four First World War howitzers. The truth was appalling: the 1st London Division, responsible for the defence of the whole of Kent east of a line between Chatham and Rye, had only eleven modern field-guns—on paper their establishment was 72. Of their supposedly 48 anti-tank guns, there were none. They received a message: *Invasion is imminent, no action need be taken.* All they saw was an Army-Cooperation Lysander crash late in the day, killing a New Zealand pilot officer and an aircraftsman.

Further down the coast, 601 'County of London' Sqdn., famed for having a lot of rather rich and influential young men amongst its pilots, received orders to meet a yellow painted Flamingo airliner and escort it to Paris. The nine Hurricanes rendezvoused with the Flamingo and formed up in sections of three behind it in the correct fashion and followed it in to land at Paris. It was only then that they realized they had been escorting the Prime Minister. Churchill came over to them, insisted on calling their Hurricanes 'Spitfires', and demanded to know where they had been because he couldn't see them during the flight. They were given instructions to wait on the airfield to escort him back at six in the evening when his conference with the French leaders would be over.

At six, when Churchill's party had not reappeared, F/Lt. Sir Archibold Hope, Bt, saw this as a golden opportunity of seeing some Paris nightlife. He put a message through to the conference that it was getting late and an escort would be no use in the dark. They would wait until seven o'clock and, if Mr Churchill hadn't appeared by then, they would go into the city. The reply came back that the PM would stay overnight and that they were released until eight the next morning. Whooping with joy, they made off for the city at once, in search of wine, women and song.

1st June. Nearly all BEF withdrawn.

At eight o'clock, nine bleary-eyed, unshaven pilots were shuffling around at Paris airport after a night on the tiles. 'Willie' Rhodes-Moorhouse* was actually being unwell behind his Hurricane when the PM arrived. Churchill, grinning happily and waving his stick, had a word with each pilot, still persisting in calling their planes 'Spitfires'. General Sir Edward Spears, one of the PM's party, later waxed lyrical about the jaded pilots in his memoirs: 'I thought they looked like the angels of my childhood . . . creatures of an essence that was not of our world. . . .' By other accounts they had done their best to be men of the world that night. For the flight back, the pilots abandoned the correct escort formation and tucked in very close on either side of the Flamingo so that the passengers could see the fighters and wave to them.

*Son of 2/Lt. W. B. Rhodes-Moorhouse, VC, who was mortally wounded when making a daring aerial attack on a railway station behind German lines in 1915. 'Willie', as a F/Lt. with DFC, was killed in aerial combat over Tunbridge Wells on 6th September 1940. His ashes were interred in his father's grave at Parnham House, Dorset.

At Hawkinge an Air Ministry press officer turned up with six representatives from the American broadcasting companies. They were going to be shown that the BEF was coming home and that the British were not finished. S/Ldr. Whitley took 245 Sqdn. off at midday and they returned an hour and a half later in an agitated state. They'd been involved in a swirling dog-fight with Messerschmitts above the armada of little ships and their pilots had claimed four—but P/Os West and Treanor were missing.

2nd June. BEF almost completely evacuated.
Sunday. 245 went on early morning patrol and reported 'Nothing over Dunkirk—apparently evacuated'. Soon after this they packed their bags, shook hands with the friends they'd made during their brief stay at Hawkinge and flew away back to Scotland. They would return in less than a week.

Hawkinge was now the nearest airfield to the enemy and changes had to be made very fast. These were started by the 'Queen Bees' of the Pilotless Aircraft Unit being removed from the aerodrome; they weren't going to be of much use in the battle to come.

3rd June. Muddled raid warning at 4 a.m. Raid on Paris. Barney's birthday (slippers).
During the darkness ships were still making their way to France to bring back troops. Destroyers came under shellfire, but never flinched from their duty.

On the bank opposite the old chalkpit above Elham, red and blue milkworts were growing.

4th June
The last ships left Dunkirk just before dawn and by 9 a.m. the Channel was empty. 338,000 Allied troops, one-third of which were French, had been taken off the beaches of Dunkirk by the seamen of Britain. Unfortunately they had brought back nothing more than the grimy clothes they stood in. Their equipment and weapons had been left behind in France.

5th June. New offensive on Somme front. Jock stripped.
The Germans resumed their offensive against France, having reinforced and reformed their forces. The French manned a 430-mile defence line along the River Somme to the Swiss border, half of which was the massively defended Maginot Line. They had, however, learnt one fundamental lesson during the *Blitzkrieg*, which was to have defence in depth. They therefore set up 'pockets of defence' with artillery and anti-tank crews ordered to stand firm when cut off and offer stiff resistance.

At Acrise Place the 64th Field Regt. RA was jubilant. Major Mayer, the 2 i/c, had been to the Arsenal at Woolwich and managed to extract four field-guns without sights. These would double their fire power.

The Smiths had two family dogs, Jock the Scottie and Dash the spaniel.

6th June. Raid warning at night—Hot.
The dawn chorus was at its peak at 5 a.m. and all the summer visitors were joining in. At

Hawkinge there seemed to be an endless cavalcade of Army officers arriving to inspect and discuss the defences. During the day they received Colonel Buchanan-Dunlop (Buffs), Colonel Fuller and Colonel Ross.

S/Ldr. Joslin had just taken over 79 Sqdn. after the battle over France. During the afternoon he circled over Hawkinge with his Hurricanes, trying to locate an unidentified aircraft picked up by radar. Nothing was seen and so they returned to Biggin Hill.

The Germans reported a new spirit in the French Army and only limited advances were made, considerable time being wasted liquidating the 'pockets of defence'. Hoth's 15th Panzer Corps with Rommel at the spearhead advanced 15 miles beyond the Somme, outflanking the remaining British troops in France.

7th June

Scottish and Canadian troops crossed into France to bolster the 51st Highland Division entrenched between Dieppe and Abbeville. 79 Sqdn., escorting three Blenheims, passed over the troops' positions. They then patrolled Abbeville inviting the Luftwaffe to scrap with them. At 2.00 p.m. they were engaged by Messerschmitts and in the hectic battle that followed, P/O Parker claimed two and F/O Davies and Sgt. McQueen one each. Joslin and his squadron returned without loss.

Rommel decided to bypass the French 'defence pockets' and push on until he was at Forges-les-Eaux, 37 miles south-west of the Somme.

8th June. Hotter—Made a cake.

At 9.45 a.m. S/Ldr. Joslin came in from over the Channel and wrecked his Hurricane making an emergency landing on Hawkinge aerodrome. He clambered from the machine unhurt, eager to hear news about his pilots who had again just tempted Messerschmitts into battle over Abbeville. Joslin claimed a victory and so did P/O Haysom, whilst F/O Jimmy Davies and P/O Stones shared a Heinkel bomber. They went over again in the afternoon but made no contact. In these tail-chasing skirmishes at moderate altitudes the Me 109s were unable to exploit their superior performance and were at a disadvantage to the manoeuvrable Hurricanes. This state of affairs made RAF pilots over-confident and prompted the Germans to develop new techniques.

During the night Rommel drove his Panzers west and the French people came out in the darkness cheering and offering refreshments to the tank crews, believing them to be British!

In the North Sea two German battleships sank two British destroyers and also the aircraft carrier HMS *Glorious* returning from Norway. On board *Glorious* were two complete squadrons of RAF fighters that had been engaged in a rearguard battle against the Luftwaffe. The news that there were few survivors was not revealed immediately.

9th June. Very hot—Mr Backhouse came to tea. Terrible battle in France.

By dawn Rommel's 7th Panzer Division had reached the River Seine and cut off the French to the north, including the British 51st Highland Division.

Later in the day, 245 Sqdn. circled and landed at Hawkinge. Their ground crews were en route from the north. After refuelling and refreshments, they flew an uneventful bomber escort mission over France.

10th June. Not so hot—Italy declares war on France and England.

The Italian dictator, Mussolini was hoping for some pickings from the French Empire. A Panzer thrust in France threatened to envelop Paris and the French government decided to leave the capital immediately.

11th June. Attack on Italian air bases. Paris in danger.

Long-range RAF bombers, intending to attack industrial targets in Italy, landed in France to refuel and were prevented from taking off by French trucks that were driven onto the airfield. The French did not want to suffer reprisal attacks from the Italian Air Force.

Reims was captured by the 2nd Panzer Division and the 7th Panzer Division turned north to Rouen and charged straight into the British 51st Highland Division. Churchill and Eden, with Generals Ismay and Spears, conferred with Marshal Pétain and Generals Weygand and de Gaulle. Weygand was despondent and said: 'the last line of defence has been overrun and all the reserves are used up . . .'

12th June. Nearer Paris—Ma and Margaret went to Canterbury and bought asparagus.

Rommel reached the Channel coast, cutting the 51st Highland Division off from the port of Le Havre. Guderian, heading the 39th Panzer Corps, thrust south-east and crossed the Champagne mountains to reach Chalon. Before the day was over, British General Victor Fortune and his staff were captured in the harbour of St Valéry-en-Caux and the whole of the 51st Highland Division surrendered to Rommel.

Brigadier Gribbon, commanding the Sandgate Platoon of the LDV, visited Hawkinge aerodrome to discuss the defence of the village telephone exchange.

13th June. Somewhat nearer—but counter attacked in one place.

Paris was abandoned by the French government. In Britain it was announced that church bells were to be rung only as a warning if enemy troops invaded.

S/Ldr. Joslin landed 79 Sqdn. at Hawkinge where they were joined by 32 and 213 Squadrons. At 6 p.m. all three squadrons make a sweep along the French coast, but nothing was sighted. Brigadier the Hon. H. St. G. Schomberg, DSO, the local Garrison Commander, visited Hawkinge and two 20 mm Hispano cannons were sited for aerodrome defence.

14th June. Capture of Paris by Nazis. Daddy puts in celery.

Another fine day. The German Army entered Paris without a shot being fired. Jack-booted soldiers stamped and strutted down the Champs-Elysées and a Wehrmacht guard of honour formed up at the Arc de Triomphe. The French government had fled to Bordeaux and the aged Marshal Pétain became President of the stunned nation.

S/Ldr. Joslin again tried to stir up the Messerschmitts by leading his squadron over Le Havre, Rouen, Abbeville and Boulogne. In the evening sunlight, 245 Sqdn. also

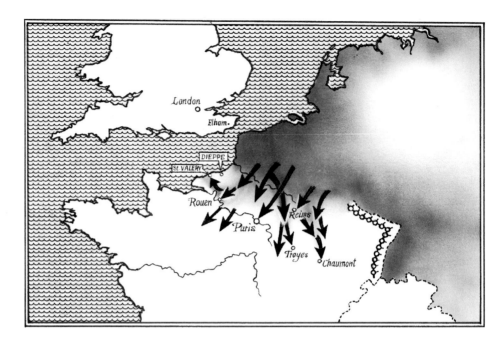

tried, but encountered nothing except some accurate bursts of AA fire which made a lot of shrapnel holes in the tail of Sgt. Banks' Hurricane.

15th June. Nazis still pushing on.

The Germans reached Langres, 150 miles south-east of Paris.

Since being rescued at Dunkirk, some 80,000 French troops had been fed, housed and transported to Plymouth, where they then embarked to sail back to France so as to continue the fight. The people of Plymouth cheered themselves hoarse as train loads of 'Froggies' came into the city, and a Royal Marine band played patriotic French music at the quayside as they departed. Thousands of sandwiches and millions of cigarettes were handed out and both municipal and private gardens were stripped of flowers so as to hand every Frenchman a bloom.

The citizens of Plymouth and the French soldiers sung the 'Marseillaise' as each ship sailed, but as they disappeared over the horizon, the French Army and Air Force became incapable of further organized resistance. The British would soon be alone in their war against Germany.

16th June. America to give all help possible but not army. French position very weak.

The weather was poor that Sunday and there was no flying from Hawkinge.

The French government collapsed and Marshal Pétain resolved to make peace at any cost, totally rejecting Churchill's offer of common citizenship between the French and British peoples to continue the fight against Germany and Italy from Britain and North

Africa. Convinced that Britain was going to be crushed quickly, Pétain said he didn't want France to be 'united with a corpse'. The Germans reach Dijon.

17th June. France gave up.

The speed of the German advance in every direction prevented any co-ordinated defence and the French Army were no longer receiving any orders. Millions of refugees stampeded along the roads in front of the enemy, panicked by German aircraft strafing attacks. It was then announced that the French had stopped fighting.

When this news came through at the officers' mess at Acrise Place, Captain Max Wilson, the MO, was amazed as his fellow officers burst into spontaneous cheering. He smiled nervously and glanced from face to face, but couldn't fully understand their sentiment. 'We had just lost our last ally—I suppose they felt the French had become a liability over the last few weeks.' It was the instinctive reaction of an island nation whose homeland had been unconquered for over 800 years. They would now withdraw into their island fortress and pull up the drawbridge.

One man who had every reason to cheer was the diligent and austere Commander-in-Chief of Fighter Command, Sir Hugh Dowding. He had created the defence system of the British Isles against aerial bombardment and had seen his fighters being sacrificed in a forlorn attempt to support a doomed ally.

General Charles de Gaulle arrived in England to lead the Free French forces.

18th June. Speech by Churchill. Hitler and Mussolini confer on terms for France.

On this day Winston Churchill addressed his nation, and indeed the English-speaking people of the world:

What General Weygand called the Battle of France is over. I expect that the Battle of Britain is about to begin. The whole fury and might of the enemy must very soon be turned on us. Hitler knows that he will have to break us in this island or lose the War. If we can stand up to him, all Europe may be free and the life of the world may move forward into broad sunlit uplands. But if we fail, then the whole world, including the United States, including all that we have known and cared for, will sink into the abyss of a new Dark Age made more sinister, and perhaps more protracted, by the lights of perverted science. Let us therefore brace ourselves to our duties, and so bear ourselves that, if the British Empire and its Commonwealth last for a thousand years, men will still say 'this was their finest hour'.

In the west Panzers reached the Loire and in the south they reached the Swiss border, trapping all the French forces behind the Maginot Line.

Hawkinge sent Hurricanes along the French coast during the afternoon, but nothing came up to meet them, although Rouen-Boos airfield appeared to be crowded with Luftwaffe planes. Two more quick-firing 20 mm guns were sited at Hawkinge and daily rifle practice was intensified.

Also on that afternoon Herbert Palmer, his shepherd and a darting black and white mongrel were on the broad sunlit uplands above North Elham Farm, moving some of the growing lambs onto new pastures. They were fattening up nicely. Fatstock would be

purchased by the government, and good prices were assured.

As the RAF practised during the day, the cacophony of sound—made up of wailing sirens, hooters and banging firearms—gave a dreadful note of preparation up at Hawkinge; but there was a blessed lull at dusk. Later the still of this warm night was disturbed when about 100 German bombers crossed the coast of Britain at various points and roamed about dropping bombs, apparently at random, on the eastern counties. However, some fell at Addington near Croydon and at 3 a.m. there was a whistle and thud when an HE (high-explosive bomb) fell on Folkestone, but failed to explode. In all some 12 civilians were killed and 30 injured.

The raids were considered little more than a nuisance, but they did give the military and civil defences a valuable opportunity to take part in a dress rehearsal for what was to come. The bombers, mostly Heinkels, had pale blue undersides and flew at about 8,000 feet, where they were easily picked up by searchlights. AA gunners were firing off a considerable number of shells that exploded harmlessly like orange stars, and British fighters were tempted to engage the raiders that could be seen in the searchlight beams.

F/Lt. Adolphus 'Sailor' Malan, DFC, of 74 Sqdn. woke his Station Commander at Hornchurch and asked permission to take a Spitfire up to engage the bombers in the AA zone over the Thames Estuary. He argued that he would use recognition flares and co-ordinate his attacks with the guns and searchlights. Climbing over the Estuary, Malan at first patrolled above Southend, protecting his wife Lynda who was in a nursing home below having just brought a son into the world; then he went after the German raiders. One fell flaming into a park at Chelmsford and another went into the sea. It was typical of this quiet, seemingly unemotional South African that he didn't tell his fellow pilots about his successes when he took them up on patrol before breakfast the next morning.

19th June. Margaret took Jock to Canterbury with Aunt Beauch to be photographed.

Eager forks turned the soil in allotments and kitchen gardens to lift the pale golden new potatoes. The growers couldn't resist taking some, despite horticultural notices asking people to leave the crop to achieve a greater yield later in the summer.

During the hours of darkness, a handful of Luftwaffe bombers returned, but they flew a little higher and made use of cloud cover. Altogether eight people were killed, but these apparently pointless raids were most important to the Luftwaffe and a secret intelligence section of the Air Ministry soon had irrefutable evidence of their intention. The Germans were testing what they called *Knickebein* and other types of target-location equipment that would enable their planes to fly along radio beams on the darkest of nights and score hits within 150 yards of a pinpointed target.

Professor Lindemann (later Lord Cherwell), who was Churchill's scientific adviser, had difficulty in persuading the RAF hierarchy that there was a real threat from beam-guided enemy bombers. However, Lindemann and his 28-year-old protégé, Dr R. V. Jones, managed to convince Churchill of the urgency to do something to counteract these beams before it was too late.

By July, No 80 Wing was formed with 220 radio specialists and they soon started transmitting false signals to confuse *Knickebein* and later more sophisticated systems. This was delightfully code-named 'Operation Headache' and it wasn't long before German bomber crews began to lose confidence in the infallibility of their radio navigational systems.

20th June

Brigadier G. M. B. Portman was inspecting Hawkinge ground defences when 245 Sqdn. returned to land with their gun-muzzle patches blasted off. Personnel rushed across the airfield to hear the news firsthand. They learnt that after days of fruitlessly trying to provoke the Luftwaffe into a fight, New Zealanders S/Ldr. Whitley and F/Lt. Mowat had taken sections of Hurricanes down to shoot up Rouen airfield at low level, setting fire to four enemy aircraft.

The Château country and the entire length of the Loire was overrun by the Germans. At the same time the Italian Army attacked France in the south with 24 divisions.

21st June. Armistice terms signed in same carriage as before. Folkestone warning.

The situation in France was one of utter confusion. At 3.30 p.m. a French delegation, headed by General Huntziger, was ushered by Germans into a railway coach standing on the track at Rethondes—the same vehicle in which the Germans had been obliged to submit to a surrender in 1918. Hitler, Hess and some of the High Command were there to hand the French an 'unalterable document of surrender'. The French party asked for time to study the document and were put into a tent to read the German ultimatum.

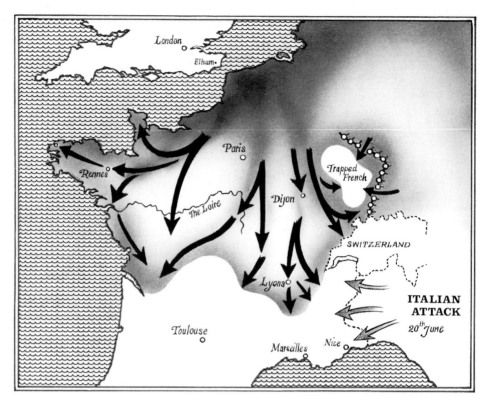

22nd June. Scharnhorst hit and damaged. First green peas.

The French delegation, still at Rethondes, tried to negotiate, but the Germans were
inflexible and advised them that, if they procrastinated beyond 19.30 hours, they would
be conducted back to their lines and the conquest would continue. The French were
obliged to enter the carriage and sign the instrument of surrender. Their humiliation was
complete.

23rd June. French armistice terms given. The Backhouse's came to tea. Wrote Mr Dryland.

Hawkinge reported: *Weather fine—A Shooting Competition was organised for both officers
and airmen of the Station. The O.C. Royal Marines AA Battery visited Station from
Dover. A concert was today given in the Camp, organised by the Station Band.* The last big
ENSA concerts were held in November 1939 when 'Bubbles' gave two performances on
the 15th and when Jack Buchanan was top of the bill on the 24th.

Jimmy Davies of 79 Sqdn., recently promoted to F/Lt., led 9 Hurricanes across the
Channel to escort Blenheims bombing German-occupied airfields, where there were
ominous signs of great preparations. AA fire was heavy, but no enemy fighters came up.
Davies, who had lived in New Jersey, USA, was dark, slim and something of a loner
compared to the hearty Empire volunteers who had permeated most RAF fighter

(Above) Formal photograph taken before the luncheon at Acrise Place in honour of the visit of Cosmo Lang, the Archbishop of Canterbury. (Left-right front) Capt. M. Ruffor, Capt. P. Talbot-Smith, Capt. T. Digby Jones, Maj. Thompson, Maj. H. B. Hall, Brig. Price (CRA), the Archbishop, Lt. Col. T. C. Burchell, Maj. Gen. Liardet (1st London Div.), Brig. Portman (OC 2nd London Inf. Brigade), Maj. G. Mayer, Capt. R. Guthrie (Adj.), Capt. Pugh, Capt. Stragger, Capt. P. Mercer. (Left-right centre) 2/Lt. K. Meikleijohn, 2/Lt. McMillan, 2/Lt. P. Barrington, 2/Lt. E. Adler, Lt. Marshall, Capt. H. D. Anderson (Padre), Lt. W. Brittain (QM), Capt. J. M. G. Wilson (MO), Lt. Hartland, 2/Lt. H. Gillett, 2/Lt. P. Gardiner, 2/Lt. C. Rowan. (Left-right back) 2/Lt. Forbes, RCS, 2/Lt. Lefann, 2/Lt. B. F. Pontin, 2/Lt. Robins, 2/Lt. G. B. Hill, 2/Lt. R. Lorimer, 2/Lt. Dawson, 2/Lt. Brigstock, 2/Lt. James, RAOC, 2/Lt. Cowley, RAOC. (Dr Wilson)

(Left) The Archbishop of Canterbury attending an open-air church parade for the 64th Field Regt. RA on the lawns of Acrise Place, 23rd June (Dr Wilson)

55

Hurricane pilots of 245 Sqdn. and Intelligence officers at Hawkinge on 25th June. (Left-right back) P/O H. J. Smith (new Hawkinge IO), F/O Hamilton-Bowyer (IO of 245 Sqdn.), P/O G. Marsland, P/O G. L. Howitt, P/O A. L. Hedges. (Left-right front) P/O K. B. McGlashan, F/Lt. Priestly (outgoing Hawkinge IO), F/Lt. J. A. Thomson, P/O J. Redman, P/O G. E. Hill. (H. J. Smith)

squadrons. His stature had risen enormously the previous November when he had brought down a Dornier photographing Hawkinge, so scoring the first victory for the Biggin Hill station.

F/Lt. Thomson brought his patrol back to Hawkinge without loss, but stimulated after having had a brisk skirmish with Me 109s over the Channel. P/O Southwell had hit one which appeared to go down out of control. Whilst this was going on the 64th Field Regt. RA held an open air Church parade on the lawns of Acrise Place, their Padre, Captain H. D. Anderson, having surpassed himself by securing the services of His Grace the Archbishop of Canterbury. Afterwards there was sherry and a luncheon for the officers in honour of the Archbishop's visit.

The armed yacht *Campeador*, crewed by the four ancient mariners, which had patrolled the Channel incessantly, struck a mine and blew up. The loss of those gallant old chaps cast a gloom over the officers of the Portsmouth patrol.

24th June. Went to Lyminge about ration book. Folkestone warning. French and Italian armistice. Took Dash and Jock for a walk.

Now the trees were in their full glory and the cottage gardens fragrant with lavender. Creamy white elder blossom crowded thickly like cauliflower heads and, in secret places, clumps of viper's bugloss rivalled the sky.

The vicarage at Elham was substantial and, since the Army needed accommodation, the Vicar had let it be known he would take in some officers. Three 'nice gentlemen' had moved in, their batmen being billeted in nearby cottages. To most people it seemed certain that the Germans were coming and the Reverend Williams had decided he was going to stay and made it quite clear to all that, if necessary, he would suffer martyrdom. If the Germans came and mindless Huns wanted to stand him up against the wall of Elham Church and shoot him, that would be his destiny. He didn't know how long he'd got, but in the meantime, with the help of the officers in the vicarage, he'd see to it that the Huns didn't get at those fine burgundies and clarets in his wine cellar. In fact there were hundreds of bottles and he would have to start getting rid of them at once—that very night!

25th June. French ceased fighting 12.35 a.m. Miss Walton wrote offering her flat. Folkestone warning at night.

The Messerschmitts of JG 51 and JG 26, based in the Pas de Calais, were being formed into a hunting pack rather like the First World War circuses. Indeed the overall operational command of the combined force was given to 'Uncle' Theo Osterkamp, the First World War ace who was dubbed *Kanalkampfführer* (Channel Battle Leader). He was ordered to gain air superiority over the Straits of Dover and then stop British convoys using the Channel by attacking ships with a force of Dorniers and Stukas. Hitler was still hopeful that he would come to a peace settlement with Britain and wanted to avoid escalating the conflict. In any case it would take time to move the bulk of the Luftwaffe to the new airfields along the Channel coast and regroup the Army for an invasion.

Among the several First World War German aces on the Channel coast trying to resavour the flavours of aerial combat were General Major Von Dörning and Oberst. von Wedel. Both had flown with Baron Richthofen's JG Nr. I and, as such, were cronies of Reichsmarschall Göring and in a position to extract favours. Professor von Wedel, with a score of 13 victories, had pursued an academic life between the wars and obtained the appointment of Official Historian to the Luftwaffe. He had inveigled himself into being attached to JG 3 for the forthcoming battle and, in order to chronicle the exploits of the Luftwaffe, intended to pilot his personal Messerschmitt with a couple of youngsters detailed to protect him.

Among the German prisoners released by the French was the ace Werner Mölders who had made a rare mistake in aerial combat against a French Morane pilot on 6th June. This extraordinarily skilful pilot had already scored 14 victories in the Spanish Civil War and 25 kills against British and French planes. Promoted to Major, he joined JG 51 as air leader to put into practice his theories on aerial combat tactics, which proved to be devastatingly effective.

26th June. Showery in evening. Margaret put out cabbage plants. Landings on enemy coast.

There were no operational flights from Hawkinge on that day.

27th June. Alice came for week-end.

This was an important day for Fighter Command and from dawn there was considerable bustle at Hornchurch and Biggin Hill. His Majesty King George VI, accompanied by

Air Chief Marshal Sir Hugh Dowding, was to present some leading fighter pilots with their decorations.

At 8.35 a.m., 79 Sqdn. joined up with 32 Sqdn. to escort six Blenheims photographing German bases in France. They passed over Elham at 10.22 a.m. and two of the pilots, F/Lt. Davies and Sgt. Whitby, were scheduled to receive decorations at Biggin Hill after lunch. Two more Hurricane squadrons went up from Hawkinge on a similar mission but neither formation encountered any opposition over France.

Meanwhile, at an investiture at Hornchurch, five Spitfire pilots received decorations. S/Ldr. J. A. Leathart got the DSO and DFCs went to F/Lts. 'Sailor' Malan, Bob Stanford Tuck and Alan Deere and P/O Johnny Allen.

79 Sqdn. were coming home when just before noon they were assailed without warning by an unseen enemy. It was all over very quickly. Sgt. McQueen's Hurricane went down belching black smoke, but he was seen to parachute from it; another Hurricane dived straight into the sea, leaving a cascade of white spray. P/O Parker just caught a glimpse of a Me 109 after his Hurricane received a burst; he was the only British pilot to see an enemy aircraft. P/O Wood dropped down and circled the figure of McQueen, who was floating with his parachute still attached, while S/Ldr. Joslin hurried his squadron back to Hawkinge, where they landed at 12.05.

F/Lt. Haysom, a South African, P/Os Murray and Millington, F/Sgt. Brown and Sgt. Whitby were at the base. Joslin yelled for the bowsers to refuel him and rushed about trying to organize rescue boats before roaring off with Haysom to relieve Wood, who was alone over the Channel and almost out of fuel. The rest of the squadron returned to Biggin Hill where they found Parker, who had limped back with his shot-up machine.

At 12.50 p.m., an hour after McQueen fell in the Channel, the Dungeness lifeboat put out with a scratch crew because most of the regulars were away fishing. They searched in vain until two aircraft led them to a point 15 miles SSW of Dungeness where they found Sgt. McQueen unconscious. He was pulled on board and given artificial respiration, which continued for 20 minutes until a Royal Navy speedboat came alongside and took him to Dover. But he was dead.

By 3 p.m., S/Ldr. Joslin had landed at Biggin Hill, where WAAFs and airmen were parading in best uniforms. But it looked as if Jimmy Davies, the pilot who had scored Biggin Hill's first victory, wasn't going to make it. At 3.15, F/Lt. Michael Crossley was awarded a DFC, followed by P/Os Daw, Grice and Stones; Sgts. Cartwright and Whitby received DFMs. As each name was called, the self-conscious recipient marched smartly to the King, saluted and stood to attention while the citation was read out. The King then attached the decoration to the man's tunic.

At the end of the ceremony, F/Lt. Davies' Cross remained on the velvet cushion and was carried away reverently, to be put into the adjutant's safe. The King listened sympathetically to all the details of 79 Sqdn.'s recent encounter and was shown the battle-damaged Hurricane by P/O Parker. Before leaving, the King spoke to S/Ldr. Joslin, offering his condolences for the squadron's bad luck.

28th June. Russia seized Bessarabia.
Rumours about spies were rife all over Britain. A Hurricane pilot returning to Hawkinge

(Above) Morning, 27th June: five Spitfire pilots, who have just received decorations from King George VI at Hornchurch, take part in the formal cheering. (Left-right) P/O Johnny Allen (killed 27 days later), F/Lt. Robert Stanford Tuck, F/Lt. Al Deere, F/Lt. 'Sailor' Malan, S/Ldr. 'Prof' Leathart. (Imperial War Museum) (Below) F/Lt. Michael Crossley receiving his first DFC from the King on 27th June. The five other pilots awaiting their decorations are P/Os V. G. Daw and Douglas Grice of 32 Sqdn., followed by P/O Stones and Sgts Cartwright and Whitby of 79 Sqdn.

from a dusk patrol reported seeing a bright light flashing from the cliffside residential area of Folkestone. P/O H. J. Smith, the Intelligence Officer, who had only been in the RAF a month, got the pilot to take him up in the station Tiger Moth to investigate, but nothing was seen. It was the first time the IO had been up in an aircraft.

29th June. Alice got rooms from Monday at Mrs Savage.
Twenty-year-old AC2 Clifford Vincent arrived on the south coast with an RAF party posted to Hawkinge. 'I recall that I was picked up at a railway station and the RAF driver couldn't find his way because all the place names and road signs had just been taken down.' Eventually Vincent was taken to a little hutted camp at West Cliff for duties at the radar station on the cliffs above Dover. He only knew it as 21 AMES and never really understood its importance.

30th June
Sunday. The Local Defence Volunteers were growing in strength (Reverend Williams had joined their ranks), but the combined fire power of the Elham Platoon would hardly have stopped a charging bull. They had been given fawn armbands with the initials LDV printed in black and were meeting one or two nights a week and on Sunday mornings, when a Regular Army sergeant major came to drill and instruct them. It seemed that field-craft and actually shooting at Germans was of less importance than stamping feet and getting into straight lines. However, it was going to be difficult when harvesting started because most of the men worked on the land and when you started harvesting, you didn't stop.

1st July. Heard from Miss Melles that her young man was missing.
S/Ldr. E. W. Whitley, the New Zealand CO of 245 Sqdn., was told to take the squadron north. Their place was to be taken by the aggressive S/Ldr. John Joslin with 79 Sqdn., who had a score to settle with JG 51.

During the day the King visited Dymchurch and Folkestone, where he inspected Army units. He probably didn't realize that if the Germans had landed in any strength with armoured vehicles, there was nothing available to dislodge them. The 2nd Armoured Division in Northamptonshire had less than 200 frail tanks and the 1st Armoured Division had returned from France with nine tanks, leaving 617 behind.

2nd July. Miss Park's medal given.
The Post Office Service Medal was presented to Miss Park by Edward Smith on behalf of the Postmaster-General.

By noon 79 Sqdn. had 12 Hurricanes sitting on the grass at Hawkinge, their ground staff having arrived by road. They were now almost within sight of JG 51's foreward base just across the Channel.

3rd July. AA fire in morning. Saw a Nazi bomber shot at over Running Hill at 3.55. Then fighter attacked one over Square. SS Andora Star sunk with aliens on board. Margaret and Alice in Canterbury shelters. Sharp storm at 7 p.m.

Hawkinge reported: *Dull early, slight rain, cloud 10/10 clearing to fine with thick cloud 2000 ft. in large patches.*

For the first time German bombers started penetrating inland on armed reconnaissance missions and, by using cloud cover, some reached the London area. There was tremendous excitement at Hawkinge when a Dornier appeared between some big cumulus clouds and only narrowly escaped six Spitfires. S/Ldr. Joslin was constantly taking off and landing and, on one sortie with F/Sgt. Brown, he sighted a Dornier, but only as it disappeared into cloud.

For 79 Sqdn., the nastiness of the previous week hadn't affected their morale and they were confident that, if the Messerschmitts had stayed to fight, they would have quickly evened the score. Tankards of ale were constantly being refilled in the officers' mess that night and there was horse-play amongst the boisterous pilots. Someone started to sing about O'Riley's Daughter and there were several choruses before the bar was closed.

4th July. Burst of gunfire and siren here for about $\frac{1}{4}$ hour in morning. Announcement of capture of French Fleet. Mr Backhouse's Sale. He came to supper and brought some eggs.

Although 79 Sqdn. were resident at Hawkinge, various other squadrons started to use it as a forward base. Just after lunch, S/Ldr. Joslin took eight Hurricanes up to investigate a plot approaching a convoy off Deal and arrived just in time to engage a dozen Dorniers. Flying amongst the puffs of bursting AA shells, with Sgt. Whitby he rushed in behind the raiders and fired burst after burst with no apparent effect, until Messerschmitts came darting in behind the Hurricanes. F/Sgt. Brown, who was attacking a Dornier, had to break off to evade three 109s and managed to fire at two others as he twisted and turned in the mêleé. At one point, he saw P/O Parker's fighter with a 109 glued to its tail and was successful in making the enemy aircraft detach itself. P/O D. Stones, DFC, had a huge hole blown out of a wing where a cannon shell exploded. Sgt. Cartwright, a DFM recipient, failed to return and the Army reported seeing a plane go smack into the sea off St Margaret's Bay. P/Os Clift, Millington and Mitchell landed without having fired their guns. After refuelling, 79 Sqdn. patrolled a convoy off Folkestone.

By evening there was still no news of Cartwright and his chum, F/Sgt. Brown, took off at 6 p.m. to search the sea for him, returning an hour later. Whilst he had been droning about off Dover, six Me 109s streaked out of clouds at 8,000 ft off Deal and attacked a section from 32 Sqdn. P/O Rupert Smythe saw one get on the tail of P/O Grice, DFC, and slanting in behind it let go two short bursts from 250 yds. The 109 streamed glycol and winged over. Smythe couldn't observe what happened to it because he had to keep turning to fend off another attacking 109. His Hurricane out-turned his assailant easily and, when the enemy fighter broke off to fly out to sea, Smythe went after it and opened fire, causing the 109 to tumble into the sea with a gigantic splash and welter of foam. Smythe circled for several minutes, but there was no sign of the pilot coming to the surface. Soon after this, a Hurricane put down at Hawkinge with the fabric blasted off its rudder. Nineteen-year-old P/O Keith Gillman climbed out hooting with laughter when he saw the damage.

All along the French coast the Messerschmitts were massing and young proven

32 Sqdn. pilots at Hawkinge. (Left-right) P/O Smythe, P/O Procter, P/O Gillman, F/Lt. Brothers, P/O Gardner, P/O Grice, P/O Eckford. (Fox)

fighter pilots were being promoted to become air leaders. They listened with respect to the advice of Werner 'Daddy' Mölders, who reasoned that, since the Hurricanes and Spitfires could out-turn their Messerschmitts, it was highly dangerous to get involved in a tail chase with them. The answer was to use the 109's faster diving speed and rate of climb to come down on the 'Tommies' fast, and then get away to climb above them again.

That evening in the dining room at Elham vicarage the air was heavy with the smoke from good cigars. A few lucky Army officers and their beaming host, mellowed by the full, round flavour of some excellent Châteauneuf du Pape, were refilling their glasses as the port decanter circulated. In the kitchens the batmen were being entertained by the household staff.

5th July. Two bangs at 6 a.m. as Nazi plane was brought down just off Hythe.
There was rain in the morning, but it brightened later. Soon after dawn, Hornchurch

Spitfires got a Heinkel bomber just off the coast. The crew swam ashore, were captured and taken to Hawkinge for interrogation. S/Ldr. Joslin was furious at having missed this chance and had sections from 79 Sqdn. on patrol all day.

The Hawkinge 'Parachute and Cable' defence system was fired accidentally. The big Schermuly rockets rose into the air, pulling up thin steel cables until, at 600 ft, small parachutes opened to suspend a screen of cables in the path of low-flying aircraft. Some of the projectiles shot off in the wrong direction, entangling wires and jerking others back to earth, where they fizzed about across the ground. From a distance, the falling parachutes looked like a miniature airborne assault and caused some alarm in Dover and Folkestone.

Late in the evening a battle-damaged Spitfire came in from over the sea and made an emergency landing at Hawkinge. The pilot, Sub-Lieutenant Francis Dawson-Paul, was a naval officer attached to 65 Sqdn. He had been on a high-flying sortie over the French coast with two other Spitfires when they were savaged by Messerschmitts. P/O Milne had been killed, but he thought the other Spitfire had escaped.

6th July. Banging at 5.30 a.m. Plane brought down off coast. Barbed wire being laid in fields.

Without any sirens having been sounded, a raider bombed Folkestone in the early morning, wrecking the Sanatorium, demolishing a house and damaging 259 other dwellings. S/Ldr. Joslin had his Hurricanes up and down all day, but there were no enemy planes about.

7th July. Mrs Bragg came to tea. I went to tea with Uncle. Distant AA fire at 9 p.m. Masses of planes overhead and were in cellar for $\frac{1}{2}$ hr.

Edith Bragg had come to Elham as the bride of Corporal Kenneth Bragg of the Queen's Westminsters and obtained lodgings at Mill House.

The weather was fine that Sunday and at 10 a.m. three Spitfires from Manston rushed to intercept a lone Heinkel off Deal and were bounced by 109s that came from out of the sun. F/O Desmond MacMullen was the only survivor.

During the evening a big formation of Dorniers went for a convoy travelling eastwards up the Channel and Messerschmitts fanned out across the coast of Kent to protect them. 65 Sqdn. from Hornchurch were the first to contact the 109s and a section of three Spitfires was shot down without the pilots ever knowing what happened to them. F/O Proudman, P/O Brisbane and Sgt. Hayes disappeared into the sea.

At 9 p.m., 79 Sqdn. went roaring off from Hawkinge to patrol Dover without their passionately keen CO. However, S/Ldr. Joslin immediately dropped his administrative tasks and ran to his Hurricane so as to join them. Minutes later Reginald Foster of the *Daily Herald* witnesses the first fighter combat to take place over Britain:

They were quite low, and we realized unpleasantly, this was the Kill. There was a burst of machine-gun fire and an augur-like glow appeared in the body of the Messerschmitt. The glow spread to a flame and the machine rocketed to earth in a shroud of smoke and flame. The whole terrible drama lasted less than a minute. I have seen scores of machines, both

(Left) Pilots of 74 'Tiger' Sqdn. at Rochford. (Left-right seated) P/O Bertie Aubert, S/Ldr. F. L. White, P/O Dowding (son of C-in-C Fighter Command), F/O 'Tink' Measures, F/O Sammy Hoare. (Left-right standing) P/O Cobden, F/Lt. Paddy Treacy, W/O 'Tubby' Mayne, F/Sgt. Llewellyn, F/O John Mungo-Park, P/O Johnny Freeborn, and Sgt. Tony Mould, who brought down Lt. Böhm's Me 109 at Elham. (Right) A bemused Johann Böhm being invited to 'quick march' between an escort (consisting of Pte. R. W. Miles, Prov. Sgt. W. F. Waterman and Piper W. MacDougall) from the London Scottish at Broome Park. (Brenzett Aeronautical Museum)

enemy and British, destroyed since, but few incidents have given me such a shock as this first close-up view of death in the air.

What the reporter actually saw was John Joslin's Hurricane being shot out of the sky by an Me 109 over Chilverton Elms, just east of Folkestone.

F/Lt. Haysom took command of the bereaved squadron, who couldn't understand how it had happened—not one of them had seen an enemy aircraft. S/Ldr. Joslin's remains were buried at Buckden. He was 24 years old and a married man.

8th July. Shell bursts over Adam & Eve just before 4 p.m. Then Messerschmitt fell at Bladbean. Little boy of 18 in it, slightly wounded in head, but otherwise all right.

The Hawkinge Hurricanes flew two patrols during the morning and, after lunch, they intercepted a Blenheim over Rye, which fired incorrect recognition flares. However, when it lowered its undercarriage, they refrained from attacking and followed until it landed at Manston.

Just before 4 p.m., machine-gun fire rang out high above Elham valley and the sounds of straining engines could be heard. Then two planes were down low banking and turning over the Downs. The chase went on, with an occasional ripping burst of fire that echoed around the hills. To observers, the little plane in front with square cut wing-tips looked different; the raucous note of its engine had a snarl and, seen in profile, its mottled fuselage made it look like some kind of fish. It was pursued by another beautifully shaped aircraft that was unmistakably a Spitfire. Then one was down.

It had belly-landed hard onto the crest of Bladbean Hill, broken its back and slithered over the grass, chopping up a few sheep before it came to a stop with propeller blades gracefully curled back. It was the first Messerschmitt down in Britain. An hour after the fight, Sgt. E. A. Mould of 74 Sqdn. was writing out a form 'F' (combat report) at Hornchurch:

I was Red Leader of 'A' Flight No. 74 Sqdn., with No. 2 of Blue Section also in company. The four of us were on interception patrol over Dover when I sighted four Me 109s flying in line astern on my starboard beam. I gave the order 'Line astern' and turned to starboard climbing up under the tail of the rear Me 109. I gave him a short 30° deflection shot and he immediately half-rolled and dived to ground level followed by Red 2.

In trying to follow him I blacked myself out and lost sight of him, but I saw another Me 109 also flying at low level so I dived on him from about 3,000 ft. He immediately dived to ground level and used evasive tactics by flying along the valleys behind Dover and Folkestone, which only allowed me to fire short deflection bursts at him. After two of these bursts smoke or vapour came from the radiator beneath his port wing and other bursts appeared to enter the fuselage. He eventually landed with his wheels up as I fired my last burst at him in a field near Elham. The pilot was apparently uninjured and I circled round him till he was taken prisoner.

This Messerschmitt on Bladbean Hill overlooking Elham valley was the first German fighter shot down over Britain (Thomson)

Whilst this action was being fought, most civilians in Elham took shelter in cellars or under stairs and the first positive information was brought to the post office by Jack Barber, the postman, who had been near the plane when it came down. He had seen a boyish-looking German, Lt. Johann Böhm, taken prisoner by troops. Böhm was slightly dazed from a knock on the head, and even more bewildered when his kilted guards expected him to march in step with them.

That evening 81-year-old George Palmer was taken up to see the plane on Bladbean, where Walter Keeler at Hillhouse Farm was bemoaning the loss of his ten ewes. Soldiers had cordoned off the aircraft from a large group of sightseers, but old George, genial but obstinate, lifted the cordon and went forward, seemingly unaware of the shouting and gesticulating guards. After peering into the plane and prodding it with his stick, he went off with Farmer Keeler to help him round up the rest of his sheep that were still wandering about the field.

The little grey-green camouflaged fighter had a shield painted on the fuselage bearing a crying bird with an umbrella tucked under its wing and Intelligence Officers soon established that it belonged to JG 51. Another Messerschmitt was found crumpled in a crater at Sandwich and two more had fallen into the sea.

On the debit side, S/Ldr. Desmond Cooke, CO of the Spitfire squadron that had lost three pilots on the previous day, went on his last flight. Messerschmitts blasted him out of the sky off Dover. He was due to hand over command of 65 Sqdn. that very day and should have been rested earlier. A little earlier, P/O Raven of 610 Sqdn., now operating from Hawkinge during the day, ditched off Dover after being hit by a Dornier's rear gunner. He drowned before he could be rescued.

To make matters worse, 79 Sqdn. hadn't avenged the death of S/Ldr. Joslin and, when on patrol over Dover, another lightning attack had come out of the sun and dispatched P/O Wood and F/O Mitchell. Wood was able to get out of his blazing plane and parachute into the sea, but was terribly burned and already dead when a boat reached him. Mitchell's Hurricane went into the ground at Temple Ewell, where the crater burned for well over an hour and no positive identification could be made until armourers had checked the numbers stamped on the twisted machine-guns.

Folkestone suffered its first death when Elsie Howland was killed as stray bullets lashed Bournemouth Road.

9th July. Trail of white smoke from invisible plane about 11.40. Three cracks of AA fire. Saw the Messerschmitt brought (down street) by RAF in evening.
Low cloud broke up soon after dawn. The contrail that Mary Smith saw was 30,000 ft up and probably made by one of a few Junkers 86 Ps that were specially adapted for high-altitude reconnaissance flights. Because they could fly so high, nothing could be done to stop them and they were immune from interception by British fighters.

79 Sqdn., now visibly fatigued from constant patrolling, were pulled out of the front line. However, they did have a final skirmish with JG 51 at 3.45 p.m. P/O Millington encountered a lone 109 at 18,000 ft and saw it fall away after discharging a burst at it. P/O Donald Stones, DFC, chased another across the Channel and had the satisfaction of seeing voluminous smoke pouring from it as it crossed the French coast. When he

landed at 4.20 p.m., Bombay transport aircraft were being loaded with his squadron's equipment and the ground crew were ready to leave.

Some newcomers entered the lists this day, when twin-engined Messerschmitt 110s of the 'Horst Wessel' Zerstörergeschwader battled with Hurricanes and Spitfires over the Channel. 43 Sqdn. came along the coast from Tangmere well over their sector boundary to engage the 110s; they claimed several shot down. Unfortunately, their CO caught a salvo of cannon shells, was blinded in one eye and had to bale out over Westgate.

Following this action, a big white Heinkel seaplane came lumbering over the Channel intent on rescuing German airmen who were in the water. The British Government had decided that these ambulance planes were unacceptable when operating over convoys or in the vicinity of the British coast and had issued instructions for them to be fired upon. The RAF had shot a similar plane down off Hartlepool the previous week, so despite the fact that the Heinkel had red crosses painted on its wings, the Luftwaffe gave it an escort of Messerschmitts. 'A' Flight from 54 Sqdn. intercepted the seaplane and P/O Johnny Allen brought it down, whilst F/Lt. 'Al' Deere, a rugged New Zealander, kept the whole fighter escort occupied with his section of three Spitfires.

In the ensuing combat, 54 Sqdn. lost two Spitfires, P/Os Garton and Evershed both being killed. The end for Tony Evershed was particularly harrowing. His Spitfire was set alight and chased by a bunch of Messerschmitts that were using him for target practice. His companions were all hard-pressed and could only listen helplessly as, just before the end, his fervent pleas for help turned into hysterical screams.

Deere was chased by two 109s, which he shook off by heaving his Spitfire up into a spiralling turn. He then had the alarming experience of making a head-on attack on a lone Messerschmitt, the pilot of which was just as determined as he. The planes flashed past each other and there was a bang as they struck. The New Zealander, unable to bale out because of a jammed cockpit cover, glided the burning machine down to crash-land at Manston and burst his way out through the perspex hood.

The German ambulance plane was towed ashore and Lt. Vedder and his crew were captured.

10th July. Machine gun fire at 11.15 a.m. More of above and AA fire at 2—fierce battle over Channel. Roar of planes overhead. Joan came to dinner and tea.
After 1940, the Air Ministry decided that the historical period of the Battle of Britain should be defined as running from the 10th July 1940 until the 31st October 1940. Only those pilots and aircrews who had flown at least one sortie with a squadron under the operational control of Fighter Command were deemed to have taken part in the Battle. Thus many Coastal Command aircrews were included, but pilots such as S/Ldr. J. C. D. Joslin were excluded.

Hawkinge reported: *Weather—fine. Station Commander prepared to hand over command to S/Ldr. H. B. Hurley and together inspected outstations at Rye and Fairlight. The funeral of P/O Wood of 79 Sqdn. was carried out by the Station.*

The first skirmishes were off North Foreland at 11 a.m. when six Spitfires of 74 Sqdn. engaged 20 Me 109s escorting a lone Dornier. F/Lt. Freeborn singled out a 109 that he thought was the leader, but the pilot was probably Uffz. Stocker of JG 51, and opened fire at 300 yards, closing to 50 yards. Bursts from his eight Brownings perforated the German plane until it dropped into the Estuary, but Freeborn and Sgt. Mould both returned with their aircraft shot up. 610 Sqdn. also got involved and S/Ldr. Andrew 'Big Bill' Smith crashed his damaged Spitfire (L1000) when landing at Hawkinge. He was to die attempting exactly the same thing in 15 days' time.

The main action didn't start until 1.40 p.m. when Dorniers of Kampfgeschwader 2, led by Major Adolf Fuchs, attacked a convoy off Dover. Their intention was to lure the British fighters out to sea where German fighters could destroy them by superior numbers. The operation was planned by Oberst. Fink and Generalmajor Osterkamp and entailed the 109s of III Gruppe JG 51, led by Hptm. Hannes Trautloft, flying above and behind the Dorniers whilst 30 'Horst Wessel' Me 110s, led by the one-legged Oberst. Huth, shadowed the entire operation from a high altitude.

32 Sqdn. intercepted the Dorniers first, but few engaged the enemy because they became separated and missed the bombers in some low cloud. British warships and the Dover guns opened up, patterning the sky with bursting shells, whilst 'Treble One' Sqdn. from Croydon went straight into the shell bursts and made firing passes at the raiders. In the fearsome battle, F/O T. P. K. Higgs made an error of judgement and collided with a Dornier flown by Fw. Umkelmann. It happened so quickly that the survivors of the crew thought they had been hit by an AA shell, but the crew of another Dornier photographed Higgs' faltering Hurricane with a wing torn off, seconds before it fell like a stone.

Numbers 56, 64 and 74 Sqdns. joined the battle and Obfw. Willi Meyer's Me 110 went into the sea. Rescue boats put out and the Dungeness lifeboat was launched again. Sgt. Carnall brought a damaged Hurricane down to skim across the grass at Hawkinge on its belly, whilst P/O Donald Cobden, a New Zealander who had played rugby for the 'All Blacks', crash-landed on Lympne aerodrome.

At 7.00 p.m., when old Etonian P/O Basil Fisher was on patrol, he was attacked by a Spitfire of 54 Sqdn. over Hawkinge. Bullets ripped through his tailplane and petrol tank, but his Hurricane didn't catch fire. He wouldn't be so lucky in a month's time.

On that day, the Elham village school had electric lighting installed.

11th July. Wrote to Mrs Comber. Picked up first fallen apples.
Hitler received from Admiral Raeder a feasibility study on the possibilities and requirements for an invasion of Britain. The report advised the Führer that no invasion fleet should, or could, venture into the Channel until the Luftwaffe had destroyed the RAF and had driven the British naval forces out of the area. Hitler agreed that this course of action was vital and Göring was complacently confident that he could clear the way for invasion with the utmost speed. However, the Führer still persisted in his hopes that the British would see the hopelessness of their situation and accept his terms for surrender. He was even prepared to offer the British better terms than the Dutch, French and Belgians had received.

Special emergency powers had come into operation throughout Britain and half of Arthur Wootten's garage business was requisitioned. There were armed guards on his petrol pumps in Elham High Street and vehicles of the 1st London Division came from miles around to draw fuel from his garage. However, since Army standing orders instructed drivers to top up fuel tanks before parking for the night, massive queues formed every evening. Because of this, canny drivers started arriving in the afternoon to beat the rush, which only resulted in the queue forming at three o'clock in the afternoon.

Arthur stood scratching his head and staring disapprovingly at the line of camouflaged vehicles, rumbling trucks, bren-gun carriers and gun tractors stretching nose to tail out of the village for about a mile. Something had to be done: every vehicle was wasting petrol in trying to reach the pumps and, more alarmingly, they made a magnificent target for German bombers. He appealed to the fresh-faced 2nd Lieutenant in charge, who explained that the job of Petrol Officer was always given to the most junior subaltern; besides, he'd only just arrived and was trying to cope as best he could. When he ordered some drivers away with instructions to return in the evening, they just drove off and motored around the countryside—wasting more precious fuel.

Most of the fighting that day was confined to Hampshire and Dorset.

12th July. Showery, windy and cool. Corporal and Mrs Bragg called. Some drunken soldiers smashed Annie's window.

S/Ldr. H. B. Hurley took over as Station Commander at Hawkinge and a conference was held to discuss the defence of the aerodrome. The remains of F/O E. W. Mitchell, which had now been excavated from the ground, were buried with full honours next to his companion, P/O Wood.

The smashed window incident of Mary's diary took place next door to King-post, the soldiers having been into the King's Arms in Elham Square.

13th July. Mr Eden came in to phone in evening. Raid warning 6–9 but nothing to hear.

Stukas attacked a convoy off Dover in the afternoon and two Hurricanes were shot down into the sea by JG 51. During the evening Spitfires engaged in a dog-fight with the 109s across the Channel; several were claimed and Lt. Lange was the only man missing. The ever-ready Dover gunners blasted away at dog-fighting Spitfires and Messerschmitts and an angry sergeant pilot from Kenley just managed to belly-land his fighter at Hawkinge, having been hit by shrapnel.

Mary Smith was leaning out of an upstairs window at King-post that evening, listening because an air raid alert was still on. To her great excitement, she saw a tall, good-looking man, in grey flannels and white tennis shoes, stride down St Mary's Road and walk straight into the post office right below her. She recognized him from his photographs; it was the Rt. Hon. Anthony Eden, Secretary of State for War, and Churchill's right-hand man. There had been rumours for some time that the Edens were staying at Park Gate, a lovely old half-timbered house in the hills just above Elham.

With great politeness he asked to use the telephone, explaining that it was an important call to London. For once Mary's father was confused about his duties. Should he be in attendance at the switchboard? Or perhaps the conversation concerned 'Affairs of State', which were not intended for his ears? Eden, looking every bit the old Etonian dressed for leisure, at once put the Smiths at their ease and carried on a telephone conversation, which Mr Smith assiduously closed his ears to.

14th July. Bursts of AA fire at 3.45. Battle over Straits. Mrs Bragg and Margaret were in Standard Hill Wood. Churchill spoke at night.

Sunday. A Hurricane crashed when trying to take off from Hawkinge, but the pilot was unhurt. When Stukas attacked a convoy, Hawkinge sent 610 and 615 Sqdns., which had brought their Hurricanes down from Kenley, and a spirited action took place in which a Stuka and an Me 109 of JG 3 were destroyed. 615 Sqdn. lost P/O Mudie, who was rescued after abandoning his blazing Hurricane, but died of his burns the next day. During the convoy attack, several ships were damaged and a destroyer hit.

15th July. It rained nearly all day.

It was St Swithun's Day and the farming people shook their heads sadly, recalling the old adage: 'St Swithun's Day, if it do rain, for forty days it will remain.' In the orchards the apples were swelling, but folk weren't able to emulate their West Country cousins, who, by tradition, always aspired to have apple dumplings on St Swithun's Day.

There was very little aerial activity because of bad weather, but Hurricanes of 56 Sqdn. encountered a formation of Dorniers that slipped under low cloud in an attempt to bomb shipping.

Anthony Eden, Secretary of State for War, visiting a Home Guard unit that had just been issued with a .300 Browning automatic rifle. (Imperial War Museum)

16th July

Fog and low cloud had spread over northern France and the UK and the curtailment of activity was just what Fighter Command needed in order to build up its fighter strength and train new pilots to replace the recent serious losses suffered over France.

Hitler issued War Directive No 16:

As England in spite of her hopeless military situation has so far shown herself unwilling to come to any compromise, I have decided to prepare, and if necessary to carry out, the invasion of England. This operation is dictated by the necessity of eliminating Great Britain as a base from which war against Germany can be continued, and if necessary the island will be occupied . . . I therefore issue the following orders :

1. The landing operation must be a surprise crossing on a broad front extending approximately from Ramsgate to a point west of the Isle of Wight . . . the preparations . . . must be concluded by the middle of August.

2. The following preparations must be undertaken to make a landing in England possible.

a) The RAF must be eliminated to such an extent that it will be incapable of putting up any substantial opposition to the invading troops.

Spitfires of 610 Sqdn. patrolling over Kent. F/Lt. Ellis is flying 'O' (R6595) in which P/O Webster was killed on 26 August; Sgt. Arnfield, a New Zealander, is in 'K' (P9495), which was destroyed by an Me 109 on 12th August. (Imperial War Museum)

71

LAC Bill Green from Bristol made the rare step from mechanic to fighter pilot with 501 (County of Gloucester) Sqdn.

b) *The sea routes must be cleared of mines.*
c) *Both flanks, the Straits of Dover and the Western approaches to the Channel . . . must be so heavily mined as to be completely inaccessible.*
d) *Heavy coastal guns must dominate and protect the entire coastal front area.*
3. *The invasion will be referred to by the code-name 'Sealion'.*

17th July. Margaret and Mrs Bragg went to Canterbury and saw a film called 'Contraband'.

Most local restaurants were functioning normally and it was quite common to see Army officers unbuckling their revolvers and placing them under their chairs before starting the meal. A satisfying three course lunch could be had for as little as 1s 6d (7½p)—an ice-cream dessert costing 2½d extra.

Single raiders flew in using cloud cover and there were some casualties. A woman and two children were killed when Ashford railway yards were bombed. More and more Luftwaffe units were reaching operational status in France.

At a football stadium in Uxbridge, Bill Green, an ex-flight mechanic—shortish, pugnacious and bearing a strong likeness to the film actor James Cagney—started a short crisp RT procedure course. On paper he was unique—an LAC fighter pilot of 501 Sqdn. who had never flown a modern combat aircraft. But he was learning quickly and was destined to visit Elham.

The stadium dressing room was used as a classroom and, after lectures and practical exercises, the class filed out onto the football pitch, which had been marked off with lots of whitewash lines and had nothing to do with soccer. A controller sat in a box above the arena and there were even plotters to simulate an operations room.

The amazed pupils were mounted on Walls' ice-cream salesmen's tricycles which had TR9 radios in the ice-boxes! Then, donning flying helmets with head-sets, they had to pedal off in threes, pretending to be a section of fighters, listening and relaying instructions. They even practised interceptions, attacking a tricycle representing a fleet of hostile aircraft.

18th July. Fine—Mrs Comber's birthday—cool and showery.

HRH the Duke of Kent visited Hawkinge by plane, piloted by Wing Commander Fielden. 610 Sqdn. Spitfires circled and flew off on Channel patrol, but returned without P/O Litchfield. Hptm. Horst 'Jakob' Tietzen, the Staffelführer of 5/JG 51 and a contemporary and disciple of Werner Mölders, had just made another classic kill using his 20 mm shell guns.

19th July. Raids round about and a lot of buzzing at 1 & 4 p.m. Aunt Beauch brought Miss Gibson to see the house. Hitler spoke in the Reichstag.

A fine morning and, before the dew was dry, 12 Defiant two-seaters had arrived from West Malling and were at readiness at Hawkinge. The Defiant was a controversial type of fighter, being a slim monoplane with all its guns mounted in a power-operated turret behind the pilot. The turret and gunner imposed a burden that made the plane considerably slower than a Hurricane and a lot slower than a Messerschmitt. These

belonged to 141 Sqdn., which had never been in action, and every plane was resplendent with a cockerel emblem painted on its side and bearing such names as 'Cock o' the North', 'Cock-a-hoop', 'Cocksure', 'Cocked for Firing', etc. At 12.30 p.m. they were sent up on patrol, but only nine took off; two had spluttering engines and one wouldn't start. They were the lucky ones.

Hptm. Hannes Trautloft, leading a Gruppe of JG 51, spotted the glint of perspex and dark silhouette of the tight formation against the silver-grey sea and his first lightning attack scattered the nine Defiants in all directions. It was then easy for the Germans to pick a target and attack from below or head-on, knowing that the British planes couldn't fire back. When the Defiant pilots banked and turned their aircraft to give their gunners a chance to fire, they presented the Messerschmitts with a better target to rake with incendiary bullets and cannon shells. It was over very quickly.

P/O H. J. Smith, the Station Intelligence Officer, had come out of the timber watch office to see the two-seaters away. It was very clear and the coast of France was plainly visible.

I kept them in view in my binoculars and when they were about two-thirds of the way across, I saw them bounced by the 109s. They had absolutely no chance against the German fighters and I watched horrified as they were picked off one by one and I saw the spouts of water as they plunged into the sea.

73

To some other witnesses on the cliffs, including pressmen, it looked as if the RAF were punishing an enemy formation—four planes were seen to fall trailing smoke, whilst another, well alight, just made it to Dover where it crashed, killing F/Lt. Donald. His Rhodesian gunner, P/O 'Arch' Hamilton, had extricated himself from the turret, but was drowned when he fell into the sea. F/Lt. Loudon, although wounded, brought his spluttering machine back after telling his gunner, P/O Farnes, to bale out; but the engine cut and he crashed at Hawkinge. P/O MacDougall also managed to return, gingerly putting his shot-up Defiant down on the grass. The turret was empty; his gunner, Sgt. Wise, had been able to get out. P/O Hugh Tamblyne, a Canadian, had his Defiant chased by two 109s east of Dover and was rescued from mortal danger by two Spitfires flown by the redoubtable 'Sailor' Malan and P/O Stevenson. 111 Sqdn., at readiness at Hawkinge, had to scramble to prevent a total annihilation.

Only one gunner, P/O Farnes, and one pilot, P/O Gardner, were rescued from the sea. When hit, the Defiant pilots tried to stay at the controls long enough to give their gunners time to revolve the turret to one side and wriggle out of a small opening in the back of the turret. It was extremely difficult and clothing and harness contrived to snag on any projections. If the traversing mechanism was hit, the gunner was virtually doomed. To make matters worse, a special black flying-suit had been designed for Defiant crews. It looked smart and efficient with lots of pockets, zippers and loose trousers gathered in at the ankles. Unfortunately, if the wearer fell in the sea it trapped air and kept him afloat—with his head under the water.

S/Ldr. William Richardson, the CO of 141, was summoned to Group HQ to explain what had gone wrong, and with ten dead and two in hospital it was decided to send the squadron back to the north again. New combat techniques were obviously needed to exploit the advantages of the turret fighter. Some wondered just what these 'advantages' were, but there were those in the 'corridors of power' who, remembering the Bristol fighters of the First World War, argued that in those days a good pilot/gunner combination had been a match for the German single-seaters.

All along the south coast convoys came under attack and ten RAF fighters were destroyed and others put out of action from battle damage. At this time the British insisted on keeping the Channel open to shipping and sent escorted convoys through, made up of various colliers, trawlers and old tramp steamers.

20th July. Swoop of machine-gun fire almost overhead at 6.30 p.m. The plane crashed at Denton. Saw pilot descend by parachute over Adam & Eve. Dash had a bit of dysentery. Mrs Bragg and Alice here.
A large convoy entered the Channel in the evening and fierce fighting took place. Only a section of three Hurricanes from 32 Sqdn. were patrolling the convoy when German dive-bombers struck and they were powerless to prevent the accurate bombing that followed. The Hurricanes went straight into the Stukas, but were chased all over the sky by the escorting Me 109s and 110s. S/Ldr. 'Baron' Worrall, CO of 32 Sqdn., with only one section of Hurricanes, tore out over the coast from Hawkinge to help in the unequal conflict, but could do little more than brief feint attacks at Stukas in between avoiding 109s that were getting in each other's way.

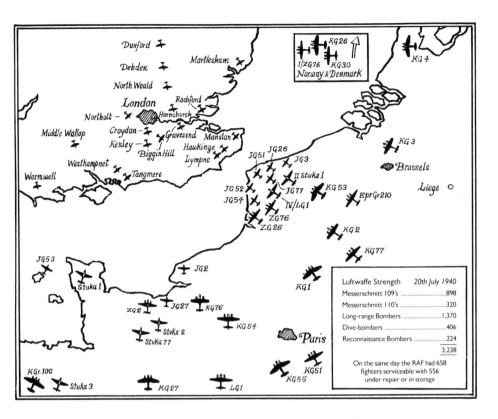

The map contains the following labels:

Duxford, Debden, North Weald, Marllesham, London, Rochford, Northolt, Hornchurch, Middle Wallop, Croydon, Gravesend, Manslon, Kenley, HawKinge, Biggin Hill, Lympne, Westhampnet, Tangmere, Warmwell, JG51, JG26, JG3, II Stuka 1, JG52, JG77, KG53, EprGr210, JG54, IV/LG1, ZG76, ZG26, KG2, KG77, JG53, JG2, KG1, Stuka 1, ZG2, JG27, KG76, KG54, Stuka 2, Stuka 77, Paris, KGr.100, Stuka 3, KG27, LG1, KG51, KG55

KG26, I/ZG76 KG30, Norway & Denmark, KG4, KG 3, Brussels, Liege

Luftwaffe Strength	20th July 1940
Messerschmitt 109's	898
Messerschmitt 110's	320
Long-range Bombers	1,370
Dive-bombers	406
Reconnaissance Bombers	224
	3,238

On the same day the RAF had 658
fighters serviceable with 556
under repair or in storage

Sub-Lieutenant G. G. R. Bulmer, RN, on loan from the Fleet Air Arm, was nailed by a 109 and sent into the sea; Sgt. W. B. Higgins was also hit, but managed to keep control and head back to Hawkinge. 'Baron' Worrall attacked two Stukas in succession but had to break off when a 110 attacked him. Evading the 110, he sighted Stukas dive-bombing a destroyer and closed on them as they made for home, hitting the nearest and making it smoke. Then he had to break off again because of an approaching 109, but shaking this off, he repeated the process. However, the next time an Me 109 got its sights on him, bullets entered his fuselage and smacked into the armour plate behind his seat. Then a couple of cannon shells hit, one in the engine and one in the gravity tank. Worrall banked the plane and steered for Hawkinge, gaining a little height just before the engine petered out. It was N5232 (his favourite Hurricane) and, rather than abandon it, he tried to glide in over Capel to reach the aerodrome. Unfortunately it came down just short and he crash-landed in a field banging his head against the gun sight. Streaming with blood, the blaspheming CO just had time to get out before the punctured Hurricane caught fire and was consumed.

P/O Procter, with a 109 on his tail, roared in low towards Folkestone, the German only breaking off when the Hurricane zoomed up over the houses on the Warren. Crossley, Procter and Higgins all claimed victories, but so did Spitfires also in combat with Messerschmitts. JG 51 lost two fighters but Hptm. Tietzen, Oblt. Priller and Obfw. Schmid claimed kills and it is probable that it was the last named who shot off the tail of P/O Keighley's Spitfire over Elham at 6.30 p.m. Keighley landed by parachute and was taken to hospital with leg wounds.

A destroyer was hit (it sunk the next day) and a 1,000 tonne collier was also sunk. The RAF had lost another eight fighters with four more out of action. Seven valuable pilots were dead.

21st July. Torrents of rain and thunder nearly the whole afternoon.

It was a brilliant Sunday morning over southern England with puffy clouds scudding over the Downs and a towering mass of cumulus here and there. German reconnaissance aircraft were about and constant patrols were flown above the westbound convoy, which was now off the Isle of Wight. At 10 a.m. a trainee pilot, Acting Leading Seaman J. A. Seed, was flying serenely over the rolling landscape of Salisbury Plain in an ancient Hawker Hart biplane. He hadn't considered the possibility of a predator over that part of Britain and certainly didn't recognize the twin-engined Messerschmitt that circled and came in close to riddle his plane and set it alight over Old Sarum. Fifteen minutes later, three Hurricanes caught up with a lone Me 110 east of Salisbury and, after a long chase, shot it down at Goodwood in Hampshire.

That day Admiral Sir William James wrote:

We have now an inner patrol line all round the coast consisting of small craft, whose job is to signal if they sight the enemy. I put no faith at all in this patrol. If the Germans decide to try invasion, they will sweep up these unarmed boats on any suitable night beforehand . . . real invasion will only be possible if a stream of reinforcements in men and ammunition and tanks is maintained, and that is where our flotillas will come into the picture. So Hitler, like Napoleon, must get rid of our flotillas and, as he is weak in surface craft, he can only do that by aircraft. I admit these Dive Bombers are disturbingly accurate and are already taking a toll of my ships, but our aircraft are now quick off the mark, and he can only succeed if he obtains complete air superiority. If he got that, our number would be up.

22nd July. Sunny most of day. Warning from 10.30–11.45—all round at night. Lord Halifax made a fine speech. Sambo [the cat] had a new bed from Auntie Annie.

The Luftwaffe bomber and fighter units were still building up their strength in northern France and now the advance units of the German Army were arriving to organize and service the invasion forces for 'Sealion'. At night the Medway towns were bombed.

When the dustman emptied the bins at Elham vicarage, he shook his head in wonderment as the green and brown bottles went clinking into the garbage truck. It had been like that every time he'd called over the last few weeks.

23rd July. Czecho-Slovak Government recognised. Good recorded speech by Miss Dorothy Thompson.

This was a cloudy and dull day with little aerial activity.

24th July. It rained most of evening.

In the morning Dorniers bombed shipping off Margate, sinking four ships and damaging others. Hornchurch Spitfires swept into them, but were absorbed by the escorting Messerschmitts of JG 26, led by Major Adolf Galland. In a vicious dog-fight, Galland sent a Spitfire down, but two 109s fell, one diving into a Margate street and another belly-landing in a cornfield.

Another battle developed over Dover, when III/JG 52, on a *Freie Jagd* (free hunt), grappled with 610 'City of Chester' Sqdn. up from Hawkinge. The fact that the Germans hadn't heeded 'Daddy' Mölders' advice was reflected in their casualties. Hptm. Von Houswald, the Gruppen Kommandeur, Oblt. Fermer, Oblt. Ehrlich and Gefr. Frank were all sent into the Channel. When 'Big Bill' Smith's Spitfires returned to Hawkinge, there was wild excitement. F/Lt. John Ellis had got three and F/Lt. Edward Smith another.

25th July. Gunfire and warning 12.10–1.20, others from 3–8.18.

Despite clear skies in the morning, a large convoy between Dover and Folkestone went unmolested. However, at noon the battle started to unfold when Messerschmitts were sent on a sweep to engage the RAF fighter patrols. Although there were about 100 aircraft in combat, making an incredible sound with their straining engines, there was little gunfire.

A big formation of Stukas, hoping to catch the British fighters on the ground refuelling, went for a convoy off Abbotts' Cliff, the dive-bombers going down in a follow-my-leader fashion and pulling out at mast-top height. Several ships were sunk during the first bombing, and then Junkers 88s attacked the convoy. British fighters trying to break through the screen of escorting Messerschmitts were mauled and four Spitfires were shot down and others damaged. Two MTBs commanded by Lt. J. B. King-Church, RN, and Lt. R. Hennessey RN, left the shelter of Dover to aid the sinking vessels and sped back and forth collecting dozens of seriously injured seamen.

In a lull that followed, the convoy reassembled, but was again assailed by Stukas. Then, soon after 4 p.m., German E-boats were reported heading across the Channel towards the stricken convoy. The Royal Navy reacted immediately, ordering the destroyers *Boreas* and *Brilliant* to put out to engage them. German long-range shore batteries then opened fire, throwing up great spouts of water, but did not deter the destroyers which steamed on towards the E-boats. The E-boats started to withdraw behind a dense white smoke-screen but *Boreas* and *Brilliant* sent their shells whining into the smoke and their attendant MTBs dashed forward in an attempt to get close to the enemy.

The Stukas returned, peeling off in perfect formation to dive vertically onto the destroyers, which fought back with AA guns and multiple pom-poms. Both destroyers received direct hits and, despite difficulty in steering, they wobbled back under a torrent of bombs, watched by a big crowd of wincing spectators on the cliff tops.

During the fighting, several squadrons used Hawkinge and from 3.40 p.m. 610 Sqdn. began to return. P/O Gardiner came back wounded in the arm and landed DW-O damaged. Then Spitfire DW-A appeared trailing a plume of black smoke; it was S/Ldr. 'Big Bill' Smith coming back wounded and on fire. He turned and came in from the north, dipping a little as he lowered the undercarriage. Coaxing the crippled fighter down to make a perfect landing, he trundled to a halt with thick smoke billowing

Cheshiremen of 610 Sqdn. (Left-right) P/O Stanley Norris, S/Ldr. Franks (killed over Dunkirk), S/Ldr. 'Big Bill' Smith (killed at Hawkinge), F/Lt. Bill Warner (killed over Dungeness on 16th August). (Heaps/Darroch)

upwards as he cut the motor.

The Station Intelligence Officer stood by the watch office transfixed, waiting to see the pilot emerge, whilst the Duty Pilot screamed at the fire tender to get out there to it. But it was too late: the 34-year-old S/Ldr. was found half out of the cockpit, presumably too weak to have got clear. Half an hour later, the IO was handed a charred wallet containing photographs of the dead pilot's family. Later that day, arrangements were put in hand to send the remains of S/Ldr. Andrew Smith to Delamere in Cheshire for burial.

After tea, F/Lt. John Ellis took 610's seven remaining Spitfires up again and set about a whole Gruppe of Messerschmitts off Folkestone, shooting down at least four and killing two staffel Kapitäne. Back at Biggin Hill in the evening, Ellis was told to assume command of the squadron.

26th July. Letter from Barney saying that she had got her A.R.C.O. Ginger [Alice] came to supper.

It was a quiet day with sporadic fighting off the Isle of Wight.

Only a year ago Britain had been at peace and Elham had held its annual flower show. In brilliant sunshine, the villagers had gathered together and with side-shows, tug-of-war and a physical training display by the Sea Cadets, there had been a carnival atmosphere. Now the war was on, and the efforts of the village were being channelled in different directions. Geo. Henry Parker and Martin Constant, important members of the Elham and Acrise Gardening Society, were now the backbone of the Home Guard. The village children had collected a ton of waste paper and the ladies, old and young, were busily knitting thick woollen socks and scarves for the 'Forces Comforts'. In any case, the roses weren't too good this year because of the plague of aphids that had feasted on the tender buds and leaves in May.

27th July. 3 Folkestone warnings that we knew of. Many planes, but that's all. Heavy thunderstorm at dinner-time.

At 2.46 p.m., almost before the storm had passed and before the Dover barrage balloons were raised, Stukas came screaming down to bomb Dover harbour. RAF fighters failed to intercept them and they sank HMS *Codrington*, the 1,540 ton destroyer flotilla leader. Also, a patrolling Hurricane was destroyed by an Me 109 over Dover. German bombers also sank another destroyer off Suffolk and, with long-range guns near Calais capable of shelling the coast, the British decided to withdraw their warships from Dover and base them at Sheerness and Harwich. This was a major achievement for the Germans, being one of their prime objectives before attempting an invasion.

28th July. A lovely sunny, cool day, but raid 2.15–3.30 and again 8.30–9.45. Heavy AA fire before that.

That Sunday at Elham Church, James and Edith Higgins had their son christened John. Meanwhile at Hawkinge, Group Captain G. E. Gibbs, MC, had arrived from Northolt to investigate the cause of 'slow turnover on 27.7.40', whilst Group Captain R. Grice, the Station Commander at Biggin Hill, came down to inspect the aerodrome dispersal points. Clearly something had gone wrong at Hawkinge the previous afternoon.

After lunch, units of JG 51 and JG 26 took off and gained a lot of height before crossing the Channel for some recreational combat. Major Werner Mölders was with them. With adequate radar warning, Hurricanes were positioned to engage the enemy bombers, whilst the Spitfires of 41 and 74 Sqdns. climbed from Manston to intercept the Messerschmitts. It was a bold tactical experiment, but on this afternoon there weren't any enemy bombers. 74 'Tiger' Sqdn. was led by the South African, F/Lt. 'Sailor' Malan, DFC and Bar, who was already indoctrinating officers more senior to himself with his views on combat tactics. Like Mölders, he was an exponent of good teamwork and believed in having height advantage before entering into an engagement. There followed half an hour of brisk duelling between the opposing fighters, during which Mölders claimed his 26th victory, which he identified as a Spitfire. However, at one point Malan observed a small bunch of 109s stalking some Hurricanes from up sun and managed to swing his Spitfires in behind them unobserved. The South African put several short bursts into a 109, closing from 250 to 100 yards, causing it to slow up and go

Pilots of 610 Sqdn. at Hawkinge, morning 29th July. (Left-right standing) F/O Norris, Sgt. Chandler, S/Ldr. John Ellis (just visible), Sgt. Ramsay, F/Lt. Warner, Sgt. Hamlyn, P/O Gardiner. (Left-right on ground) F/Lt. E. B. B. Smith, P/O Pegge, Sgt. Parsons, Sgt. Corfe. (Imperial War Museum)

into a series of gentle right-hand turns, as if the pilot were hit. A second 109 that floated across his path received three well-aimed deflection bursts from within 100 yards range.

Then the battle spread out over the Downs. Sgt. Mould, who had brought down Lt. Böhm at Elham on the 8th July, was enveloped in flames when his petrol tank was hit, but he succeeded in baling out and was rushed to Dover Hospital badly burned. P/O Young was killed when he fell in his Spitfire and a Hurricane crashed on Hawkinge.

It would be sheer conjecture to state that Malan and Mölders definitely duelled with each other, but someone nailed the German ace with a good burst and sent him down wounded to crash-land on the French coast. In fact, if it hadn't been for Oblt. Leppla, who picked off a Spitfire that was pursuing Mölders, he most probably would have been finished off. No less than seven pilots of 74 Sqdn. claimed Messerschmitts. 41 Sqdn. also entered the fray, Bennions and Webster both hitting 109s.

When three Heinkel ambulance planes arrived over the Channel to pick up German survivors, Hurricanes took off from Hawkinge, shot two of them down and punctured a third.

29th July. Siren at 7.20 a.m., another in morning that we didn't hear and another ditto at dinner-time. Attack on Dover harbour—heavy Nazi losses.
501 'County of Gloucester' Sqdn., now based at Gravesend with Hurricanes, arrived at Hawkinge and 610 Sqdn. came down from Biggin Hill. At 7.20 a.m., before the morning mist had cleared, a big formation of Stukas dive-bombed vessels in Dover harbour. 41 Sqdn., attempting to intervene, were assailed by a vast number of Messerschmitts. F/O Gamblen was killed and another four Spitfires were forced to return to Manston as write-offs. 56 Sqdn. arrived with Hurricanes from North Weald, but they too were bounced by 109s, killing F/Sgt. Cooney. However, 501 Sqdn. raced into the Stukas and brought down several, despite having to run the gauntlet of bursting AA shells discharged at them by the Royal Navy. For a short period the noise of bursting bombs and banging AA guns was deafening. Then, quite suddenly, it was almost silent as the buzzing sound of aircraft receded back to France.

Further down the coast, another British destroyer, HMS *Delight*, had been sunk by bombs.

On some farms harvesting had started; the clanking machines, which were a combination of reaper and binder, cut a sward through the ripening wheat, leaving the bound sheaves littered in its wake. The sheaves had to be picked up and propped up in groups to make stooks, or 'shocks' as they were known in this part of Kent. The sweat poured down the faces of the workers, as the orderly lines of shocks began to pattern the landscape. Ten sheaves made a wheat shock, with six or eight for barley and four for oats. Haymaking and harvesting were times when every spare pair of hands was needed, and now with so many soldiers in the area help was available.

30th July
Activity was minimal on that day, because of rain and low cloud. Aerial reconnaissance over the French ports showed an alarming fleet of barges being assembled for the invasion of Britain.

31st July. Very distant gunfire in morning. Warning from 3.50–7 p.m. Machine-gun fire about 4 p.m. and slight AA later. Barrage balloons over Running Hill.
At 3.45 p.m., Me 109s and 110s attacked the Dover balloons, several of which descended in flames. Five RAF squadrons were sent to the area, but only 'B' flight of 74 'Tiger' Sqdn. was disastrously engaged, Blue section being bounced by Hptm. 'Jakob' Tietzen with some of the up-and-coming aces of JG 51. The 109s divided into two groups and slanted down unobserved, one group coming in from the beam, using their cannon from long range. Sgt. Fred Eley's Spitfire burst in flames and fell close to Victoria pier, Folkestone, whilst P/O Gunn went into the sea a little further out. Only F/Lt. Dillon Kelly survived—and he was extremely lucky. At one point he was hemmed in, whilst one particular Messerschmitt was allowed to shoot at him from behind. The armour plate behind his seat was dented, his port wing damaged and holes pierced through his upper petrol tank and cowling. Nevertheless, he escaped along the coast, going into a spin and diving towards Hastings. Hptm. Tietzen, Oblt. Foezoe and Lt. Hohagen all claimed victories.

1st August. Cold and dull. Wore brown tweed coat to meet M. Pegden at night. Leaflets dropped in night, giving Hitler's speech of July 19th.
At Marshal Kesselring's forward command post at Cap Gris Nez, Major Adolf Galland brought his heels together with a snap to receive the coveted Knight's Cross. At this time, he was leading the III Gruppe of JG 26 and had just notched up his seventeenth kill. 'Uncle Theo' Osterkamp, who had increased his World War I score, was also awarded the Knight's Cross to replace the 'Blue Max' he had received from Kaiser Wilhelm. He wore both—with the 'Blue Max' in front. He also received a direct order from Hitler to stop operational flying. At 48 he was too old for the swirling dog-fights that were being fought at great heights and for diving at speeds five times faster than his First

World War Albatros. In any case, there was no need for him to be concerned with leadership in the air; Werner Mölders was recovering well and would soon be back in harness.

Mölders had devised a new combat formation that was later to be emulated by all air forces. At this time, the RAF used fighters in combinations of three, a section leader and two wingmen. A full squadron consisted of four sections—usually called Red, Blue, Yellow and Green—all twelve aircraft keeping in an orderly tight formation, with two rear machines weaving so as to watch the sky above and behind. Invariably, the novice pilots got the job of weaving and, time and time again, British squadrons were bounced by enterprising Messerschmitt pilots, who would dive in pairs very quickly, fire and disengage. One would be the marksman and hunter, the other his No 2 guarding his rear.

Mölders advocated that two such pairs made an ideal combat formation when flying loosely in what was called a 'Schwarm'. In an engagement, the 'Schwarme' endeavoured to stay together, but, if necessary, it broke down into pairs: a lone fighter was ineffectual and vulnerable. When a Jagdgeschwader, consisting of 40–60 planes was in flight, it was made up of a cluster of 'Schwarme' that were able to dart and turn quickly. When a formation turned, the inside pairs crossed over those on the outside so as to reverse positions, completing the manoeuvre quickly and not having the problem of speed differentials on the inside and outside, as experienced by British formations during a turn.

2nd August. Cold and dull still. Warning and buzz 7.15–7.30 p.m.

The German High Command issued orders to the three Luftflotten. These were detailed operational orders for commencing destruction of the RAF prior to landing forces in Britain. This was scheduled to begin on August 12th—'Eagle Day'. In England, the Prime Minister urged General Ismay to get on with having uniforms made for the Home Guard.

3rd August. Sunny and coolish. Mr and Mrs Bowes and Tim called in evening, also Mrs Castle. Short warning about 6.55–7.10.

Hawkinge reported: *Weather fine . . . All WAAF personnel of AMES Dover were today evacuated and posted to RAF Station Dyce for duty at AMES Schoolhill.* This move was highly significant, following immediately after the Luftwaffe secret orders for the attack on Britain—an attack that was to start with the destruction of the radar stations.

As the result of some consternation in Elham, because the Vicar had been seen marching about with the Home Guard, the Rev. Williams put a letter in the parish magazine:

The Secretary of State for Foreign Affairs, Lord Halifax, said in his recent broadcast to the Nation: 'We realise that the struggle may cost us everything; but just because the things we are defending are worth any sacrifice, it is a noble privilege to be defenders of things so precious.'

Surely we feel the truth of this in our inmost beings, for we know that we are fighting, not for any imperialistic advancement or material gain, but for the things of the spirit—liberty, straight-forward dealing, freedom to worship God as we think right, family life and the brotherhood of nations. These are things which Nazi Germany has trampled under foot wherever her iron heel has trod, and which, in the event of a German victory here, would be lost to our children and our children's children. To preserve our heritage then, as Lord Halifax says, is worth any sacrifice—even life itself.

It is for this reason that I have thought it right to offer my services to the LDV, which is now to be known by the much more picturesque name of 'the Home Guard'. I hasten to add that I have done so with the knowledge and approval of the Archbishop of Canterbury, and under the two provisos that have kindly been allowed to the clergy by the War Office, viz : (1) That I should not bear arms. (2) That my military duties should not interfere in any way with my spiritual duties as Vicar of the parish. I hope that you will pardon my mentioning what in a sense is a purely personal decision on my part, and I should not have thought it worth mentioning, had I not also duties and responsibilities as Vicar of the parish. It is, therefore, for this reason that I am anxious that my position in the Home Guard should not be misunderstood by parishioners. We are a jolly crowd, but I doubt not will be able to give a fierce account of ourselves in an emergency.

Bill Green, the ex-flight mechanic who had become a pilot, still hadn't flown a modern type of aircraft, even though he was technically on the strength of a 501 Fighter Squadron. He was supposed to have had some lessons at Biggin Hill on a Miles Master trainer, but this was out of service and he was sent over to Hornchurch with P/O Aldridge to use their Master. He stood around waiting whilst some officers all did a couple of circuits, each with a flying instructor, followed by at least one solo flight. But there was only time for Bill to do one dual circuit in Master (N7570) before he had to return to Biggin Hill.

4th August. Hot and Sunny. Aunt Beauch came to tea and supper.

That Sunday the BBC news broadcasts started with the national anthem to commemorate the Queen's birthday. About an hour after dawn six Hurricanes bearing the letters JX banked over Elham, losing height in a gentle descent to land on the damp grass at Hawkinge. For one of their pilots F/O N.P.W. 'Pat' Hancock, it was a special day—his 21st birthday—and his parents had arranged an evening dinner party in London. Hancock came from Purley and after training had been posted to No 1 Sqdn. in France, where within weeks he'd seen his squadron fight to a standstill in a vain attempt to stem the German *Blitzkrieg*. They were now based at Northolt on the western periphery of London.

From the plateau of Hawkinge there was no sign of activity from France. The Channel was as still as a millpond, shimmering slightly under the diffused sunlight that penetrated a thin blanket of cloud. At noon, the Northolt Squadron was stood down, the pilots going to their messes to have a beer and a midday meal. At the same time at Elham, Mary and Margaret were enjoying Sunday dinner with their parents in the living room behind the post office. But for them, life at Hawkinge, only three miles away, was a world they knew nothing about.

At 3 o'clock, No 1 Sqdn. returned to Northolt for some airgunnery practice. This was thought necessary because three of their pilots had expended all their ammunition on a lone Dornier the previous Wednesday and failed to shoot it down. After refuelling, they flew up to Buckinghamshire to make some practice attacks on RAF bombers, but an unfortunate tragedy took place when one of the Blenheims dived into the ground near Aylesbury, killing the crew of three and a Spitfire pilot who was on board.

Back at Northolt, 'Pat' Hancock had tea whilst his Hurricane was refuelled for a flight down to Tangmere in Sussex. During the evening he was on a dusk patrol over the Solent and, after a wash and a quick change back at Northolt, he travelled into London on the Underground for a memorable birthday celebration with his family and friends. It had been a happy day for the young man, but it had only needed one of the young hawks of JG 51, over Elham that morning, to have spoilt it irrevocably.*

5th August. Hot. Warning 9.40–10.30. One loud explosion. All went down cellar. Bomb near Fir Tree Farm, Stelling—no harm done.

In the morning, Hornchurch and Kenley both dispatched a squadron of Spitfires to patrol Dover-Folkestone and there was the sound of a considerable dog-fight when JG 51, accompanied by the 'Greenheart's' Messerschmitts, met them over the coast. Honours were about equal as two plumes of spray marked the end of Obfw. Schmid of Germany and Sgt. Lewis Isaac of Wales. A Hornchurch Spitfire came back spewing fuel from a holed petrol tank; the wounded pilot was very lucky to have got down at Manston without being incinerated. The Spitfire of P/O A. G. Donahue, an American, limped into Hawkinge making a high-pitched whine as the slipstream whistled through big holes made in its fuselage by cannon shells. In exactly a week's time, he would fail to reach Hawkinge in another shot-up Spitfire.

Farmers crowded into the village of Lyminge for the Monday fatstock sales. There was brisk selling, especially of the splendid lambs fattened on the lush grass of Romney Marsh. The railway authorities had an inspector and a team of men at the sidings to help load the wagons, which often numbered more than a hundred.

6th August

This turned out to be an extraordinarily quiet day over Kent.

7th August. Italian troops massing against Egypt. Auntie Jennie came to dinner from 58 Broad Street, Canterbury.

References to aunts and uncles in Mary's diary are not to be taken literally, since it was a custom in the Smith household for the daughters to attach these prefixes to friends of their parents. 'Auntie' Jennie had been Mrs Smith's bridesmaid.

Hawkinge reported: *Weather—fine. Group Captain Reverend H. Beachamp, R. C. Chaplain, visited the Station. The body of ——— was recovered from the sea at Folkestone by RAF of Hawkinge during salvage of Spitfire down in enemy action. F/Lt. E. E. Arnold, DFC, reported on posting from Base Personnel Office, Hendon Hall, to command RAF Station Hawkinge.* The name of the fighter pilot was left blank in the Hawkinge

*Wing Commander N. P. W. Hancock, DFC, survived the war and in the 1970s he became Hon. Sec. of the Battle of Britain Fighter Association.

Operational Record Book, but it was Sgt. Fred Eley, whose Spitfire had gone into the water like a blazing torch when 74 'Tiger' Sqdn. had been attacked by JG 51 the previous Wednesday. Troops, sailors and local boatmen all helped pull the wreckage ashore. The heavy engine broke away and was left in the mud, but the remainder of the scorched and twisted machine was dragged onto land. As the water ran out of the cockpit section, the figure of the pilot was revealed, still strapped to his seat. The body of Fred Eley was returned to his family for burial in Wrenbury Churchyard, Cheshire.

8th August. Several warnings—Lots of planes about. 53(60) Nazi planes brought down in attack on convoy. 16 British pilots missing (3 found) M of I talk in street at 8.30 p.m.

Mary's reference to shot-down planes was taken from overestimated British figures released by the press. The true figures, assuming that the Luftwaffe Quartermaster General's returns are complete, were 24 German planes lost, including two that collided, compared with 20 RAF fighters lost and 15 RAF fighter pilots killed.

From noon onwards, the heaviest air fighting took place off the Isle of Wight, but JG 51 and JG 26 swept in over Kent and some pilots indulged themselves shooting down Dover balloons. 65 Sqdn. were attacked by Messerschmitts over Manston and the Spitfires of Sgt. David Kirton and F/Sgt. Norman Phillips tumbled out of the sky in flames, whilst a third shot-up Spitfire managed an emergency landing. Back at JG 26's

86

base, Oblt. Muncheberg, Lt. Willy Fronhöfer and Obfw. Gerhard Grzymalla celebrated with champagne. Even they had to admit it was easy stalking the patrolling 'Tommies' when flying well above them.

About an hour later, Hptm. Trautloft took III/JG 51 down to make a surprise attack on Spitfires patrolling Hawkinge. One wounded RAF pilot crash-landed at Capel and another dived away over Romney Marsh to make a belly-landing. Nineteen-year-old P/O Peter Kennard-Davis of 64 Sqdn., although seriously wounded, abandoned his blazing fighter and opened his parachute, but died in Dover Hospital two days later. At the same time, an obsolescent and vulnerable Blenheim fighter became involved in the dog-fighting; it flew over Ramsgate, burning from nose to tail, and fell into the sea. F/O Dennis Grice and his two crewmen did not bale out.

Bill Green, the untrained fighter pilot of 501 Sqdn., was still hanging around Biggin Hill's Training Flight waiting to be taught to fly a Hurricane. A tall officer inclined his head and asked Green what experience he'd had and, upon learning that he'd been an aircraft fitter, the instructor raised the palm of one hand and said 'Oh! Then you will know all about them if you were a fitter. Look, there's one over there.' He pointed to Hurricane P2549. 'Go and sit in it, and when you feel happy, take it up!' Bill Green did just that and had two exhilarating and rather frightening flights in a fighter that wasn't destined to spend its days as a training hack.

Following the loss of their organ virtuoso, who was wooed away by St Alphage's in Canterbury, Elham Church appointed Miss Ongham from the village school to perform the duties. At this time Elham Church notes reminded worshippers: *Now that hymns and canticles are started much more promptly, members of the congregation are in danger of missing the first line and so losing the sense of the first verse, through not being ready to start singing with the choir. If the congregation stands directly the organ starts to play over the tune, all is well. Further, when saying the Psalms a distinct pause should be made at the colon, in the middle of each verse, long enough to count 'one, two'. This is a great help in following the sense and also in keeping people together.*

9th August. Sunny and windy. Warning 6.40 to about 7.30.

64 Sqdn. were bounced over Hawkinge by 109s and two shot-up Spitfires force-landed whilst another limped back to Kenley, rent open by a shell. Margate and Dover were bombed that night.

10th August. Mrs Bragg's birthday. Margaret went there to supper. Dash had a sore and red skin.

All over southern England, harvesting was getting into full swing and yields were going to be good despite the terrible winter. Powerful friendly horses worked alongside the tractors hauling wagons and pulling harvesting machinery: machines, men and horses were being worked to the limit. Pegden's, the Elham engineers, were servicing, hiring and repairing equipment continuously. Fred Pegden was a wizard at improvization and on one occasion big George Benefield had demonstrated his enormous strength when a long shaft, weighing nearly a hundredweight, had to be lifted and delicately positioned for coupling bolts to be inserted at either end. To the astonishment of Pegden and

Herbie Palmer, George had grasped the middle of the shaft with his huge hands and held it out horizontally whilst they fumbled with the couplings.

At breakfast time a lone Dornier flew over Kent in low cloud and made two bombing and strafing attacks on West Malling aerodrome, killing a workman and wounding 16.

11th August. 3 lots of AA and buzzes during morning attack on Dover balloons. Heavy attack on Portland. At least 50 Nazi planes destroyed, 19 British.

Sunday. Three Dover balloons were shot down by Me 109s of fighter-bomber Gruppe Epr 210 soon after dawn, then the Me 110s of the same Gruppe bombed the harbour. There was heavy fighting all along the coast, but no attacks on airfields. Bill Green, teaching himself to fly a Hurricane, had logged three hours and was over Kent when he was recalled and warned of the presence of 40 Me 109s in his area.

74 Sqdn., led by 'Sailor' Malan, who had been promoted to squadron leader, was involved in four combats that day. P/O Stevenson had to bale out soon after destroying a 109 and drifted some eleven miles out to sea. He nearly drowned, entangled in his parachute cords, but 1½ hours later, after firing his revolver and frantically waving to attract their attention, he was picked up by a Royal Navy MTB.

In the afternoon they had a swirling fight over the sea with the Me 110s of Epr 210, both sides making grossly exaggerated claims. P/O Denis Smith and P/O Donald Cobden, a New Zealand rugby star, were both killed when their fighters were hit by the heavy fire power of the Me 110s. It was Cobden's 26th birthday. Two Me 110s went into the sea.

At Hawkinge and Lympne, RAF personnel worked late that evening sweeping, painting, polishing and gardening, because the Inspector General of the RAF, Air Chief Marshal Sir Edgar Ludlow-Hewitt, was to inspect both aerodromes on the next day.

12th August. Raids nearly all day. Nazi plane down on Running Hill about 8.30 a.m. Horrid odd AA bangs all morning. Heavy battle overhead 5.30–6 p.m. Down cellar. Tiles off Hemsley's and Butchers.

Lympne aerodrome was bombed at 8.16 a.m., cratering the landing ground and damaging a hangar. Feverish work was started in an attempt to clear up and make temporary repairs before the Inspector General arrived. At 8.20 a.m. there was a big dog-fight over Elham, during which an abandoned Messerschmitt continued to fly in circles over the village. The inhabitants came out of their houses to watch as the plane, chased by a frenzied group of Spitfires, flew wildly about the sky with its undercarriage lowered. After scything in low over the village, it flew into Running Hill, where it cartwheeled across a meadow and disintegrated in a cloud of dust without catching fire. The pilot, Oblt. Friedrich Butterweck of JG 26, was found dead in a field six miles away. The wreck lay unguarded on the hill for days and people feasted on it for souvenirs.

At 9.15 a.m., AC2 Clifford Vincent was on watch duty on the platform of a radar mast, perched 575 ft above Dover. He had a marvellous view of the sparkling Channel and could see out to Dungeness. Minutes later, Hptm. Rübensdörffer, the Swiss-born leader of the élite Epr 210 fighter-bomber Gruppe, divided his mixed force of Me 110s and Me 109s and sent them streaking in at low level to attack the vital radar stations at Dover,

Rye and Pevensey. Vincent just had time to marvel at the sight of the three rapidly approaching fighter-bombers before the masts rocked from the explosions around their bases and shrapnel went clanging through the girderwork. As the dust and smoke cleared, he looked below to where F/Lt. Peter Axon was shouting and gesticulating to him to climb down. Distant explosions could be heard coming from Brookland on Romney Marsh and also from further west where Fighter Command was having its radar eyes put out.

During the lull that followed, there was a series of unexplained explosions without any German aircraft being overhead. In Folkestone and Dover several houses crumpled up into heaps of rubble and a few civilians were killed or maimed. There were two explosions at Hawkinge and veterans of the previous war asserted that they sounded like shells. And shells they were—from the long-range German guns across the Channel. There was more airfighting at 11 a.m., then a bomber formation attacked Manston catching 65 Sqdn. on the ground.

At Hawkinge things were very quiet, except for the presence of the Inspector General and his entourage. Visiting fighter pilots lolled in deckchairs or spread themselves out on the grass in easy reach of their fighters. The catering arrangements had changed dramatically. Orderlies now came to the dispersal points with thick corned beef sandwiches and an urn of tea, which was consumed in the sunlight.

Among the 501 Sqdn pilots down from Gravesend was a slim, pink-faced Yorkshire sergeant with unruly fair hair that was inclined to stick up in spikes. His youthful, unprepossessing appearance belied his age and skill. Later, when someone in the Air Ministry started totting up the victory scores of various pilots, lots of senior officers, were saying 'Who's this chap Sgt. Lacey, he seems to top the list?'

J. H. 'Ginger' Lacey, from Wetherby, had worked as a pharmacist before becoming a professional flying instructor and RAF Volunteer Reserve pilot. He had an independence of spirit, preferring to doze in his reclining chair, rather than smarten himself up for the Air Chief Marshal's inspection. In the event, 501 was scrambled to intercept raiders coming in over Ramsgate.

Wing Commander Jimmy Jeffs, a former controller of Lympne aerodrome, chose this day to make a nostalgic visit to his old base. The place had changed since those halcyon days of the Cinque Ports Flying Club, when sheep had to be driven off the field before aircraft could take off. Jeffs spotted the ramrod figure of ex-Sergeant Major Dupe of the Royal Flying Corps and together they went to the old Civil Aviation transport office to reminisce. Suddenly, Jeffs felt an urge to have a souvenir from Lympne before it was all gone and the barograph that had been in his office for years seemed ideal. With scrupulous care he made out a 108 receipt form and the faithful Dupe carried the instrument to the Wing Commander's car.

Just before leaving, Jeffs telephoned a colleague at HQ Fighter Command. The voice came back: 'I advise you to get out of Lympne—at once!' He didn't need telling twice, but before going he found Dupe, who had quarters on the aerodrome, and told him to get himself and his wife away at once. The Wing Commander was on the old Roman Road driving to Canterbury when he heard the din and saw smoke billowing up from his old base. At least he had his souvenir from the Amy Johnson days.

The remains of Oblt. Butterwick's Messerschmitt after it cartwheeled over Running Hill, Elham. (Horace Cook)

At teatime the Air Chief Marshal left Hawkinge and was driven to nearby Lympne, where he was greeted at 5.35 p.m. by the Station Commander, S/Ldr. Montgomery. Five minutes later a large force of bombers arrived overhead and proceeded to wreck the aerodrome before the Inspector General's eyes. Simultaneously, Hawkinge got the same treatment from a formation of Junkers 88s that came in over Folkestone at medium height. The big bombs penetrated the soil and went deep into the chalk before erupting in a line of fearsome explosions across the airfield and detonating amongst the buildings. Most of the personnel dived for cover and gun crews were taken by surprise, leaving only the two Hispanos to spray their small shells at the raiders. A few minutes later a wave of Dorniers passed over both aerodromes releasing a stream of smaller bombs. Sir Edgar cancelled his inspection at Lympne, saying he had every intention of returning in a few days' time. The airfield had 242 craters, making it quite unserviceable.

Meanwhile at Hawkinge, No 3 hangar received direct hits. The towering iron doors came off their top runners and crushed to death an airman and two civilian employees, Brisley and McCaister. Within the hangar Corporal McColl and three more airmen were killed and six seriously injured. Two Spitfires under repair were wrecked and others perforated by splinters. The workshops and clothing store were destroyed and two houses were demolished amongst the married quarters. Fires burned in various places, including the main stores where ammunition was exploding.

Spitfires of 64 Sqdn. engaged the Dorniers over Hawkinge and the pilots were severely critical about the complete lack of AA fire. Flying with them was an American, P/O Donahue, who jumped from his Spitfire when it streamed a banner of fire over Sellinge. Floating down by parachute in the evening breeze, he nursed his burns in the cool air.

Some Hurricanes were obliged to return to the cratered airfield at Hawkinge to refuel. Sgt. Lacey collapsed his undercarriage as he put down and F/Lt. Gibson had his fighter tip up on its nose. Others that put down safely had to stay the night. P/O Barton of 32 Sqdn. didn't take the risk and chose a nearby field in which to crash-land his shot-up Hurricane.

The aerodrome fire-fighting squads were augmented by firemen from Folkestone. Section Leader R. R. Fry reported later: *A chaotic scene greeted our arrival. There were fires in several places. The water tower, supplying pressure for hydrants, had been holed by splinters in many places and water cascaded from it, reducing our mains supply to a trickle as we watched.* Section Leader Fry with his team, consisting of Bill Willis, Percy Sutton, Ted Beeching, Geo. Rumsey and Geo. Kelly, were sent to tackle No 3 hangar, which was ablaze at several points.

An ammunition store was also on fire and there were explosions at intervals as boxes went off in the heat. Some fighters were in the debris, but no attempt was made to salvage them, the main priority being to get the landing field operational again. Throughout the night soldiers, airmen and civilians shovelled and scraped the chalk and russet-coloured soil back into the craters, taking short rests at a mobile canteen serving an endless supply of tea and sandwiches.

The Inspector General of the RAF, Air Chief Marshal Sir Edgar Ludlow-Hewitt (portrait by Sir William Rothenstein)

13th August. Nazi bomber overhead about 7.15 a.m. Very sharp AA. It came down across railway just beyond Barham station. Air battle at 4 p.m. Nazi airman down at Parker's by parachute. Leg wound.

In the pale light of dawn the toilers at Hawkinge speculated on how long it would be before the Luftwaffe returned to undo their night's work. Folkestone firemen, who were still on the aerodrome, were exalted when they heard the sound of Merlin engines warming up and saw three Hurricanes race across the grass and filled craters to climb away with undercarriage legs retracting under their wings. They wanted to cheer and some found their eyes watering—not entirely because of the smoke and dust. Hawkinge was back in action.

This was to have been 'Eagle Day', when the Luftwaffe started the concentrated bombing of RAF aerodromes, but it was cancelled soon after dawn because of cloudy weather. However, some units were not notified in time and as a result escort fighters arrived over Britain without bombers and vice versa. By 6.20 a.m. the 60-plus Dorniers of KG 2 had already started and the twin-engined Messerschmitts that were to have escorted them were withdrawn. But because of different radio frequencies, the leader of the escort fighters couldn't communicate and one-legged Colonel Joachim Huth, leading the escort, zoomed up in front of the leading bomber, turned over and dived past its nose, gesticulating to the crew. Colonel Fink in the Dornier didn't understand and was irritated by what he thought was a dangerous display of overexuberance.

Then the fighters left and Fink led his Dorniers north, skirting Kent to fly up the Thames Estuary to pulverize Eastchurch airfield. They were intercepted by Malan's 74 Sqdn. and four bombers succumbed quickly and eight more were shot-up. One Dornier, flown by Oblt. Heinz Schlegel, came towards Elham on one engine and with a wounded crew. It came down on the railway track near Barham school, then bounced and slewed, leaving its tail on the line, and entered woodland beside the track with a rending splintering crash. The crew were extraordinarily lucky to get out of the wreck alive. At Elham, the station master was informed by the railway's factotums, Jack Heathfield and Joe Fox, that an enemy aircraft was blocking the line.

Soon after 4 p.m., Uffz. Hans Wemhöner of JG 26 baled out over Elham and parachuted down near Henbury, wounded in the leg. His Messerschmitt dived into the ground at Denton. About an hour later, a flock of crank-winged Stukas, clasping 500 kg bombs under their bellies, slipped in over the coast using cloud cover and arrived over the RAF station at Detling, north of Maidstone. With fiendish precision they dive-bombed and strafed for several minutes and then flew back to France without loss or damage.

Behind them Detling lay in ruins. The operations room, the cookhouse and messes were all destroyed and hangars were wrecked and set on fire. Casualties were very heavy, especially in the crowded canteen, where airmen and soldiers were having tea. The Station Commander was dead, but the Adjutant, F/O Anthill, had survived, despite being blown off his feet twice by bursting bombs.

14th August. Dover attack about 12 noon. Plenty of buzzing, but only one burst of machine-gun fire near. Margaret cut her first kohlrabi.

During the night, RAF bombers struck at the barges in French harbours and at dawn the Dungeness lifeboat searched for the crew of a British plane down off Hythe. Two survivors were rescued by a fishing boat and another was saved by Miss Peggy Prince, who had put out in a small canoe (she was awarded the OBE).

Again the dull weather curtailed 'Eagle Day', but at midday Stukas crossed the Channel, principally to act as decoys to draw British fighters into combat with JG 26. From Hawkinge, 615 Sqdn. engaged the Stukas that had sunk the Goodwin lightship and 610 Sqdn. engaged others over Folkestone. However, Major Galland's Messerschmitts intervened and 615 Sqdn. lost F/O Collard and P/O Montgomery, one or other of them receiving a lethal burst from the Major. 32 Sqdn. were surprised by Messerschmitts near Dover, but P/Os Wlasnowalski and Barton were unhurt after forced-landing their shot-up Hurricanes. However, P/O Rupert Smythe, who came from Dublin, did rather better when he caught up with Fw. Gerhard Kemen just behind Dover and fired two withering bursts. Kemen's 109 started to break up and went down vertically, the pilot baling out badly injured. Smythe's Hurricane was then hit, but he escaped in cloud and landed at Hawkinge. Manston suffered low-level bombing by Epr 210, where three Blenheim fighters were destroyed, but for once the Bofors' gunners were on target and two Me 110s were shot down.

Sir Edgar Ludlow-Hewitt returned to Lympne and inspected the battered airfield. Meanwhile across the Channel, Luftwaffe intelligence officers were examining reconnaissance photographs taken the previous day and decided Lympne and Hawkinge both needed another dose.

15th August. One raid (nothing much) early morning, another before dinner, heavy for a time, another 3.30 p.m. Very heavy (bombs at Palm Tree Inn—no harm done).

The sky was clear at dawn and it promised to be a fine day when 501 Sqdn. arrived at Hawkinge. The aerodrome was preparing for the return visits of both the Inspector General and the Luftwaffe.

At 11.30 a.m., 501 Sqdn. were patrolling high above Hawkinge and failed to see the single line of Stukas approaching the airfield from the east and which for ten minutes delivered individual dive-bombing attacks from all directions. The sound of screaming aircraft and deafening explosions of 1,000 pound bombs mingled with the constant banging as two of the aerodrome's Bofors guns blasted shell after shell at the raiders. The other two guns had jammed after a couple of rounds. Hangars received direct hits and caught fire, a barrack block collapsed in a pile of rubble and again the landing ground was dotted with craters. Then the Hurricanes fell on the Stukas.

Sgt. Farnes met one over the aerodrome and thumbed off a long 8-second burst, watching the target rocking under the hail of bullets before it spun, emitting a thin trail of

Anti-aircraft shells bursting over Elham on 15th August as bombers attack Hawkinge. (Horace Cook)

Landing ground →

Hawkinge Aerodrome under Attack

1	Station Commander's house	24	Married quarters
2	Officers' Mess	25	Warrant Officers' quarters
3	Paint store	26	Fuel dump
4	Salt store	27	Power house
5	Bijou Cottage	28	Municipal cemetery
6	Water tower	29	Shooting butts
7	Reservoir	30	No. 5 Hangar
8	Fire station	31	Gymnasium
9	Sergeants' Mess	32	Haskard target building
10	Guard Room	33	Lecture hut
11	Station HQ	34	Vehicle sheds
12	Old Officers' Mess	35	Workshops
13	Barrack block	36	No. 3 Hangar
14	Barrack block	37	Parachute store
15	Ambulance shed	38	Main stores
16	Sick bay	39	Offices
17	Cookhouse and dining room	40	Armoury
18	Ration store	41	Operations block
19	Parade ground	42	No. 2 Hangar
20	Children's playground	43	Watch hut
21	NAAFI	44	No. 1 Hangar
22	Boiler house	45	Fire tender hut
23	Store huts	46	Fuel dump

smoke to disappear behind a hill. Sgt. Don McKay, another of the veterans from France, went up to only 50 yards from another Stuka and gave it 1,200 rounds, which caused it to turn over onto its back and fly through some HT cables just before smashing into a row of houses at Shorncliffe. F/O Witorzenc, bent on revenge for everything the Germans had done to Poland, saw a Stuka scurrying away low after dropping its bombs and caught up with it out to sea. The German's rear gunner hosed back a stream of tracer, but that soon stopped as the Pole's eight machine-guns hit it from dead astern. First it belched white smoke, then the dive-bomber put its nose down and bored into the Channel with a gigantic splash.

Armed with two foreward-firing guns, two Stuka pilots showed a very aggressive spirit when they turned into F/Lt. Gibson soon after releasing their bombs and fired at his Hurricane. He evaded them and nailed one with a good burst. Then there was a considerable bang underneath his fighter, which caught fire immediately, forcing him to bale out. Sgt. Glowacki saw a parachute open in front of him as he went for a Stuka climbing over the hangars. He distinctly saw the buildings lurch as flashes lit them up from the inside and whirling sheets of metal lifted off in all directions.

Sgt. McKay, having expended all his ammunition, was about to land, but noticing lots of Messerschmitts above Hawkinge he prudently decided to rearm at Gravesend. F/Lt. Putt lost his Hurricane in the sea off Folkestone, where quite a number of Stukas were seen to disappear.

The noise had hardly died away when a high-level attack came over from the west, scattering a pattern of small bombs. Lympne suffered an identical attack and was virtually destroyed. Huts and hangars were annihilated, the orderly room and sick quarters were wrecked and water, telephone and electricity supplies were cut off.

Sir Edgar Ludlow-Hewitt, who by this time had become quite adroit at getting into shelters quickly, insisted that Hawkinge should be made ready immediately. S/Ldr. H. B. Hurley was actually in the process of handing over command of the station to S/Ldr. Arnold, and together they made contingency plans to disperse the station staff off the airfield into nearby houses which would be requisitioned. These plans were accelerated when at 3.25 p.m., high-altitude raiders pattern-bombed Hawkinge whilst the heavy AA guns engaged them from Swingfield. Many bombs fell across Folkestone, where 19 houses were wrecked.

After intense fighting over the whole of southern and eastern England, right up as far as Newcastle, both sides counted their losses. The RAF had lost 32 fighters, with 28 damaged but repairable. A total of 13 RAF pilots were killed and ten were in hospital, whilst three had been captured as the result of coming down over the French coast. The Germans had lost or written-off 72 aircraft and 165 of their aircrew were killed or taken prisoner. Amongst the German dead was Hptm. Rübensdörffer.

The Luftwaffe regarded Hawkinge as being destroyed, but Royal Engineers and civilian work parties toiled away repairing the surface.

16th August. Buzzy raid at 12 and another at tea-time—not nearly so heavy as yesterday. Nazis reached outer London.
S/Ldr. E. E. Arnold DFC, formally took over command of Hawkinge and the station

administrative staff were moved off the aerodrome into a large house half a mile away. Arnold was 46 years old and had retired from the RAF in 1934, but volunteered to rejoin when the war started. The energy, drive and inventiveness of this resourceful officer was just what Hawkinge needed.

At 12.20 p.m. a tight formation of Dorniers passed over Elham with a huge umbrella of Messerschmitts above. Within ten minutes vicious air fighting exploded across the skies of Kent. No 266 Sqdn. lost five Spitfires fighting a mass of 109s and three pilots were killed, including their CO, S/Ldr. Wilkinson. Amongst the German casualties was Hptm. Karl Ebbighausen, a great bull of a man with seven kills, who disappeared into the Channel in a 109 that was festooned with emblems and badges all along the sides of its fuselage.

In one of the Spitfires was Sub-Lieutenant Henry 'Sinbad' Greenshields, a naval pilot from Axminster, Devon, who carried on fighting the 109s right across the Channel before he was shot down and killed over Calais by Lt. Müller-Dühe. In one of Greenshields' pockets German intelligence officers found an unposted letter to his parents describing his experiences when his squadron was bombed on Eastchurch airfield whilst making a temporary stop. Although this was a serious breach of security, it inadvertently had a positive effect because the Germans assumed Eastchurch to be a fighter station and, to the surprise of the RAF, they persisted in wasting a considerable tonnage of bombs on what was a Coastal Command base.

West Malling airfield was badly hit and, further down the coast, the vital station at Tangmere was devastated by Stukas. However, German bomber formations, sent to

Sgt. Kozlowski of 501 Sqdn. reporting to the Hawkinge Intelligence Officer on 16th August. Hurricane (V7234), flown by Sgt. Hugh Adams, was shot down by Messerschmitts on 1st September. (Central Press)

(Above) Two Hurricanes of 501 Sqdn. lift off from Hawkinge (bomb-damaged No. 5 hangar is visible in the background). Two days later both these fighters were shot down by the same Messerschmitt flown by Oblt. Gerhard Schoepfel. P/O Kenneth Lee baled out of 'N' and P/O John Bland was killed in 'T'. (Imperial War Museum). (Right) A Hurricane of 615 Sqdn. (KW-B) being replenished at Hawkinge. The ACs are wearing gym shoes to avoid damaging the wing surfaces. (Central Press)

attack the fighter aerodromes of Duxford, Northweald, Debden and Hornchurch, failed to find their targets because of cloud and harassment from snapping fighters. One Hurricane collided head-on with a leading Dornier, filling the sky with whirling pieces.

After a lull during the afternoon, the raids started again in the late afternoon. S/Ldr. McDonnell flew off from Hawkinge leading 64 Sqdn. and engaged raiders over Sussex, whilst 610 Sqdn. went into action against JU 88s and Me 109s in thick haze over Romney Marsh. F/Lt. Bill Warner, only 21 years old, spiralled into the sea, with a brace of 109s taking it in turns to fire at the Spitfire as it fell.

Dr Hunter-Smith took surgery in Hawkinge village twice a week, where he rented some rooms in a large house belonging to Mr Churchley, a fine horseman and hunting enthusiast. When the doctor arrived that day, he found the Churchleys in a state of shock following the bombing. There was continuous activity at the aerodrome and every time there was the sound of an aircraft coming in low, people crouched down or scurried off to take shelter, because there had been no warnings before the attacks. The RAF were moving into private houses off the aerodrome and the place was no longer fit to live in. So the doctor suggested that the Churchleys pack a few things and come to stay with his wife in Elham. This they did and never returned.

Sub-Lt. Henry le Fone Greenshields, RNVR. Rejected by the RAF because of weak eyesight, he joined the Fleet Air Arm and trained as a pilot. Attached to 266 Sqdn. during the Battle of Britain, he was shot down and killed near Calais by Lt. Gerhard Müller-Dühe of JG 26. (Dennis Knight)

17th August. Daddy sent R.P. wire to Offens to see if safe. A lovely sunny and quite normal day. Mr Duff-Cooper broadcast on RAF successes at night.

This day provided a welcome lull for both sides. German radios throughout the Third Reich and at military bases right across occupied Europe started booming out a hideous patriotic song: 'Bomben auf EN-GE-LAND'. The brass and percussion blared out the martial rhythm, onto which they dubbed the sound of roaring aircraft. The Luftwaffe aircrews didn't like it at all, but it had the right psychological effect on ordinary people who worked in factory and field to supply the needs of the triumphant 'Master Race'.

18th August. Heavy raids at dinner time and after tea. Bombs round about. Attack on London driven off.

Anthony Eden contrived to spend his weekends at Elham and he visited battered Hawkinge. There had been several warnings, but on that Sunday the Germans were attacking inland aerodromes and the coastal airfields further west. At midday the raiders came streaming back and there was airfighting over Elham. Two twin-engined Messerschmitts crashed on Romney Marsh and a Heinkel, savaged by Hurricanes, released its bombs on Rye, before turning back to crash-land on the Marsh.

No 266 Sqdn., led by F/Lt. Dennis Armitage, were sent from Hornchurch to patrol Manston. Many of their Spitfires were brand new, having been delivered the previous evening and prepared overnight. Things were not going well for the squadron—bombed at Eastchurch, their CO killed and half their number shot down. At 2 p.m. they were diverted to intercept Dorniers and, after a brief action, they returned to refuel at Manston. Eleven Spitfires taxied across the big grass airfield, trailing a huge backwash of swirling chalk dust towards the shelters and bowsers of the Servicing Flight. A few other planes were down, some of No 65's Spitfires and the odd Hurricane or two.

99

Pilots stood around, the shimmering vapour distorting vision as the fuel was sent gushing into the fighters' tanks. Belts of ammunition were threaded into the guns, oxygen bottles changed, the whole operation moving swiftly. Overhead the sky was full of planes and the pilots and airmen hoped that someone knew what was going on. The first they knew of the impending attack was the thump of cannon and the rattle of machine-gun fire: spurts of chalk dust darted around their Spitfires as 20 109s streaked over the field and were gone. Pilots and erks rose from where they had been crouching, except for a few men who were moaning on the ground; some planes were burning.

Then the 109s came again—shooting at everything. Joseph Lister, a private soldier in the Border Regiment, had emptied his Bren gun at the raiders when a Messerschmitt lashed him with a burst of fire and down he fell. As the dust and smoke swirled and the sound of Daimler-Benz engines receded out to sea, the pilots got to their feet, cursing as they surveyed the damage.

Many planes were burning with an incandescent brilliance. Four Spitfires and a Hurricane were totally destroyed and seven shot-through Spitfires would have to be rebuilt. One airman was killed and 15 injured, but the only casualties among the pilots was one needing treatment for shock and Sgt. Don Kingaby with a bullet-nicked finger. Private Lister was carried to an ambulance with five bullet wounds. Despite the amputation of his right leg he survived and was subsequently awarded the Military Medal. When S/Ldr. D. G. Spencer arrived to take command of 266 Sqdn. at Hornchurch, there wasn't very much left for him to command and they were withdrawn to reform at Wittering.

At 5 p.m. the seven remaining Hurricanes of 501 Sqdn. from Gravesend appeared over Hawkinge. Amongst them was F/Lt. Stoney, flying Hurricane P2549, which had been taken from Biggin Hill's Training Flight and had given Bill Green his maiden trip in a fighter. It had been a black day for 501. That morning 'Hawkeye' Lee had baled out wounded. Kozlowski the Pole went down seriously wounded and Sgt. Don McKay was also in hospital with burns after parachuting into a tree. Thirty-year-old P/O John Wellburn Bland, the son of a Bristol parson, was still buried in the ground in the remains of his plane. All four of these Hurricanes appeared to have been shot down by the same Messerschmitt, flown by Oblt. Gerhard Schoepfel of JG 26.

In the afternoon, returning to Gravesend, 501 had again been in combat near Biggin Hill. Tall, dashing Bob Dafforn had to abandon his fighter and F/Sgt. Morfill also went down. Fortunately they were both unhurt.

Now, whilst circling above Elham, they sighted some 58 German bombers with a heavy escort of Me 110s coming in over Deal. The seven Hurricanes rushed to engage them. However, only George Stoney ignored the JG 51 Messerschmitts that came out of the sun, scattering the rest of 501. He went on alone, trying to reach the bombers, until a few seconds later Hurricane P2549 was blasted from behind and plummeted in a screaming dive. During this action Hptm. 'Jakob' Tietzen and Lt. Lessing were killed, possibly falling to 501's revengeful Poles, Witorzenc and Zenker. Stoney's remains were sent to Sefton churchyard in Lancashire.

During the evening, Galland's 109s swept in over Elham again and tangled with 32

Sqdn., who were still flushed with their success in helping rout the raiders that had bombed Kenley and Croydon at midday. This time, 32 Sqdn. lost three Hurricanes, the pilots all escaping by parachute. However, at the top end of the valley they got Lt. Walter Blume, whose Messerschmitt hit a field full of cows at a shallow angle and ricocheted back into the air, giving the pilot just enough time to jump out and open his chute. Another 109 went into a wood upside down, taking Lt. Müller-Dühe to his death. It was the latter who had dispatched Sub-Lt. Greenshields over Calais the previous Friday.

At the end of the day, 31 British fighters had been destroyed and 22 others damaged. The Germans had lost 67 aircraft with many damaged.

19th August. Quite a normal day. All Britain declared a defence area.
The weather was mainly cloudy. Göring, far from satisfied with the progress of the battle, made recriminations and ordered a reorganization of his Jagdgeschwader.

20th August. Buzzy raid 2.30–3.30 p.m. Heavy guns Dover way. Churchill spoke on the war situation. It rained in the evening the first time for ages.
Major Gottardt Handrick, a Spanish Civil War ace, relinquished command of JG 26 in favour of Adolf Galland. To the intense irritation of the International Olympic Committee, Handrick, having won a Gold Medal at the Berlin Olympics, chose to decorate his Messerschmitt with five interlocking rings. The Committee regarded the unauthorized use of their registered symbol as an illegal act.

Weather conditions were again poor, but during the afternoon 27 Dorniers, escorted by JG 51, attacked Eastchurch once more. Also that afternoon, Sgt. Bill Green delivered a new Hurricane (R4222) to 501 Sqdn. at Gravesend and bumped into S/Ldr. Hogan, who was desperately short of pilots. The ex-fitter had been a protégé of 501 and when the CO learned what the sergeant was doing, he said 'Look, you come back here and we'll train you a lot faster.' That night Green returned with his kit and blundered about in the dark until he was directed to a hut where he got a cup of cocoa, some bread and cheese and was introduced to a Sgt. 'Ginger' Lacey, who was in the bed next to him. At that time, Bill Green had experienced just seven hours in a Hurricane, had never fired any guns, and had received no instruction on aerial combat.

21st August. Two bursts of AA during morning. Explosions—some AA during the afternoon. Ginger came to tea.
Full-scale Luftwaffe operations were curtailed because of bad weather.

It was just getting light at Gravesend when Bill Green was woken by someone shaking him and telling him to get up. He tried to explain: 'No, no, I'm new and my name is Green.' He was told: 'That's right, you're Green 3—Arsend Charlie.' Within half an hour he was up on his first operational patrol. He arrived at Hawkinge alone, having lost his squadron when he tried to carry out his weaving manoeuvre as 'Arsend Charlie'.

22nd August. Heavy bangs during gun fire attack on convoy in morning. Raid warning 1–2.50 p.m.—nothing but a few distant bangs and buzzing. Another

7–8 p.m. A Spitfire crashed in flames on Adam & Eve. Pilot landed. Dover shelled at 9.30—awful bangs.

In the morning about 100 shells were fired at a convoy off Dover, but no ships were hit. When bombers threatened to attack in the early afternoon, two Spitfire squadrons warded them off, but were themselves bounced by 109s. Sgt. D. F. Corfe of 610 Sqdn. brought his burning Spitfire down to crash-land at Hawkinge and jumped clear before it exploded. Sgt. Collett of 54 Sqdn. was shot down into the sea and killed. Sixty miles away at Kenley, 616 Sqdn., newly arrived from Yorkshire, were unwinding after having been at readiness all day under rain-threatening clouds. At teatime the pilots were released and several had gone off swiftly to bath and change, intent on having a night in London. However, a little later, the tannoy speakers in the officers' mess instructed them to return to their dispersal point. There the disgruntled pilots were told that Winston Churchill had arrived and was going to visit them.

Churchill had specifically come to Kenley to see the parachute and cable defence system that had claimed a Dornier making a low-level attack on the airfield the previous Sunday, but the Station Commander sensed that the PM wouldn't have appreciated seeing young pilots deserting the aerodrome for a night on the tiles in London. After ambling around the dispersal areas with his face set in an expression of sternness, Churchill went through the ritual of shaking hands with all the pilots and then, as if prearranged, 616 Sqdn. was scrambled to patrol base at 5,000 ft.

The washed and powdered officers, about to go on a spree, had to pull on oil-stained kit and straps over their best uniforms and put on a good show for the 'old boy'. All 14 of their Spitfires were taken up for what they thought was a demonstration. F/O Hugh 'Cocky' Dundas, one of those chafing to get away to London, thought they would circle a few times and land, but to his irritation the formation were ordered to fly east and start climbing towards distinctly brighter weather.

At 7.15 p.m. Dundas found himself at 12,000 ft over Folkestone, looking for an unidentified aircraft reported to be above Hawkinge. Over Elham, the villagers saw some puffs of smoke around the Spitfires and heard a high-pitched whine as 'Cocky' Dundas's fighter went out of control, started to spin and caught fire in quick succession. Later, he recalled the event:

White smoke filled the cockpit, thick and hot, and I could see neither the sky above nor the Channel coast 12,000 feet below. Centrifugal force pressed me against the side of the cockpit and I knew my airplane was spinning. Panic and terror consumed me and I thought 'Christ, this is the end'. Then I thought 'Get out, you bloody fool; open the hood and get out.' With both hands I tugged the handle where the hood locked onto the top of the windscreen. It moved back an inch, then jammed. Smoke poured out through the gap and I could see again.

I could see the earth and sea and the sky spinning round in tumbled confusion as I cursed and blasphemed and pulled with all my strength to open the imprisoning hood. If I could not get out I had at all costs to stop the spin. I pushed the stick hard forward, kicked on full rudder, and opened the throttle. Nothing happened. The earth went spinning on, came spinning up to meet me. Grabbing the hood toggle again, I pulled with all my might, pulled for my life, pulled, at last, with success.

(Far left) During the evening of 22nd August, Hugh 'Cocky' Dundas parachuted from his crashing Spitfire over Elham. (Imperial War Museum). (Left) Capt. J. M. G. 'Max' Wilson, MO of the 64th Field Regt. RA, rescued Dundas from civilians who wanted to entertain the injured pilot

I stood up on the seat and pushed the top half of my body out of the cockpit. Pressed hard against the fuselage, half in, half out, I struggled in a nightmare of fear and confusion to drop clear, but could not do so. I managed to get back into the cockpit, aware now that the ground was very close. A few seconds more, and we would be into it. Try again; try the other side. Up, over—and out. I slithered along the fuselage and felt myself falling free.

Seconds after my parachute opened, I saw the Spitfire hit and explode in a field below. A flock of sheep scattered outwards from the cloud of dust and smoke and flame.

Pilot and aircraft were on Adam & Eve, a hill at Elham, so-called because of two big trees that stood there at the turn of the century. George Parker, the opulent Peckham building contractor, who was second in command of the Home Guard, reached the spot just before the Army and the limping Dundas was found in the charge of a local man armed with an ancient hammer-gun.

Parker was delighted with his catch, a fine RAF officer with curly russet hair, in an immaculate uniform and polished shoes—he should be taken back to Henbury, displayed to the household and plied with refreshments befitting a hero. But when the Army arrived soon afterwards, Captain J. M. G. 'Max' Wilson, MO of the 64th Field Regiment RA thought otherwise. The tall pilot was in a shocked condition and was stooping strangely.

A discussion took place in the field, which soon developed into a heated argument. Dundas, although in pain, was willing to be taken away to accept George Parker's hospitality, but when the civilians started to lead him off, Captain Wilson felt obliged to restrain them with a direct order. The doctor, a shrewd Scot, was proved right, because when he examined the pilot at Acrise Place, he found his shoulder was dislocated. By nightfall Dundas was in the Kent and Canterbury Hospital.*

It was the general opinion that Dundas had been shot down by local AA guns, but the gunners claimed they had fired at enemy aircraft only. The matter was resolved when P/O Casson's Spitfire returned from the same patrol with a cannon shell hole in one wing and it was discovered that at about the same time as Dundas's mishap 65 Sqdn. were similarly attacked over Dover when three Spitfires were hit and Sgt. Keymer was killed.

23rd August. Quite normal except for a little very distant gunfire. Made Sambo [cat] a pillow out of my old dressing-gown.

For the second day running P/O Pfeiffer, one of 32 Sqdn.'s Poles, crashed a Hurricane landing at Hawkinge.

The Home Guard was being issued with a cheap denim copy of an Army battledress. There were only one or two sizes available and short, stocky Herbie Palmer was issued with a massive pair of trousers, the waist of which came up to his armpits. At first he tried to devise special braces to hold them up, but eventually his wife cut them up and remade them several sizes smaller. This kind of improvization was going on in homes all over Britain and, after a week or two, about one and a half million men of the Home Guard were kitted out in these curious uniforms.

Some ancient or obsolete rifles and automatic weapons started to be issued. Mostly American types that had been in storage since the First World War, there were also quite a number of Canadian Ross rifles that were extremely long and had a breech like a miniature naval gun. It was a proud occasion when the Home Guard were sent home with their greasy rifles and a clip of five rounds to keep at the ready—but out of the reach of children.

LAC Ronald Tudball was one of twelve flight mechanics who arrived at Folkestone by train. They clambered onto the platform in bright sunlight dragging kitbags, greatcoats and gas-masks and asked a porter what they should do to get to RAF Hawkinge. His reply was: 'The best thing you could do is go right back where you came from.'

The twelve had left Kinloss where everything seemed a complete muddle, their aero-engine maintenance course having tailed off when the station became inundated by hordes of dispirited airmen returning from France with depressing stories of the

---

*After recovering, Dundas rejoined his squadron and was groomed in new airfighting techniques with the Tangmere Wing, then commanded by Wg. Cdr. Douglas Bader. On 8 May 1941, four Spitfires, which included Dundas and Bader, were experimenting with a 'finger four' formation off Folkestone, inviting some 109s to attack. Werner Mölders obliged and Dundas became the Colonel's 82nd victory, but managed to survive a high-speed crash-landing at Hawkinge.

Dr J. M. G. Wilson volunteered to join the Airborne Forces and was parachuted into Normandy with the first assault troops several hours before the D-Day landings. After the war he had a distinguished career in the Ministry of Health.

'Blitzkrieg'. Tudball had been at school with a boy called John Cunningham, who made model aeroplanes. Cunningham had gone into the RAF after leaving school and Tudball wondered if he would bump into him somewhere. Within two years everyone in Britain would have heard of 'Cat's-eyes' Cunningham when his achievements as a night-fighter ace were given widespread publicity.

The weary and ravenous airmen, creased and crumpled after their long journey, soon found themselves in a truck leaving the almost deserted seaside town and grinding up the steep gradient skirting Sugerloaf Hill to deposit them outside the guardroom at Hawkinge. It was late afternoon when they arrived and were greeted by the sight of bricks and glass scattered all over the place and the big hangars in ruins. After a long wait, a senior NCO announced that they were to join No 11 Servicing Flight, whose job it was to keep fighter planes ready for battle. There were no proper quarters, but they would be issued with palliases and could kip down on the concrete floor of the gymnasium, which still had a roof.

The newcomers queued for bully-beef and beans and a big mug of tea at the airmen's mess. Everybody seemed to be carrying helmets or wearing them, and they were impressed to see that even the robust cooks were ladling out victuals wearing steel helmets.

24th August. Ghastly—Raids incessantly from 8.10–5.30 p.m. Bombs at Dreals! Terrific AA fire. Shelling over Dover.

At dawn there was heavy mist north of the Thames Estuary when the dew-covered Defiants of 246 Sqdn. took off from Hornchurch to fly to Manston. Their outgoing CO, S/Ldr. Hunter, was eager to vindicate the reputation of the two-seater fighters following the débâcle of 141 Sqdn. in July. Over Kent the mist cleared to reveal a perfect morning with a crystal clear sky and fighting started from 8.15.

F/O Cambell-Colquhoun was delayed in taking off on patrol with 264 Sqdn. because of engine trouble and when he eventually climbed over Manston, he tried to join up with a formation he assumed were Defiants. To his chagrin he discovered they were Messerschmitts and, as he made a 'run for it' with the sluggish two-seater, a burst of fire hit his aircraft behind the turret, igniting a box of signal cartridges. Green, crimson and white balls of fire leapt about in the fuselage and gunner P/O Robinson, sitting amidst a veritable firework display, was very lucky to escape serious injury.

Aircraft recognition was equally bad on the German side: Uffz Delfs of JG 51, rescued from the Channel by a seaplane, asserted that he was attacked by a Messerschmitt. Over Calais an Me 109 of JG 3, sporting bright yellow wing-tips and markings to aid recognition, was savaged by another 109. Fw. Oglodek of JG 51 was killed when his aircraft was seen to collide with an RAF fighter, the identity of which was obscure, but it may have been the irascible Pole, P/O Zenker, who showed no regard for the welfare of his plane or himself when fighting the Luftwaffe.

Raiders were over Manston at 10.30 and an hour later Ramsgate and Broadstairs suffered severe bombing. Thirty-one people were killed and there was considerable damage to civilian property. At 12.55 p.m. another big formation arrived over Manston, when only three Defiants were patrolling overhead. Despite a Homeric battle, the three

(Above) F/O Rupert Smythe warming up his Hurricane at Hawkinge. (Fox). (Right) Australian troops amused by the badge on Obfw. Beek's Messerschmitt. Although this plane crashed near Dover, it was deposited in an aircraft dump at Elham. (Dennis Knight)

were quite unable to prevent the airfield getting a pounding from JU 88s. However S/Ldr Hunter managed to get most of his squadron into the air and nine Defiants went into action. The Hurricanes of 501 Sqdn. rushed from Hawkinge and helped punish the Junkers, but Sgt. Bill Green was hit by the Manston AA guns before he had a chance to engage the raiders. Fortunately he left the fray just as a host of 109s joined in. Three Defiants disappeared into the sea and the gallant Philip Hunter, with recently commissioned Freddie King, his air gunner, were never seen again. Major Lützow, Kommodore of JG 3, had shot down two Defiants, and was hoping to meet up with them again.

Bill Green limped back to Hawkinge with his screen and hood covered in dark engine oil. He landed L1659 with a dead engine, and was shocked when the plane spun out of control as it touched down and pirouetted to a halt with its nose dug in the ground. Only one undercarriage leg had come down. As the 109s left, they used up their ammunition shooting down some of the Dover balloons.

AC2 Cliff Vincent, with his hut mates from the Dover radar station, were sauntering along the cliff-top road near East Langdon when a Messerschmitt came gliding in fast with a dead engine to make a perfect belly landing in a field close by. Within seconds a black Wolseley saloon drew up and and two flat-capped policemen entered the field to arrest the German pilot. Oil-splattered Obfw. Beek, who was on his second sortie that morning, was conducted to the car and driven away.

During the afternoon Heinkels went for Hornchurch and 32 Sqdn., led by S/Ldr. Crossley, battled twice with Messerschmitts over Elham valley. Unfortunately they lost another five Hurricanes.

At Elham post office the Smiths came out to watch the air battles. Suddenly there was excited shouting: 'Look! there's one going down . . . Yes, I can see it, look—he's baled out!' Arthur Wootten, standing in front of his petrol station, saw a parachute blossom behind a descending Hurricane. Jumping into his Austin Ten, he raced along the lanes until he arrived on the hillside at Shuttlesfield. There he found an officer with a small sandy moustache suffering from cannon shell splinters in his shoulder and legs. Dr Hunter-Smith soon arrived with his medicine bag and, after examining the pilot, established that his wounds were rather more painful than serious. Surgery was necessary to remove all the little slivers of metal and the doctor could do no more than apply sterile dressings.

For F/O Rupert Smythe, it was the fourth time he'd been shot down over the district, but on previous occasions he had managed to reach Hawkinge. He cheerfully accepted a little hospitality at Lower Court, where Martin Constant was famed for his generosity with whisky. However, the wounded pilot made it quite clear that he wasn't going to be taken back to Hawkinge: he felt much safer in the cockpit of a fighter than on the ground at the aerodrome. His benefactors were sympathetic and by nightfall he was being made comfortable at the Royal Masonic Hospital in London.

By the evening, wrecked Hurricanes were scattered around Lyminge. S/Ldr. Michael Crossley had escaped from one fighter that skidded across a field near Valley Farm. At the time he was the RAF's leading ace, having been credited with 20 victories. That day's score was 38 Luftwaffe planes for 25 British fighters, and from 5.30 German shells started to fall in the district, one or two just missing the aerodrome.

At Manston something had gone seriously wrong with morale. Some airmen were refusing to leave their shelters during daylight for fear of being caught in the open when the Messerschmitts made their lightning strafing attacks. Others were hiding away for days, only coming out to make nocturnal foraging trips. An administrative officer couldn't get a pay parade organised as the airmen weren't bothering to read daily orders or were unwilling to stand in the open for half an hour to salute an officer and collect a few shillings. The absence of several personnel went unnoticed for days because it was assumed they were casualties from the bombing and were either dead or in some hospital.

25th August. Quite nice—nothing but a slight buzz 6.30–7.30 p.m. Lord Halifax and Mrs Eden at Church in morning. Saw them drive away.

Many, including the King, thought Halifax should have been given the premiership following Chamberlain's resignation in May of that year. Mary noticed that the immaculately dressed 'Lord Holy Fox' always wore a grey glove on one hand.

That Sunday the battle switched to the West Country, but during the evening there was fighting over Kent when Dorniers came over with a strong escort. 32 Sqdn., scheduled for a rest, battled for the last time. P/O Gillman disappeared into the sea and P/O Rose had to parachute when his rudder was shot away. However, someone blew Oblt. Heinrich Held's 109 to pieces.

At Elham a burning Hurricane flew low down the valley and suddenly flicked on its back, allowing the pilot to drop out and open his parachute. Arthur Wootten said 'It was one of the neatest things I've ever seen.' The pilot hit the ground heavily in a cornfield at Ottinge, the silk canopy settling over the prostrate figure. After a pause, the hump sprang into life and a flailing man, cursing in Polish, struggled to get into the sunlight. Being Sunday, people appeared very quickly until there were about a hundred attending the tall Pole who spoke very little English and gesticulated wildly in an endeavour to explain that he'd baled out over the district the previous day. When a car came to take him back to Hawkinge, the local people formed a passage for him to reach the car and spontaneous clapping broke out—just as if he were a batsman returning to the pavilion after a spirited innings.

A couple of days later an interpreter extracted the following report from P/O Karol Pniak, better known to the pilots of 32 Sqdn. as 'Cognac'.

I was flying No 3 of Blue Section when we met 12 Me 109s at about 2,000 ft; they were above us and attacked us. I was attacked by an Me 109 from head-on and above. I circled round on his tail and closing to 150 yards gave him two 2-second bursts. He started to smoke from the engine, I followed him and gave him two more bursts; much black smoke came from the aircraft and he was diving. Just after this I felt my machine vibrating and saw smoke coming from the engine and right wing, flames also appearing from the right wing. I switched everything off and put my aircraft into a dive to land, but when I reached 5,000 ft the flames were so big, that I turned my plane on one side and jumped. I landed very fast because my parachute was not properly open and full of big holes. I landed 3 miles NW of Hawkinge, my ankle and knee were injured and I was taken to hospital.

26th August. Raids at 12 & 3 p.m. not bad here but bombs on Folkestone. Letter from Joan telling of dreadful time in Ramsgate on Saturday.

During the night code-word 'B' was sent to all Service units in the south-east and thousands of servicemen were armed and went out into the darkness expecting invasion. Sgt. Bill Green, who had survived his first few days of air fighting, was Duty Pilot at Gravesend that night. He was roused by an Army officer on the telephone who passed him on to a more senior officer, who in turn said the Brigadier-General was going to speak to him personally. The Brigadier asked Green to identify himself and, when satisfied, said: 'I have the most important message you will ever have in your life and I want to be certain that you will take it to your Commanding Officer at once. Now this is the message—Unnatural fog has been observed out to sea stretching from Yarmouth to Beachy Head. Believed enemy Invasion Force behind it. All forces to stand to.' Inflamed with a sense of urgency, Bill Green found S/Ldr. Hogan and shook him from a deep sleep. After grunting and listening to the message, his CO informed him: 'OK! give it to the Station Defence Officer and go back to bed.' Soon after dawn, code-word 'B' was cancelled.

Having lost two pilots the previous evening, it was another disastrous day for 616 Sqdn. from Kenley. Blue and Yellow sections were sent to intercept a lone Heinkel which escaped in cloud over Elham. Then Blue section were detached to look for a loose barrage balloon over Romney Marsh and were ambushed by a massive force of Me 109s. All three were shot down. Meanwhile 'A' flight had also come down from Kenley and were caught unawares by Messerschmitts of JG 51. By lunchtime, F/O George Moberley and Sgt. 'Marmaduke' Ridey were dead, F/O Teddy St Aubin, an ex-Guards officer was burned and P/Os Walker and Marples and Sgt. Copeland were all in hospital. Jack Bell was also shot down but unhurt.

When 610 Sqdn. went into eight 109s over Folkestone, Spitfires and Messerschmitts started to fall. P/O Frank Webster, son of an Isle of Wight publican, smashed into the ground flaming near Hawkinge, whilst Sgt. Else baled out seriously wounded before his Spitfire crashed on Castle Hill. Another Spitfire went down at Paddlesworth and was burned out. On the credit side S/Ldr. Ellis and F/O Wilson sent a 109 into the sea and Sgt. Hamlyn attacked two more, one of which dived into the sea. The day's score was 30 RAF for 42 Luftwaffe: at that ratio the British had no hope of winning.

27th August. Quite decent. A few pops at a stray Jerry about 12 and a buzz at 1 p.m.

This was a day of rest for the Luftwaffe.

28th August. Terrible all day. Bombs at Park Lane. Alice slept here.

There were air battles all day. 79 Sqdn., Joslin's old squadron reformed and refreshed, came down to Biggin Hill from the north led by S/Ldr. Heyworth. At 8.25 they were sent to Hawkinge and were immediately embroiled in a dog-fight over Elham. At 9.05 Oblt. Erich Kircheis, the adjutant of JG 51, became separated from the Staff Flight and seconds later his 109 caught in the shot-gun blast of eight Brownings was sent into a screaming spiral dive. Hunched behind his armour plating, he was spared being pierced by bullets, but had great difficulty leaving the plane and broke a leg landing by parachute.

Churchill arrived in Dover by special train, accompanied by some US naval and military observers. He had made it clear to them that the British were going to hold Dover and stop any invasion. The Americans toured the coastal defences and were given lunch in Dover Castle. During the afternoon they witnessed a dog-fight and Colonel Raymond E. Lee described it to his wife in a letter:

> . . . *as we were inspecting we saw one German plane take its death dive, whirring down almost vertically with a whining note, finally ending in a dull 'Whoomph' as it hit the ground. The pilot had forsaken his machine just under the clouds and came swaying down in a large white parachute as rotund and delicate-looking as a bubble. At the same time a German bomber came tumbling down into the sea, where it disappeared with a good-sized splash, while a British motor boat put out to capture what might be left of the crew.*

The Prime Minister had visited Ramsgate and Manston and was angry at the senseless destruction of shops and homes. In the evening he stopped to see the wreck of a Messerschmitt at Whitfield. The whole party boarded the train again at 7.45 and, talking through his cigar, Churchill told the Americans that Berlin was going to be bombed hard that very night—a snap decision made in what appeared to be a fit of pique. The Prime Minister was certainly in a highly-charged emotional state, angry because Manston had become untenable and deeply moved by the councillors of smashed Ramsgate. His intake of alcohol during the day had not been inconsiderable, but during a hearty dinner on the train he recovered his composure and acted the garrulous host to the American observers.

The sky above Elham was a turmoil of planes for most of the day. At one point Major Galland, with JG 26, scattered the Defiants of 264 Sqdn. just as they were about to slide under a formation of Heinkels to fire into their bellies. At Petham, a Defiant and a Messerschmitt fell in adjoining meadows. Sgt. Geof Goodman, a very experienced Hurricane pilot, who'd been grounded for a long time following concussion, was led in action twice that day by S/Ldr. Peter Townsend. In his second combat Goodman managed to turn in behind a 109 and opened fire, but he was tensed up and his shooting was wild and inaccurate. On his return to Croydon, he made a detour to fly over his home town of Horley in Surrey.

At teatime Sgt. George Smythe of 56 Sqdn. abandoned his burning Hurricane three miles up above Elham. It came screaming down with its engine at full power and flew splintering through Ladwood before exploding in a great fireball. Finally that evening a single Messerschmitt came down Elham valley trailing smoke with a Spitfire close behind. From Truckshall Cottage below Beachborough, Sid Eade and his 14-year-old son watched them roar over Newington and out to sea where the RAF pilot, S/Ldr. Denholm, gave the 109 another burst. Executing a perfect U-turn, the German put on power to clear the terraced slopes of Hythe, just missed Saltwood Castle, and then flew through high-tension cables with a terrific flash before belly-landing near the railway tunnel. The pilot, with bullet-grazed face and head, leapt from the burning machine and walked calmly towards the Eades' cottage, adroitly jumping a fence en route.

29th August. Only two raids. Saw a plane fall and parachute come down.

A quieter day, but bombers came over acting as decoys for groups of 109s waiting to pounce from above. 603 Sqdn. from Edinburgh lost five Spitfires quickly over Romney Marsh. Purely by chance, P/O Hillary crash-landed in a field into which his chum, Colin Pinkney, descended by parachute. After seeing Pinkney off to hospital, Hillary ended up getting stoned at a regimental cocktail party in a nearby country house.

In the evening, 501 patrolling Gravesend at Angels 15 were ordered to climb south to patrol Hawkinge. There were no clouds and visibility was good. Some Spitfires were up and were involved in an engagement. At 6.45 Sgt. Beardsley made a beam attack on one of six Me 109s at 25,000 ft and it went down in a steep turning dive over Hawkinge. Sgt. Baker attacked another at 15,000 ft and saw it go into a dive smoking heavily.

At about the same time, 501 Sqdn. were either attacked in the rear or hit by AA shells over Elham and two planes were shot down before the squadron scattered. Lacey spotted a 109 and after a long chase nailed it with an accurate burst.

Bill Green was in one of the Hurricanes that went down. He recalled later:

Without warning a hole appeared in the $1\frac{1}{4}$ inch plate windscreen as big as a tennis ball and the noise of the splinters shattering around the cockpit will always remain with me. I was immediately covered with glycol liquid and the control column was just like a piece of stick disconnected to anything and quite useless. The engine stopped and I realised that I had to get out.

Sliding back the hood and pulling the pin from his Sutton harness, Green stood up and found himself free of the aircraft and rotating forward with his legs apart. Both flying boots came off and a considerable time passed as he fumbled for his rip-cord. When he pulled it he saw the little pilot chute deploy and detach itself from the main chute, which started to come out between his legs—still folded like a roller-towel. Then as the folded silk came apart, it wrapped itself about him, enveloping him as he plummeted down at terminal velocity. He pushed and tugged, resorted to prayer and thought about his wife Bertha, with whom he'd spent the previous night—she had knitted the warm socks he was wearing. As he realised that he was only seconds from oblivion, there was a jolt and a secondary tug as the parachute lines were ripped from the tangled pack and he floated free. After the terror of the fall with rushing air and flapping silk the silence was 'noisier than any noise I have ever heard'. He saw electricity pylons, relaxed and thudded down on a hill overlooking Elham.

For a while Bill Green stayed still, contemplating the beauty of the landscape, and then became concerned at the prospect of walking in his new socks across a field covered with thistles and cow manure. But he was rescued by Helen Goldup and taken off to Millhill Farm. When troops came to collect him, he was sitting in a comfortable chair having tea. After fainting when the MO at Hawkinge dug a piece of metal out of his knee, he was reunited with F/Lt. Gibson, who had been shot down at the same time, and later that night a staff car took them both back to Gravesend.

Green's fighter had landed in Ladwood, which had received a flaming Hurricane the previous day. Across Romney Marsh other squadrons were bounced that evening and, over Rye, Peter Townsend lost a Hurricane which fell like a comet to hit the ground

Sgt. Bill Green went into battle as the most inexperienced pilot in Fighter Command—and survived when his Hurricane was blasted out of the sky over Elham. (W. Green)

beside Camber Castle. The pilot, F/Lt. Harry Hamilton from Canada, was buried in Hawkinge cemetery.

30th August. Terrible—Raids nearly all day.

This was a day of massive air fighting during which the battle became particularly ferocious over Surrey. F/O Teddy Morris, a South African of 79 Sqdn., flew into a Heinkel, knocking a wing off. Two Messerschmitts collided when a Kenley pilot was being machine-gunned to death whilst descending by parachute. S/Ldr. Denholm 'Uncle George' of 603 Sqdn., lost another two Spitfires, including his own called 'Blue Peter', from which he parachuted over Brenzett. And 222 Sqdn., just down from the north, obviously weren't employing the right tactics: although only one of their pilots was killed, they lost nine Spitfires.

After making a formation head-on attack at Heinkels over Bethersden, Sgt. Geof Goodman of 85 Sqdn. found himself under a great canopy of Me 110s that were not inclined to attack the RAF fighters below them. He pulled his Hurricane (VY-V) up, singled out a target for a longish burst, and was delighted to see it trail smoke and leave the formation. He then sighted a lone Me 110 and went after it over Hythe. His first burst at the fuselage was rather wild, but Goodman settled down to concentrate on shooting accurate bursts at the engines, both of which started to smoke nicely. He followed the enemy as it lost height and watched it turn back over the sea in an attempt to reach land. When some 4–5 miles off Sandgate the 110 flopped into the sea near a launch its wings folded up as it sank, leaving no trace of the crew. To celebrate the occasion, Sgt. Goodman flew back over his home town of Horley and executed a series of rolls which kept them talking for weeks. The people knew who it was and waved sheets and towels at him.

Lympne aerodrome got another pasting at 3 p.m. when the one remaining hangar was destroyed. At the Elham Valley ARP report centre at Lyminge, the heavy explosions were heard some few minutes before a telephone message came through with a request for ambulances to be sent at once because an air-raid shelter had been hit. Mrs Harrowing, the attractive wife of a major in the Duke of Cornwall's Light Infantry, was on duty as a volunteer ambulance driver and she completed the five-mile journey in record time in the green Austin car that was used for sitting casualties. However, as soon as she reached the scarred airfield, she was hustled down a shelter because raiders were still overhead. She spent some time in a very stuffy dugout crowded with silent soldiers and airmen clasping rifles. When at last it was safe for her to emerge, she was told there weren't any sitting casualties. But Stan Woods and the other ambulance drivers brought the remains of several men back to Lyminge mortuary.

On that day 28 RAF aircraft were down for 48 Luftwaffe.

31st August. Not quite so bad. Fierce scrap overhead at 9 a.m. Nazi came down by parachute in Hog Green. Saw him. Only slightly wounded.
At breakfast time Messerschmitt pilots displayed skill and bravado by weaving amongst

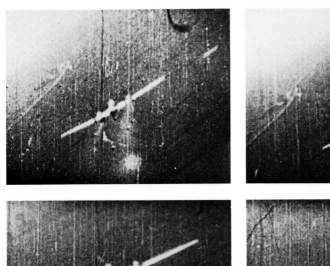
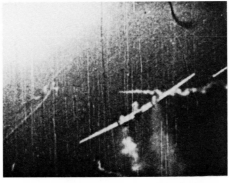
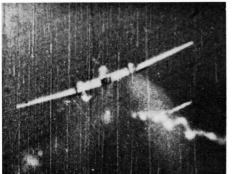
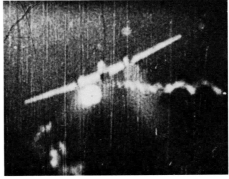

Camera-gun pictures recording the end of an Me 110. The spirals of smoke mark the path of tracer bullets. (Imperial War Museum)

113

(Above) Air ace Oblt. Eckhart Priebe, just before he was shot down over Elham. (Priebe). (Above right) Priebe descending over Elham, photographed by Dr Hunter-Smith. (Dr Hunter-Smith)

the Dover barrage balloons for about half an hour and firing incendiary ammunition. The balloon crews seethed with anger as, one by one, all the great silver gas bags sagged and crumpled into a burning mass. Roofs were burned and it took days to unravel miles of steel cable from the chimneys. In monetary terms, it had cost the equivalent of $1\frac{1}{2}$ fighters.

JG 51 had been reinforced by attaching I/JG 77 to form a fourth Gruppe. Among their pilots was the ace Oblt. Eckhart Priebe (Iron Cross 1st class), one of the golden boys of the Luftwaffe. Exceptionally well educated and the son of a famous churchman, Priebe had been a member of the 'Göring Kadetten' élite and had shot down two Russian Ratas in the Spanish Civil War before being wounded. He had returned to Germany to become the personal aide of Feldmarschall Milch who, after Göring, was the Chief Executive of the Luftwaffe and its prime mentor. Although ordained for advancement by staff appointment, Priebe had managed to get in some combat flying over Poland and France, where he shot down two French aircraft and a Hurricane.

The eager pilots of I/JG 77 took off after breakfast and climbed over the Channel in loose formation to pass over Elham at combat altitude. Each fighter bore the emblem of a worn-out boot painted on the cowling, an allusion to the group's nomadic moves between Silesia, Poland, France, Germany and Denmark. The pilots thought the Battle of Britain was nearly over and they were anxious to score kills before it was too late. The *Freie Jagd*, led by Oblt. Erick, penetrated deep into Kent before they tangled with RAF fighters. And then things started to go wrong for Priebe.

Yorkshireman Denys Gillam, who attacked and crippled Eckhart Priebe's Messerschmitt. At the time he was a F/Lt. with 616 Sqdn. (Fort Perch Rock Aviation Museum)

Having selected a target he found his guns wouldn't fire, probably, he believed, because of too much oil, but he continued to lead his *Staffel*, taking them into lunging attacks and then pulling aside at the last moment to observe how his comrades were doing. 'It worked only partly as, inevitably, I got deeper involved than planned. Finally, heading for the Channel, I had some assorted Spits and Hurricanes on my tail, obviously aware of my calamity. To my luck they were crowding each other, as everybody wanted my scalp and thus their shooting was somewhat erratic, to say the least.'

However, his plane flew through a spray of bullets and the complicated maze of pipes and rubber hoses that circulated the vital cooling fluid was pierced. Very soon the bellowing engine started to protest. Another burst caught his plane and the missiles entered the slender fuselage behind the cockpit, one bullet entering the cabin and ricochetting back, striking him on the forehead. It is uncertain who shot Priebe down, but the New Zealander, F/O Brian Carbury of 603, and F/Lt. Denys Gillam of 616, both seem to have assisted in his downfall.

At 12,000 ft above Elham, Priebe jumped out and opened his parachute. His first fleeting impression was of an RAF fighter zooming around him, discharging bursts into space as if intended as a victory salute. By this time the cut on his head was bleeding freely and he had to wipe blood from his eyes to see his watch face, which showed 10.23 (9.23 a.m. British time). For the next seven minutes he contemplated the few thousand feet that separated him from captivity and marvelled at the incredible beauty of the Kent countryside. As he drifted in the morning breeze, down below he saw little figures running across fields and, to his amusement, he noticed that his 'reception committee' was so intent on looking up as they ran, that several of its members stumbled and fell headlong. He saw the church spire and then experienced a moment's anxiety as he came dangerously close to some electricity cables. 'I tried to accelerate my fall by pulling the lines in on one side of my chute. It worked, but I released too late and, as a result, I landed not in a forward roll as you are always told you should, but with my hands still on the chute lines on my back, thus getting bent and twisted in various parts of my body and legs. I also conked out for a few seconds.' Just before he landed in the King George playing field, Dr Hunter-Smith clicked the shutter of his camera and then returned to his surgery.

Eighteen-year-old Enid, the Vicar's cook, was one of the first on the scene and there was one woman waving a big stick. Mrs Grace Champion ran to the airman carrying a cupful of water. PC Hampshire came jogging along the road at a brisk trot from the police house and he described the situation as 'chaotic'.

Strong hands lifted Priebe to his feet and the villagers came forward to peer, as if he were an apparition from outer space. He was just what they expected of a Jerry ace— smart flying boots, black leather jacket and even an Iron Cross. People kept touching him to see if he was real and, after taking a sip of water, the onlookers were astonished when Priebe said 'Good morning' to those who came near him. Within seconds the villagers were reciprocating the greeting.

The Reverend Williams presented himself wearing a strange mixture of priestly attire and battledress, with the buttons of his blouse done up incorrectly and giving him a peculiar hunchback appearance. When the Vicar tried to effect some preliminary first-aid, Priebe completely misunderstood and thought he was trying to administer the last rites.

An entourage escorted the posturing Priebe to the vicarage via the tennis court path, where a vintage sedan car appeared with Army driver to take him to Sibton Park. When PC Hampshire decided to travel in the car and get a proper signed receipt for the prisoner he discovered to his surprise that the German spoke perfect English.

That night Priebe went to sleep not knowing that JG 77 had lost seven Messerschmitts that day and that he would shortly be reunited with his friend, Oblt. Erick.

Werner Mölders was back on form and just before 9 a.m. claimed three Hurricanes in quick succession. The fighting was now almost demonic and the Poles of 303 Sqdn. could not be restrained from queuing up to fire bursts at Oblt. von Perthes as he descended by parachute over Surrey.

1st September. Scrapping and parachute down at North Elham. Sudden violent AA fire at 3.30. Tiles off Uncle's roof. AA at snooping Jerries at night.
On this Sunday, Air Marshal Dowding was desperately worried because yesterday's figure of 39 RAF fighters destroyed was not good. He would have been even more worried had he known the Germans had lost only 38. The battle had now become a flat-out contest between the dwindling forces of Fighter Command and the might of the Luftwaffe. The entire weight of the German effort was exclusively concentrated on destroying the British fighter defences and, with one or two exceptions, all attacks on factories were directed to disrupt production of fighter aircraft. Fortunately for the British, the Germans did not know that there was only one drop-hammer in Britain that was capable of forging crankshaft stampings for the Rolls-Royce 'Merlin' aero engines, situated at the Vickers' works in Sheffield. The 15 ton steam hammer was kept constantly in operation month after month by two teams of eight men, producing an average 84 stampings per shift.

The Germans believed that once they had eliminated the British fighters, the Royal Navy and the whole of Britain could be systematically bombed into submission and softened up for operation 'Sealion'. Indeed it was true that in some tired RAF squadrons morale was getting low, especially in those that had received a succession of replacement leaders. Also, what the people of Britain did not know was that Dowding and the Chiefs of Staff had a contingency plan to withdraw fighter cover from the south of England, including London, if and when the strength of Fighter Command fell to a certain level that was considered the minimum requirement to give air support to the forces opposing a German invasion.

Dowding, and only he, at the lonely pinnacle of his Command, could make that decision. He had husbanded a dozen reserve squadrons and had nine first-line squadrons in the Midlands, which he was loath to use until the invasion started. In any case, many of the reserve squadrons were those that had been rested after suffering heavy losses and their inexperienced—and often inadequately trained—replacement pilots were being decimated when fed into the battle. He decided to continue, where possible, the rotation of squadrons between the front line in the south and the comparative quiet of the north. But statistics were beginning to show that exhausted squadrons of experienced pilots tended to suffer less casualties than re-formed units with novice pilots from the north. The Cabinet and Chiefs of Staff had no real idea of how desperately concerned the introverted Commander-in-Chief really was; they only noticed that he didn't have the personal buoyancy and vigour that they expected.

At 11.30 a.m., dozens of people living just north-west of Elham came out of their homes to watch the extraordinary flying display put on by a lone Hurricane. Harold Pilcher, the Head Warden and village storekeeper of Stelling Minnis, came out of his shop with his wife and staff to watch the antics of the demented aeroplane as it circled overhead. It was obviously out of control, twisting and turning, climbing and diving, and it was only a matter of time before it would fall out of the sky—as far away as possible, so the villagers hoped. After ten minutes it flew off to the north but, when nearly out of sight, the wretched machine turned and came back on a reciprocal course. As if guided by some ghostly hand, it came down in a gentle descent over Bossingham, flew between two trees, and made straight for an isolated bungalow, where it landed straight on the roof. The plane was almost undamaged, except that the huge engine broke out of its mountings, crashed through the kitchen ceiling and extinguished the life of Mrs Elizabeth Boughton. The cockpit was empty.

Now that Peter Townsend was in hospital with a shot-off toe, P/O 'Sammy' Allard, DFM, an ex-sergeant pilot, found himself leading 85 Sqdn. over Hawkinge. He sighted a *Staffel* of 109s about to attack the Dover balloons and positioned his squadron so as to attack from out of the sun. With them was Sgt. Geof Goodman, who was flying a brand-new Canadian-built Hurricane (P5171). He went after four 109s flying in line astern and joined up close behind, apparently unobserved. Taking very careful aim, he took a dead bead on the last aircraft, flown by Lt. Strasser, and fired. His Hurricane jawed viciously, because only the four guns on one side were working. But it had been enough to chop pieces off one wing of the 109 and Goodman was so fascinated by the antics of the crippled plane that he made the mistake of not glancing in his mirror. There was a terrific noise and stench of cordite as his Hurricane caught the full blast of a burst at point-blank range. His new fighter was riddled and part of the hood was blown off; two bullets had actually entered the cockpit and passed through. Goodman could find no way of escaping the enemy fighter sitting on his tail and finally put his Hurricane into a deliberate spin to make it seem as if it was out of control. Since he was near the ground, this was a very dangerous thing to do because to get out of the spin he was forced to put the

(Left-right) Sergeants Webster, Geof Goodman and Berkley, and S/Ldr. Peter Townsend, C O of 85 Sqdn., shortly after having had a toe shot off by a cannon shell. (Imperial War Museum)

fighter in a flat-out dive. As the speed mounted up alarmingly he put his feet on the instrument panel and pulled back on the control column with both hands. He pulled out, but in so doing the air pressure on the underside of his machine was so great that the fabric covering burst in several places. Perspiring profusely, he flew back to Croydon very gingerly, prudently deciding not to indulge in any aerobatics over Horley.

Back at Croydon, everybody agreed he was lucky to have returned in such a badly damaged plane. Soon afterwards, Goodman learnt that 85 Sqdn. were being moved out. In a big battle soon after lunch three more pilots had died and five Hurricanes were missing. P/O Lewis had crashed his shot-up fighter on the aerodrome.

At 3.32 p.m., Lympne was bombed again and two mechanics were killed as they tried to repair a Hurricane that had made an emergency landing. At 5.30, five Messerschmitt fighter-bombers passed low over Hawkinge dropping bombs that detonated amongst the wrecked hangars.

2nd September. Raids nearly all day.

In August 1940 the *Daily Telegraph* had appointed Harry Flower as special correspondent to gather news of the air battles over Kent. This affable and urbane reporter spent a lot of his time in the hotels and bars at Dover and Folkestone, where

'Daily Telegraph' special correspondent Harry Flower was present when Gefr. Schockenhoff was captured after parachuting from an Me 110. The officer and sergeant-major were from the 34th Searchlight Regiment

correspondents gravitated from both sides of the Atlantic, and during September the front page of the *Telegraph* was dominated by Harry Flower's prose, his stories having been gleaned from chatting with Hawkinge officers or by observing dog-fights over Dover. However, when the main fighting moved inland, he decided to share the expenses of a car and driver with a photographer from the Fox agency.

Clad in voluminous tweed plus-fours and wearing a steel helmet, he became a well-known figure around east Kent.

On this Monday morning, the two pressmen were above Elham watching some 20 Dorniers in 'V' formation, with an escort of Messerschmitts, fly over the coast unhampered, except for puffs of smoke from bursting AA shells. As the Dorniers were booming over Acrise, a small formation of Hurricanes engaged them. Flower reported:

The British fighters, tiny by comparison with the big black Dorniers, weaved in and out above and below them and, in a matter of two minutes, the bombers were broken and dispersed. . . . Two went hurtling down in volumes of dense black smoke and I was about to make in the direction of one of them, when a Hurricane began to speed all round a twin-engined Messerschmitt 110 in ever decreasing circles.

Harry Flower watched the two fighters through binoculars and, as the Hurricane's machine-guns rattled out a burst, he saw an airman jump from the German plane. This was just what was wanted. The pressmen leapt into their car and raced through the deserted country lanes in the direction of Alkham where the parachute was descending. Screeching to a halt under a shady hedgerow, they clambered into a field simultaneously with soldiers and police—just as the airman dropped to the ground. Both pressmen rushed towards the parachutist on the heels of a burly sergeant major of the 34th Searchlight Regiment, an enormous .45 revolver in his hand.

The young German, Gefreiter Schockenhoff, once he had been assisted to stand up, looked rather concerned about his welfare as a ring of armed men converged on him. However, after being given a cigarette and a swig from a soldier's water bottle, he became more composed. Just before being taken away to captivity in a truck, he was obliged to make an effort to read a letter thrust at him by a local woman whose son had been taken prisoner in France. The smouldering remains of the Me 110 were found beside the ancient ruins of St Radigund's Abbey. Somehow the pilot, Lt. Schipper, had survived.

By this time there were the carcasses and twisted remains of crashed aircraft scattered all over the county and, later in the day, the two pressmen toured behind Romney Marsh, where at Bilsington they stopped to photograph an Me 110 that had belly-landed quite whole the previous day.

72 Sqdn., recently down from the north, operated from Hawkinge this day. Their previous CO, Wing Commander Ronnie Lees, had permission to spend a week's leave flying with his old squadron and, returning to Hawkinge after his first combat, ground personnel had to lever and wrench his cockpit open as a cannon shell had welded the frame to the windscreen. On his next sortie, he was wounded in the thigh and had to crash-land. S/Ldr. A. R. Collins, the current CO, was shot down twice this day and also ended up in hospital, wounded in both the knee and hand.

3rd September. Not quite so bad. Odd waves of Jerries coming back from London. 50 American destroyers for Britain.

Fighting started at 10 a.m., when heavily escorted Dorniers crossed Kent and made for North Weald aerodrome in Essex. Once over target, they unloaded their bombs, hitting hangars, the motor transport yard and stores. Two Hurricanes and a Blenheim were set on fire and many vehicles were burned out. The station was fortunate in only having two killed and 37 injured—one bomb actually detonating on the reinforced concrete roof of the operations room without penetrating. A huge air battle developed between the

P/O Richard Hillary shortly before his features were burned away in a blazing Spitfire. Hillary recovered, after protracted surgery, and wrote 'The Last Enemy' before perishing in a flying accident

opposing fighter aircraft. Just prior to the attack, the Blenheims of 25 Sqdn. took off and, being mistaken for enemy aircraft, two were promptly shot down by Hurricanes.

One of the first to intercept the raiders was P/O Richard Hillary who, although epitomizing the handsome product of a typical upper middle-class English education, was born in Australia of Australian parents. He was a descendant of Sir William Hillary, the founder of the Royal National Lifeboat Institution. In four days this young and idealistic officer had sent down four Messerschmitts, then at 10 a.m. one got him. He fell, trapped in the cockpit of his blazing Spitfire, for several thousand feet, whilst a blow-torch of flame seared his fine features and shrivelled his hands. When he finally managed to clamber out, much of his uniform had been burned away and he parachuted into the sea in agony. Nearly two hours later, the crew of the Margate lifeboat pulled the young man out of the water. The RNLI report stated:

1015 AM Coastguards reported airman in sea 7 miles NE of Reculver. The sea was smooth with light N.W. wind. 10.25 Life-boat 'J. B. Proudfoot' launched—11.45 she found airman. He was badly burned and was on the point of collapse, after having been in the sea for over an hour. Mr. A. C. Robinson the honorary secretary was aboard and bandaged the airman and gave him stimulants. Another boat was asked to wireless for medical help to be ready to receive the airman when the Life-boat came ashore—after a journey at high speed the Life-boat landed the airman at 1 p.m. and he was taken to Margate Hospital. (Rewards £5-12-6) The parents of the airman sent the crew a letter of thanks.

At the hospital doctors and nurses started cutting the charred clothing from the swollen white flesh, whilst Hillary mumbled his name and that of his next of kin before being given morphine. That evening he lay suspended in straps whilst the skin around his eyes was smeared with gentian violet and the rest of his burned flesh was coated with tannic acid, which coloured it black and made it go quite hard.

By the end of the day, 27 RAF fighters had been destroyed or were in need of repair, and the same number of Luftwaffe aircraft had been put out of action. It was about this time that the Elham Home Guard started to raise money for the Spitfire Fund and the Vicar wrote in the parish magazine:

We have seen some of the splendid work of our fighters over-head, and as a thanks-offering for our protection everybody will be glad to give something—But a complete fighter plane costs about £5,000, which is more than we could raise; but why should we not aim at providing some particular part of a Spitfire, e.g. a wing? Possibly either Lyminge or Barham might provide the other.

Up at Stelling Minnis, where the red, white and blue hydrangeas were in bloom, an RAF recovery team pulled the Hurricane fighter off the roof of Cherry Garden Bungalow. The house wasn't badly damaged, but to get the great engine out of the kitchen, walls had to be taken down. The body of Elizabeth Boughton was brought out and, because of insufficient funds, she was buried in the churchyard without a gravestone.

That evening Mary Smith's father took the Elham Parish Council down to the King

George playing field to inspect the repairs carried out after the Sea Cadets had gone on the rampage a few months previously. The work was thought 'not entirely satisfactory' and more substantial repairs were considered necessary.

4th September. Joan came to dinner and tea. Quite quiet after 2.30 p.m.

Women were coming under fire all over the country and their courage and calmness came as a surprise to many of Britain's men, conditioned to thinking of women as panicky creatures in constant need of male protection and supervision.

At noon the previous Friday, Biggin Hill had received a shower of HE bombs from Heinkels coming in from the west harried by fighters. Then at 6 p.m. it was dive-bombed by Junkers 88s, causing severe damage. Many buildings were wrecked and over 40 aerodrome personnel were killed, the heaviest casualties being in a crowded shelter which received a direct hit.

A near miss beside the WAAF's shelter caused it to cave in, burying the girls or trapping them in the dark. Digging swiftly, willing hands came from everywhere: airmen, soldiers, the old civilian gardener from the officers' mess, and even some pilots who ran to help as soon as they had landed their fighters between the bomb craters. The

Three Biggin Hill WAAFs who received Military Medals for bravery. (Left-right) Sgt. Joan Mortimer, Corporal Elspeth Candlish-Henderson, and Sgt. Helen Turner. (Imperial War Museum)

P/O 'Snowy' Winter, one of three Spitfire pilots shot out of the sky over Elham on the afternoon of 5th September. From South Shields, he joined the RAF as a 15-year-old apprentice and at the time of his death was credited with four victories

WAAFs were extricated cut, dazed and dusty, but there was no screaming or panic. Section Officer Felicity Hanbury was there, helping her girls out and checking them as they shook the soil out of their clothes and hair. Although a few had to be sent to hospital, there was only one death. Corporal Lena Button from Australia was buried with full honours with many of the airmen at St Mary Cray cemetery.

Two days later, when the defences were saturated, a bomber formation slipped through to Biggin Hill again and in the Operations Room the WAAF plotters could see the plot moving remorselessly towards them as Observer Corps posts telephoned in their sightings. All fighters were engaged and there was nothing the Controller could do. The Station Commander, Group Captain Grice, ordered non-essential personnel to the nearby shelters and told the rest to put on their steel helmets. A few minutes later the building leapt and shuddered to the explosions; then a bomb detonated on the reinforced concrete roof, cracking the structure open and severing many of the communication lines. Most of those inside flung themselves to the floor, but some stayed at their posts, coughing and spluttering in the dust and fumes. The Station Commander recovered his helmet from the floor, lit his pipe and noted the extraordinary behaviour of the WAAFs. Sergeant Helen Turner, a First World War veteran, was still fumbling about with the wires at her shattered telephone switchboard and Corporal Elspeth Henderson, although covered in dust and slivers of glass, was resolutely keeping communications open to Sir Keith Parks' Group HQ. Both were awarded the Military Medal.

5th September. 2 raids. 3 planes down, near—probably Spitfires.

72 Sqdn., on their fifth day of combat, were very short of fighters. After lunch at Croydon their seven Spitfires went down to Hawkinge and, after topping up the fuel tanks, they went up to patrol the airfield at 25,000 ft. At 2.45 p.m. two formations of 109s came over Kent at 27,000 ft and set about the Spitfires over Elham. P/O 'Snowy' Winter, a fine pilot and superb marksman, was the first to go down but, characteristically, he tried to control his riddled plane and left it too late when he baled out. A twin-engined Messerschmitt joined in the dog-fight and, with its battery of four machine-guns and twin cannons mounted in the nose, it got its sights onto Sgt. 'Mabel' Gray's Spitfire and, in the words of one of his fellow pilots, 'he was seen to catch a terrific packet, apparently being killed instantly, his aircraft dived vertically into the deck'.

F/O Desmond Sheen, an Australian who already had the DFC, was hit and wounded:

My next recollection is coming to and finding my Spitfire going down at great speed. Panels and bits were missing from the port wing and I had no flying controls whatsoever. I had no idea of the height but released my harness to bale out when I was immediately sucked out of the cockpit. Unfortunately my boots caught on the top of the windscreen with me lying on top of the fuselage. After what seemed an age my feet came free and I at once pulled the rip cord and my parachute opened with a terrific jerk and I just had time to see tree tops underneath when I was in them. These broke my fall and I landed on my feet as light as a feather. But for the trees I am sure it would have been a different ending.

People on the ground had heard the long lethal bursts ring out in the blue sky and, by

124

shielding their eyes from the glaring sun, they saw the slender pale shape of the twin-engined 110 bank away, after raking the little Spitfire with concentrated fire. At first the Spitfire fell out of the sky, but after a while it flattened out and, spiralling down in small circles, went into Elham Park Wood near the wreckage of Priebe's Messerschmitt.

At Beveridge Bottom the two strapping Wood brothers, Walter and William, flung down their tools and dashed through the trees to find the blazing Spitfire at the base of a chestnut tree. No one could have been alive in that heat, but they had to make sure. Protecting their faces, they ducked into the inferno from either side of the fuselage and looked into the cockpit for a long painful second. William, with his eyebrows gone and singed hair, called over to his brother 'He's not there Walt.' Fred Gammon arrived and they reasoned that the pilot had either jumped or been thrown out, but a search revealed nothing.

Much later, when the fire had died down and with cartridges exploding only occasionally, an RAF motor-cyclist arrived, having accounted for the other two Spitfires. He nodded towards the burning plane and said: 'That's number 3093 and Sergeant Gray has copped it!' When the glowing wreck had cooled a little, they approached and discovered a charred corpse crammed into the small space under the instrument panel. The remains of 20-year-old Sgt. Malcolm Gray were buried in Fulford cemetery near his home in north Yorkshire.

Sgt. 'Mabel' Gray perished when his Spitfire went into Elham Park Wood and burst into flames

6th September. 3 raids but only bad in morning—Rang Dickie up to wish him many happy returns at night.

It had only just gone nine and Walter and William Wood were digging a pit at their home near Clavertye. For the second day running, as they looked up at the sound of straining engines, they saw an RAF fighter pilot receive the *coup de grâce* right overhead. This time it was a Hurricane flying north-east and coming right up behind it was a Messerschmitt 109. 'I wish we could have shouted a warning to the poor chap—the German's burst was spot-on and it looked as if he'd shot the side right out of the Hurricane's fuselage.'

The British plane banked and turned a full 360 degrees before it started to drop, bits and pieces falling off it. Something large came away and hurtled towards Park Wood as the plane spiralled into Beveridge Bottom Wood. P/O Hugh Charles Adams, probably still wearing his sergeant's uniform, thudded into the hard ground and died instantly.

That very morning in Tandridge, Surrey, Adams's commission had just come through from the Air Ministry, but his parents were never to enjoy the proud moment of seeing their son wearing his officer's uniform. It is not clear what really happened in that dangerous piece of sky behind Folkestone. What is known is that 501 Sqdn. split up in disorder when they were bounced by 109s over Westwell. Two sergeant pilots, Houghton and Pearson, were killed immediately and Adams, who might have been wounded, found himself all alone.*

*Forty years later there were none of his family living in Tandridge and, because Adams's grave was neglected, it was tended by Air Chief Marshal Sir David Lee, GBE, CB, who had no knowledge of what had befallen the pilot.

Pilots of 501 Sqdn. at Hawkinge. P/O Hugh Adams (extreme right) fell over Elham with a burnt parachute on the very day his commission came through. Other pilots are (left-right) F/O Witorzenc, P/O Dafforn, Sgt. Farnes, F/Lt. Stoney (killed 18th August), P/O Lee, Sgt. Kozlowski, F/Lt. Gibson. (Central Press)

Minutes after Adams's death, two Me 109s were seen to crash into the sea off Sandgate and Hythe and at Lydd soldiers felt obliged to use their rifles to put a German pilot out of his misery when trapped in the cockpit of his blazing fighter with no hope of rescue—a reluctant service that occasionally had to be performed for RAF pilots.

At 6 p.m. there was considerable excitement when Fw. Gottschalk arrived over Hawkinge in a combat-damaged Messerschmitt. Very daringly he made a proper landing with wheels and flaps down on the aerodrome. Immediately the defences opened up, the pilot scampered from the plane to hide in a wrecked hangar until the shooting stopped. The mottled grey fighter had white wing-tips and rudder and a blue tip to the spinner.

7th September. Terrible. Attack on Hawkinge in morning. Masses of raiders over 5–6 p.m. Terrible night attack on London. Alice went to Mrs Swains.
The Saturday dawned bright and clear again and anxious controllers watched the plotting tables for the expected onslaught. Some single high-flying reconnaissance

126

planes came over, but by 10 a.m. there were no raiders and still nothing at 11 a.m. However, 20 minutes later, a small mixed bunch of Messerschmitt 109s and 110s came in at wave-top height, well below radar surveillance, heading for Hawkinge. Flashing over Sandgate, they climbed to top the Downs and made a fast diving attack on the aerodrome. Bombs straddled the officers' mess, hit the one undamaged hangar and scored a direct hit on the evacuated Station HQ. There was some strafing and a soldier was killed and about a dozen personnel injured. One of the last bombs fell on Hawkinge village, where it struck an air-raid shelter, killing PC Parker, Constable Kettle and his family and two women.

As the dust settled, troops and civilians went to work shovelling the clods of chalk and red soil back into the new craters, whilst the rest of Britain bathed in sun and peace. During the afternoon, troops and airmen were involved in organized games and, all along the south coast, civilians came out to shop or relax. Deckchairs were put up in gardens and behind the fortified seafront the Spitfires and Hurricanes waited on airfields, their camouflage paint baking in the sunlight, whilst the pilots lolled on chairs or stretched out on the dry grass.

It all ended just before teatime. The sun had been seen to glint on polished perspex above the haze over France from 4 p.m. and now radar stations were reporting massive echoes and plotting tables showed cohorts of raiders heading for Kent. Sector controllers

A Luftwaffe warrant officer gives particulars to a Kent policeman as his captors pose for a photograph. The Home Guardsman appears to have put on his uniform in some haste. (Imperial War Museum)

sent up squadron after squadron to make 'angels' on specific patrol lines, which would enable them to cover the vital fighter bases. Just across the Channel from Dover, Reichsmarschall Göring, wearing a pale blue uniform designed by himself, was watching the Luftwaffe armada pass over.

As the raiders crossed east Kent, the sky filled with the vibrating sound of almost a thousand aircraft. The first RAF squadrons that intercepted were powerless against such odds and controllers were unwilling to bring forward any squadrons protecting specific airfields until the raiders split up to make for their allotted airfield targets. Only then could they be committed to interception. As the tense minutes ticked by and excited Observer Corps posts telephoned in the numbers of aircraft passing over, some reporting that they were 'still counting', HQ 11 Group and Fighter Command came to the same conclusion simultaneously—they weren't going to split up, the whole lot were going up the Thames heading for London! Within seconds, Sector Controllers were giving their orders. Humpbacked Hurricanes came bellowing across Sussex and Surrey from Tangmere, to be overtaken by the swifter Spitfires from Middle Wallop that normally battled over Dorset and Hampshire.

But it was all too late. The docks and the East End of London took a pounding that sent gigantic clouds of smoke into the air that could be seen from 40 miles away. The nipping attacks by RAF squadrons, each consisting of about ten fighters, could do nothing to deflect such an armada and there were so many Messerschmitts about that they got in each other's way trying to snap at the British machines. Some of the most experienced and aggressive RAF pilots were shot out of the sky in the battle that followed. The Hampshire-based 234 Sqdn. lost their CO trying to break up a Dornier formation and the Australian F/Lt. Pat Hughes was so infuriated that he climbed under the formation and smashed into the leading Dornier, losing his own life in the process. The famous S/Ldr. Douglas Bader, the legless CO of 242 Sqdn., nearly had his career ended by a Messerschmitt that reefed in onto his tail and blasted a lot of holes in his Hurricane.

As some of the last raiders passed over Elham troops at Acrise discharged their rifles at the smoking Messerschmitt of Oblt. Gotz, that crashed near St Radegund's Abbey. Two more 109s went into the sea just off the coast and the Dungeness lifeboat rescued Uffz. Melchert who was suffering from a head wound. Forty German aircraft had been destroyed for 36 RAF planes shot down. However, 11 of the British planes were repairable.

That night, the Luftwaffe from bases in France, Holland and Belgium converged on London to stoke up the raging fires that were burning in dockland. It was the start of the so-called Blitz. Drew Middleton, an American war correspondent, was in London that night and wrote:

I dined that night, very tired and shaken, with a Colonel of the United States Army Air Force I had met recently. His name was Carl A. Spaatz and he had been in London for some weeks watching the battle. We dined at Rules and, midway through the meal, we heard the high, keening scream of a bomber in a shallow dive. Paddy, the waiter, volunteered that the Germans were 'at it again'.

'By God', Spaatz said, 'that's good, that's fine. The British are winning.' I remarked that it hadn't looked like it that afternoon. 'Of course they're winning,' he said vehemently. 'The Germans can't bomb at night—hell, I don't think they're very good in daylight—but they haven't been trained for night bombing. Nope, the British have got them now. They've forced them to bomb at night. The Krauts must be losing more than we know.'

I suggested that night bombing in the end might succeed in beating the British to their knees.

'Not in a million years,' Spaatz said. 'I tell you the Germans don't know how to go about it. And look at this bunch here. Do they look worried or scared. We're both a damned sight scareder than they are. The Germans won't beat them that way. Nope, the Germans have been licked in daylight.'

Dowding and his pilots were far less confident and certainly didn't appreciate the fortuitous change of German tactics that had been brought about as a reprisal for the RAF raid on Berlin. In 1942 General Carl Spaatz returned to Britain to command the mighty US 8th Air Force.

8th September. Day of Prayer in England and America. It rained for first time in about six weeks. Mr Eden reviewed the Home Guard. Ginger's birthday.

There was singularly little activity from the Luftwaffe on that Sunday. The 'Day of Special Prayer' was in fact held throughout the UK and its Dominions.

The usual Sunday morning muster parade for the Elham Home Guard turned into a rather special occasion. Anthony Eden, Secretary of State for War, and his wife turned up in the village and before going into church, Eden expressed a desire to inspect the Elham platoon. The men were formed up in the square whilst buttons were fastened, then the crumpled contingent was marched into the High Street and stood in a long line in front of the 'Abbot's Fireside' tea shop, facing the Rose & Crown.

Major Kingsley Dykes, with complete ease, conducted the Edens along the single rank of agricultural workers and tradesmen, who stood clasping shotguns or rifles. It was Anthony Eden who had conceived the idea of the Home Guard and personally made the BBC appeal, asking for men to come forward and volunteer. We shall never know what he really thought of his creation—maybe the need for another 'Day of Special Prayer'.

9th September. Slight raid in evening, but lots of shelling. Joan arrived to stay.

A very heavy raid attempted to reach London coming in over Sussex and there was fierce fighting over the outskirts of London, where the raiders were repulsed. Twenty-eight Luftwaffe planes were destroyed, including 13 Messerschmitts, for 17 RAF fighters.

At this time a German officer was being held in Hawkinge guardroom and an 'erk' was on a disciplinary charge, having swopped his sausage and mash for the infinitely superior meal he was conveying to the prisoner from the kitchens of the officers' mess.

10th September. A little more rain. Joan and Margaret went for 2 walks.

Low cloud and rain precluded daylight operations, but London was subjected to bombing regardless of the weather. In some areas of London the ordinary citizens were not taking too kindly to air-raid wardens who were often a little overzealous in the

(Above) A Spitfire circles
above as Fw. Friedrich's
Heinkel burns on Romney
Marsh. (Fox). (Right) For
Heinz Friedrich and his crew
the war is over—they were
lucky to have survived multiple
fighter attacks. (Fox)

130

execution of their duties. In fact magistrates' courts had been dealing with quite a number of incidents where people had become aggressive to officious wardens during the early night raids on London. For instance, a warden who instructed a man to close up a small chink of light showing through his blackout curtains, and then ordered him to take cover, had his steel helmet knocked off and his glasses broken. On another occasion, a man who was forced to evacuate his home and enter an air-raid shelter was repeatedly cautioned for using foul language. He became so irritated that he seized the warden's helmet and beat him over the head with it. At Stoke Newington, a man came out of a shelter and accidently switched on his electric torch. However, a citizen decided that the man was signalling to an enemy agent and promptly attacked him with his walking-stick. ARP personnel were not always above reproach. One night a stretcher-bearer became hopelessly drunk and being denied entrance to public shelters, went windmilling around the empty streets until arrested by the police. Punishment for such convictions was usually a fine of about 20 shillings.

11th September. Warning from 3 onwards. Fighting overhead at 6.30 p.m. Churchill spoke about invasion.
The day dawned cloudy with some rain showers, but by midday the weather had

Harry Flower of the 'Daily Telegraph' chats to Fw. Friedrich as he is taken into captivity at Burmarsh. (Flower)

brightened considerably and the massed Heinkels of the 'Hindenburg Geschwader' and the 'Löwen-Geschwader' took off for London.

Harry Flower, the *Telegraph* special correspondent, was again sharing a car with the Fox photographer and they were touring behind Folkestone waiting for something to happen. After a pub lunch, they drove out to Lympne with its commanding view of Romney Marsh, but could see little because the main attack had gone over North Foreland and was going into London again via the Thames Estuary. However, a massive air battle took place over north-west Kent and Surrey and soon the raiders were streaming south in disorder. Flower reported:

A dozen Heinkels and Dorniers were heading back seawards in half a dozen different directions. On the tail of each was a Hurricane or Spitfire. And then they began to fall. Three Dorniers with tell-tale wisps of smoke showing from their engines as they came lower dived for the sea in the hope of reaching the opposite coast . . . A great Heinkel passed over my head flying low and in obvious distress following a rattle of machine-gun fire up in the sun. A Hurricane slipped over some tree-tops on a hill, poured a short burst into the Heinkel, which caused the bomber to lurch wildly and then 'hedge hop' across field after field trying to find a safe landing.

The pressmen hurried off in their car towards Burmarsh where the bomber had disappeared behind some trees. They spotted a lone fighter flying back and forth over its victim and using it as a guide arrived to find an armed policeman and an entire column of troops had also reached the field where the bomber had crash-landed. They all surged forward together to apprehend the crew, who emerged after setting the plane alight.

Four Germans climbed out and lifted out a fifth crew member who was wounded. One of the crew was a thick-set sergeant pilot whose swagger was very obviously causing some embarrassment to the rest of his crew. The sergeant and at least one other crew member was wearing the Iron Cross ribbon. Harry Flower chatted with the pilot, whilst the photographer took a series of unique photographs, one showing the burning bomber with an RAF fighter circling above.

Soon afterwards, Flower recorded an incident when a formation of Messerschmitts had been engaged overhead, one aircraft falling like a stone to hit the ground a short distance away. When he reached the spot, all that remained was a smoking pit made by the aircraft that had plunged deep into the earth, leaving only a few pieces on the surface. It was a Hurricane and nobody had seen a parachute come down. Several columns of smoke were rising over the marsh and at Camber two Heinkels were burning in the same field.

A favourite haunt of members of the Press was the Grand Hotel in Dover. That evening Harry Flower got back there late and missed being in the building when it received a direct hit. Guy Murchie, a colourful American journalist on the *Chicago Tribune*, and Stanley Johnson from the paper's London office, were with friends in a room on the fourth floor when the bomb exploded right above them. Miraculously they survived the fall as the building collapsed around them.

12th September. Dull and windy. Joan went. Officers came round about billeting.

The raids were limited because of heavy cloud, but individual raiders bombed London.

Police and ARP notices were displayed warning people not to tamper with spent German cannon shells which were falling all over southern England. Many were harmless solid projectiles, but others were highly dangerous and contained more explosive than a grenade. A soldier at Clavertye lost the tip of his nose when he hurled a shell at the ground to explode it and PC Roberts, the Stelling Minnis village policeman, was maimed when he attempted to unscrew the brass nose-cap off another. An armourer at Hawkinge, who should have known better, was half way through a shell with a hacksaw when it blew up removing some of his fingers. He had intended to convert it into a cigarette lighter.

13th September. It rained hard in morning. Buckingham Palace attacked.

Throughout the night the RAF bombed the flotillas of German invasion barges at Antwerp, Calais and Boulogne, repeating the process the night after. From breakfast time single German bombers roamed over Britain concealed in the heavy blanket of cloud, dropping low to release their bombs on any attractive target. During the morning, a raider released bombs that straddled Buckingham Palace, two actually detonating in the courtyard whilst the King and Queen were looking out of the windows. They were badly shaken and lucky not to have been cut by flying glass.

That morning, Sgt. 'Ginger' Lacy, DFM, had just returned from a week's leave and he volunterred to go on patrol in the atrocious weather. Control directed him about over Kent to intercept a Heinkel that was almost certainly the 'Buck House' raider. He sighted the bomber flitting through the mist and, with extraordinary tenacity, stayed with it in the thick vapours across Kent. During an exchange of close-range fire, he shot the top gunner who was replaced by another gunner, who in turn hit Lacey's Hurricane and set it alight. In one final burst the sergeant emptied his guns at the Heinkel before baling out—slightly singed—over Leeds Castle. The bomber, with dead and wounded on board, crashed in France.

14th September. Raids 3.40–5.15 p.m. and 6.10–7 p.m.

It was a glorious bright morning with quite a lot of cloud. A small bombing force made for London during the afternoon, accompanied by a big force of 109s. By the end of the day, Major Galland's score stood at 32 and Colonel Mölders claimed a Spitfire south-west of London at 4.40 p.m., bringing his score to 37.

At Sittingbourne, the football season started at the Tunstall Road ground with a match between Lloyds and the Old Bordenians. Instead the crowd watched 253 Sqdn. duel with JG 26. After about 15 minutes of play, the game was called off because of airfighting overhead, during which Sgt. Higgins was killed when his flaming Hurricane fell at Bredger and Sgt. Anderson baled out with severe burns over Faversham. However, Sgt. Dredge got his sights on Oblt. Dähne's Messerschmitt and blew it to pieces.

An incredible incident took place over Tilbury when the Hurricanes of 73 Sqdn., led by S/Ldr. M. W. S. Robinson, were attacked and chased south by Spitfires. Messerschmitts then joined in and, in all, the squadron had six Hurricanes shot down.

S/Ldr. Robinson and Sgt. Griffith both baled out injured and Sgt. J. J. Brimble went into the ground at Sutton Valance. During the day the RAF lost 10 fighters for 8 German aircraft.

15th September. Roars and fighting at 11.45 and 2.20 p.m. Mrs Bragg came to supper.

This Sunday was another fine sunny day with a lot of fluffy cumulus about. At 11.40 a.m. the first wave of Dorniers crossed the coast with an enormous escort of Messerschmitts, all heading for London. As the course of the formation was predictable, Air Vice-Marshal Sir Keith Park was able to plan the progressive interception of the raiders by more and more squadrons until, at the culmination, they were assailed by a huge formation of five squadrons brought down from Duxford in Cambridgeshire by S/Ldr. Douglas Bader. The German bomber formation broke and many wheeled for home, jettisoning their bombs.

Flying with the Messerschmitts of JG 3 on that day was 47-year-old Professor Hassel von Wedel, the Luftwaffe's Official Historian. In a swirling dog-fight over Maidstone the Staff Flight, led by Gunther Lützow, split up and von Wedel didn't even see the Hurricane that got him. In a frantic few seconds, he kept control of his crippled fighter and let it go down in a series of turns, trying to coax power from a spluttering engine, and then headed for Romney Marsh. However, his motor seized as he came over the ridge of hills overlooking the marsh and the Professor was obliged to put the plane down straight ahead in the first available field. An ARP message received at the Report Centre in Maidstone at 1230 hours, told only the basic facts:

German aircraft crashed at Horne Farm, Bilsington MR 27/83. Pilot taken prisoner. One child killed, 1 or 2 people injured. (1 woman seriously injured (died), 1 suffering from shock). Three farm sheds extensively damaged; 1 small car completely wrecked.

The small farm, properly called Hans Farm, was occupied by William Daw, who was about to take his family out for a Sunday jaunt in their car. Alice Daw and her four-year-old daughter were waiting in the car that was garaged in a shed when the Messerschmitt came sailing down fast and smashed the building into matchwood, giving the little car a terrific blow that mortally injured Alice Daw and her daughter. The Professor was so distraught at what he'd done that he wandered about with tears in his eyes trying to apologize and was finally led away by PC Eyres and given a cup of strong tea.

Later there was some scratching of heads by the RAF Intelligence Branch. The double black bars painted on the Messerschmitt's fuselage had not been seen before and they found themselves interrogating a scholarly man who said he was Colonel von Wedel and had apparently been a First World War fighter ace flying with Baron Richthofen's Circus! (In 1943 von Wedel was repatriated back to Germany in exchange for certain prisoners. He perished during the Russian attack on Berlin in 1945.)

After lunch the Luftwaffe came again with progressive waves of Heinkels and Dorniers, all on course for London and all to be engaged by a host of British squadrons. Many German fighter units were ordered to stay close to the bombers and in so doing were unable to engage the RAF planes to any advantage and suffered as badly as the bombers. By nightfall the British had counted the German wrecks scattered across

A reassuring word from Clementine. Winston Churchill, showing signs of distress when travelling on the Thames to see London's bomb damage. (Imperial War Museum)

south-east England after the day's fighting. There were 41 on land with many others having fallen into the sea.

The RAF announced a loss of 25 fighters with 16 pilots killed and claimed the destruction of 185 German aircraft. However, from examination of official records, it has been established that the true figures were 61 Luftwaffe aircraft for 27 RAF fighters, and even in the light of the amended figures, the overwhelming victory achieved by the RAF on this Sunday is in no way diminished. The effects were decisive: the stunned German High Command postponed the invasion of Britain indefinitely.

That evening Colonel Raymond E. Lee, US Military Attaché to Ambassador Joseph Kennedy, wrote in his journal:

If there was ever a time when one should wear life like a loose garment, this is it. I particularly admire the little tarts who wander about the streets of Mayfair every afternoon and evening in their finery. When everyone else is hurrying for the air raid shelters, they are quite indifferent and continue to stroll unperturbed . . . In the air raid of today, which was quite a lively one, with brisk fighting overhead, a number of German machines were brought down. One landed at the entrance of Victoria Station, a complete wreck, another on the roof of a house a couple of blocks further on and firemen were trying to get it down . . . 8.15 p.m. just as I finish writing this, the heavy guns commence giving tongue—Wha-a-am! Wha-a-am! Wha-a-am!—and the little Irish maid comes in to turn down the bed. She went to Victoria to see the plane which crashed there and is very pleased because she saw the dead German crew extracted from the wreckage.

It has been a rather good thing that Buckingham Palace was bombed. The people feel that the King is in the same boat with them all and is being as unperturbed and dogged as a British King should be. What a chance Windsor has missed.

16th September. Roar, but only distant scrapping at 8 a.m. Odd Jerries over rest of day. Loud bangs, which we thought at first were bombs, at 6 p.m. A soldier came in.

Individual raiders came over using cloud cover. The sirens were sounding so often now that people just carried on with what they were doing and only took shelter if raiders were overhead. Many didn't even bother to do this and preferred to watch the dog-fights. Up at Hawkinge there was the menace of low-level attacks by fast fighter-bombers coming in from the sea to release bombs over the aerodrome. There was insufficient warning for personnel to enter shelters and they just threw themselves flat or dived into slit-trenches.

17th September. Gale in early morning and most of day. Invasion plans affected. Heaps of apples off. Raid (slight) in afternoon. Loud bangs at night.

LAC Tudball, now acclimatized to life at Hawkinge, had seen helmeted cooks in the airmen's mess drop their ladles and leap through open windows when the Bofors opened fire. Most of the day he was on duty at the dispersal point near Killing Wood with a team of 30 men. They were equipped with petrol Bowsers with long arms and pipes to refuel fighters, starter batteries on trollies and an endless supply of ammunition and oxygen bottles. Hawkinge wasn't like other aerodromes where the ground crews looked after their own pilots—it was purely a servicing station and the same customer was rarely serviced twice.

Quite a lot of Me 109s came over at teatime. Three were shot down and a fourth belly-landed on the sea-shore.

18th September. Heavy raids 9.45, 12.45 and 4 p.m. Alice came to tea. Some glare from attack on Calais 10 p.m.

There were several fighter skirmishes during the day and a massed formation of Junkers 88s made for the London docks during early evening. Major Kless, the raid leader, was among the casualties. Twenty German aircraft were lost during the day for 12 RAF fighters.

The Vicar of Elham lost another of his stalwarts this day when Frank Verney joined the forces for the second time in his life. He had been vice-chairman of the Parochial Council, a church warden and deputy leader of the bell ringers.

19th September. Rough and wet on and off. A nice, reasonable day, except for loud bangs overhead at 9 p.m.

Extensive individual bombing and reconnaissance missions were flown over Britain. At Hawkinge the London Rifle Brigade made a mock attack on the aerodrome defences and the Commanding Officer sited positions for the so-called 'disappearing pill-boxes'. These were sited around airfields and consisted of precast concrete cylinders, about 5 ft in diameter, that were installed so that, when lowered into a hole, the top was flush with the ground. A pneumatic jack was fitted at the base and the crew could raise the cylinder out of the ground and fire their weapons out of a gun slit. The devices were rather like big letter boxes and were not popular with the troops.*

20th September. Buzzy raid in morning. Otherwise quite decent. Mrs Thorp brought her rent and some tomatoes. Jock pitched over while chasing a rabbit.

A *Freie Jagd* swept in over Kent in the morning and Werner Mölders obtained his 39th and 40th victories soon after 11.30 a.m. Sgt. Peter Eyles of 92 Sqdn. disappeared with his Spitfire and P/O Howard Hill, a New Zealander, fell to his death at West Houghton. Witnesses on the ground saw Hill's Spitfire flying slowly along the coast stalked by four Messerschmitts. They darted in behind and shot the wings clean off the British aircraft, which tumbled down slowly. There is some suggestion that Hill was already dead, having been killed by a burst of fire several minutes earlier.

The fighters landed quickly at Hawkinge, bumping over the grass towards the dispersal points with grumbling engines, until the pilots cut the ignition off. That was the signal for the erks to swarm out to the planes and make them ready for further combat. There were no proper anti-blast bays or shelters and pilots mostly stayed in

*Two young engineers involved with the installation of these 'disappearing pill-boxes' were Alan Madeley and Donald Campbell, and it was the last named who, after the war, broke both the world's land speed and water speed record, before being killed on Lake Coniston in his jet-propelled boat.

their cockpits, anxious to get away from Hawkinge as quickly as possible. They often went off with holed aircraft without having them properly examined to see if the structure had been weakened. LAC Tudball saw one such fighter with a couple of holes through a propeller blade. For a few minutes a small group debated with the pilot the wisdom of taking it up again, but the pilot decided to go. So an erk said 'Hold on a moment,' took the chewing-gum from his mouth, and plugged the holes.

21st September. All night till 6 when heavy AA at a crowd of Jerries, but nothing much developed. Mr Eden's detective called about the phone.

That night raiders released a large number of parachute mines over London and Kent. These fearsome weapons were really ordinary sea mines and, when detonated in residential areas, they caused tremendous devastation by blast.

Dr Hunter-Smith had managed to keep his 14 horse-power Flying Standard going for his rounds in Elham valley, but the bright sunlight of that glorious summer had faded the maroon paintwork, and it had gone matt with a whitish bloom on it. There were no spray shop facilities in the area so he made the mistake of accepting someone's offer to do a good job by brush-painting it. Unfortunately the finished job was smothered in brush marks and it was never the same after that. A short time later, he bought a Humber for £12 from Fred Pegden the agricultural engineer.

22nd September. Ghastly—Bombs on Kennels Bank—Had a fire at 4.15 p.m. Ma had a nice lot of birthday presents.

It was a dull grey Sunday afternoon when George Butcher walked past the Rose & Crown, all spruced up to court Ethel Williams. He stopped when he heard the unmistakable sound of a German bomber and saw a Dornier slip out of cloud, fly right over Elham, and then circle to come back with its bomb doors open. Ten seconds later all hell was let loose as a stick of bombs detonated in a line along The Row and across the Kennels of the East Kent Hunt. The Kennels were split open and collapsed, the terrified beasts leaping out in all directions. George Butcher, on his hands and knees in the High Street, saw a bunch of them with wild staring eyes go flying past him and make off up the Canterbury Road. It was days before they got them all back and it was extraordinary that only five of the hounds were killed.

The villagers' explanation for this raid was that 'The Jerries knew Eden was up at Park Gate'. However, what the villagers didn't know, was that in a paddock just above 'Autumn Cottage' in The Row, there was a dump containing the remains of many wrecked Messerschmitts, and it was this that the Germans were bombing, probably mistaking it for an aircraft repair works.

It was the Methodists' Harvest Festival and it was a matter of pride for them to put on a better display than the Anglicans. The sombre grey church was transformed: a massive table in front of the altar groaned under a magnificent array of produce and around the walls was a profusion of flowers in rows of vases. The evening was unusually dark and the congregation was nervy following the afternoon's attack. Suddenly the electric lights failed during a hymn. The organ groaned and stopped and the singing tailed off, until all that could be heard was the soprano voice of Mrs Webb singing faultlessly: 'Come ye thankful people, come.' As she progressed, candles were lit and the congregation, recovering its composure, joined in again with renewed vigour.

23rd September. Slight raids in morning and after tea.

By 10.00 a.m., Spitfires were fighting Messerschmitts over various parts of Kent. German fighters, belonging to JG 26, fell at Biddenden and the Isle of Grain and over Folkestone F/Lt. Cosby and Sgt. Glen of 72 Sqdn. followed an ailing 109 down as it circled with one undercarriage leg dangling before flopping into the sea close to the harbour pier. Uffz. Dilthey of JG 2 was badly injured and only just got out of his fighter before it slipped under the green waters. An Army officer, Lt. M. E. Jacobs, and a Lance Corporal stripped off their jackets and dived into the sea to help the wounded pilot into a fishing boat. Another 109, flown by Obfw. Knippscheer, went into the ground in a power dive near Broome Park, Barham, and two more were shot down over the Channel.

The Reverend Williams, realizing his big Austin 18 h.p. used too much fuel, had resolved to buy a motorcycle. Arriving in Canterbury by train, he found a dealer and was

With one undercarriage leg dangling, Uffz. Dilthey puts his Me 109 down off Folkestone harbour. (Peter Cornwell)

(Above and right) Unknown to the local population, a dump containing the wreckage of crashed German aircraft was situated in a paddock in Elham. The Messerschmitt bearing the numeral 10 was that of Obfw. Beek that crashed at East Langdon on 24th August. (Imperial War Museum)

soon persuaded to buy a large BSA sports model, with hand gear change. He had never ridden a motorcycle before and the salesman was in the process of explaining how the machine worked when the sirens sounded and the apologetic young man ran off to fulfil his ARP duties. As it was getting late, the Vicar decided to forgo further lessons and, as the machine seemed to work rather like a car, he would try to play it by ear. He forced the kick-start lever down a few times, and at last the engine fired properly and continued to run with a fine thumping sound. Wobbling at first, he soon gained confidence as he gathered speed.

Leaving Canterbury by the Dover road, the Vicar revelled in the sensation of speed and surging acceleration, oblivious to the sound of a dog-fight right overhead. It seemed a divine means of travel and, with no other vehicles about, there was nothing to impede his homecoming as he thundered down the valley. However, it was when he reached the war memorial that he realized he couldn't locate the brake levers. Entering the High Street with his shoes scraping along the ground, he flashed past several incredulous parishioners with the clutch held in and free-wheeled fast into Vicarage Road, through his magnificent gateway and, beaming with exaltation, plunged into the soft clipped hedge bordering the lawn.

24th September. Daddy had nice presents on a tray. Two roaring raids in morning. Margaret had a bad cold and I went in the shop.

A fine and bright morning over south-east England. At 8.25 a.m., high-flying German aircraft came in over Dover, leaving contrails as they flew north. Major Adolf Galland scored his 40th kill over the Thames Estuary, for which he was to receive the 'Oak Leaves' to decorate his Knights' Cross and so become the third member of all the German armed forces to receive this decoration—Mölders had beaten him to it by three days. It seems likely that Galland shot down P/O Bird-Wilson, who parachuted from his Hurricane suffering from burns. Lympne aerodrome was bombed again.

25th September. Quite a reasonable day. Attack on Bristol. I took the dogs out.

Opposite the chalkpit, the dogs scampered and played on the grassy banks dotted with red field gentians. During the previous night London received a heavy attack and a Wren church and five hospitals had been hit.

Lord Lovat, an extraordinary Scottish nobleman who had formed one of the first commando units choosing gillies and gamekeepers for its personnel, was up to his tricks in Elham during 1940. He arrived wearing a major's uniform with a tam-o-shanter and, after inspecting the Home Guard, was closeted for a long time with Major Kingsley Dykes, to whom he presumably outlined his plans for the formation of special squads. These units, in the event of a German invasion, would stay behind on Romney Marsh or in the hills, hiding during daylight and creating havoc behind enemy lines at night. For these suicide squads, he was looking for men who had special qualities and knew the ground like the backs of their hands.

After his visit, it was noticed that leathery, reliable 'Foxy' Sturmey the huntsman, shepherd George Austin and the immensely powerful George Benefield no longer trained with the Elham Home Guard platoon. Nobody asked questions and the little underground bunkers with camouflaged steel lids still exist on Romney Marsh and in the coastal hills.

26th September. No big raid, but odd, buzzing Jerries about. Dover shelled in afternoon. Margaret back in shop, but not up to much.

At 11 a.m., Kenley Hurricanes fought JG 15 over Dungeness and, although Fw. Meudner was shot down, 253 Sqdn. lost two fighters. F/Lt. Gerry Edge was rescued from the sea by fishermen, but Samolinski the Pole was killed. During the afternoon, the Spitfire factory at Woolston was severely damaged by bombing.

Major Galland flew to Berlin to receive the 'Oak Leaves' from Hitler at the Reich Chancellery and was surprised to find himself sitting alone with the Führer, who was eager to discuss Britain and the war situation. Galland, with predictable frankness, voiced the opinion that he and his pilots had a great admiration for their enemies across the Channel and felt rather bitter about the condescending and presumptious way the German radio and press belittled the RAF. He expected the Führer to contradict him or even get angry, but instead he listened intently, repeatedly nodding his head and finally said that Galland was confirming his own views of the situation. Galland was then whisked away to the Ministry of Propaganda to be interviewed and photographed by international pressmen, including some Americans who were just beginning to realize that the British were not going to be beaten.

27th September. Mass raids at 9.30, 12, and 3.15 p.m. Terrific battle just before dinner right overhead. Heavy shelling after dinner. Germany, Italy and Japan signed a mutual assistance pact.

This was a day of fierce fighting with German and RAF aircraft falling all over southern England. One Spitfire pilot to score his first victory this day was Sgt. M. A. Lee of 72 Sqdn., who pressed home his attack on a Junkers 88 at very close range, oblivious to the Messerschmitts that were around him.

At 12.30 p.m., P/O Dexter of 603 Sqdn. was returning from a chase over the Channel when he saw his friend, P/O 'Pip' Cardell, having trouble trying to control his shot-up Spitfire. He could do nothing to help and watched in horror as Cardell jumped out over Folkestone and plummeted into the sea with an unopened chute. After repeatedly zooming over the harbour and rescue boats that were slow to put out, Dexter lowered his flaps, crash-landed his Spitfire on the beach, and ran to help the six men who didn't seem to have his sense of urgency. He helped launch two boats and went aboard the last, but when they reached Cardell, he was found to be dead, having been killed by the impact of hitting the water. He was buried close to his home in the churchyard of Great Paxton, Cambridgeshire and, instead of a headstone, he has a sundial that was actually made by Philip Cardell for his parents' garden.

Major Galland, eager to get back into the battle now that he and Mölders were level-pegging with 40 victories each, had been obliged to spend a couple of days in East Prussia as the personal guest of Göring at his Reichsjägerhof. This huge Gothic hunting lodge was situated within earshot of the biggest and finest stags in Europe, especially reserved for Reichsjägermeister Göring. A well-placed bullet from Galland dropped a massive stag, and his host ordered its head to be severed so that the Major could take it back to his fighter base on the French coast.

At 4 p.m. over Maidstone, Colonel Mölders came in behind a Spitfire that was piloted by a 35-year-old sergeant, who was one of the oldest operational pilots flying with Fighter Command. With consummate skill, Mölders sent the riddled plane spinning into the ground to become his 41st victory. About an hour later, Göring received the first reports of the Luftwaffe's very active day over England. The German losses were devastating and Galland thanked the Reichsmarschall for his hospitality and left him depressed and quite unable to understand how the RAF were still able to inflict such losses on his fighters and bombers, after having sustained such heavy losses themselves. If he had been able to see how hard the British people were working in their factories, he would have understood.

28th September. Buzzy raids at 10 a.m. and after dinner. First American destroyers arrived.
During the course of this very unsatisfactory day for the RAF, Messerschmitts repeatedly bounced patrolling British formations, shooting down 17 machines for only two German fighters. The 'American destroyers' of Mary's diary refers to some obsolete and decrepit warships leased from the USA.

The well-meaning Vicar of Elham, as platoon padre of the Elham Home Guard, was supposed to be non-combatant and capable of rendering first aid, although he had little knowledge in that direction, despite the fact that his wife was a doctor. So Dr Hunter-Smith found time to instruct the Vicar on the treatment of fractures, haemorrhages, and other possible injuries. The Doctor's lurid descriptions of gunshot wounds in the abdomen caused the Vicar to become unwell and pass out, and 'Doffy' Hunter-Smith had to be on hand to bring the padre hot sweet tea during these instruction sessions.

29th September. Harvest Festival. A few bangs at 8 a.m. Otherwise nothing but a couple of snoopers. Margaret went to tea and supper with Alice.
The Dover AA guns claimed to have shot down a high-flying raider at 11 a.m. that Sunday morning and, during the later afternoon, there was dog-fighting over Surrey and Sussex. At dusk, Heinkels made their way to Liverpool by flying close to the coast of Ireland. Hurricanes intercepted and two were shot down for one bomber. The pilot of a third Hurricane, who landed in the Irish Republic because of damage, was temporarily interned and his plane impounded. The 'snoopers' referred to in Mary's diary were solitary raiders that didn't drop any bombs.

30th September. No big raid, but naggly with some loud AA shelling before dinner.
This was to be the last day on which big formations of Luftwaffe bombers flew over the British Isles in daylight. Forty-six of their aircraft were destroyed, including 32 Messerschmitts, for the loss of 20 RAF fighters. Two Hurricanes crashed at Lydd and a burning Spitfire put down at Hawkinge, but most of the fighting was well to the west of Elham this day.

At one point in the day, P/O Alan Wright of 92 Sqdn. arrived back at Biggin Hill after leave, to find his squadron was airborne. However, as there was a spare serviceable Spitfire, he took off on his own. Meanwhile at Northolt, Group Captain Stanley Vincent, a veteran fighter pilot from the First World War, took up an armed fighter to 'observe tactics'. Four miles up between Reigate and Dorking, the Group Captain saw an Me 109 shooting at another Messerschmitt and decided to join in, opening fire on the rearmost machine, which went down out of control. When P/O Wright appeared on the scene, he saw two 109s attacking a single British fighter and he closed on one of the enemy machines and shot it down. Uffz. Limpert of JG 51 went into the ground at

Nutfield and Gefr. Strasser of JG 52 baled out of his blazing aircraft over Walton on the Hill.

1st October. Nothing much all day, but some heavy AA about 10.15 p.m. Cold and windy.

From this time, the Luftwaffe concentrated on systematically bombing British industrial cities at night, whilst sending over a few heavily escorted fighter-bombers during daylight. The 109s generally flew at extreme altitudes that were beyond the climbing ability of the RAF's Hurricanes.

2nd October. Raid on nearly all day till 5.30 p.m. when I took the dogs out. Heavy AA close at 3.30 p.m. Cold till evening. Wore a viyella frock.

When the Messerschmitts adhered to 'Daddy' Mölders' doctrines, they were extremely successful, but when the 8th Staffel of JG 53 tried to mix it with Spitfires they were punished, losing their leader and three others. Lympne was bombed again and a shelter was hit for a second time.

3rd October. Very dark and cloudy. A nice quiet day. Nothing over at all except the autogyro. Lovely presents and 10/6 each from Daddy, Ma and Margaret. Alice came to supper.

Today was Mary's birthday.

4th October. Not bad. Stray Jerries about in the clouds. Very rough with wind and rain at night. Hitler and Mussolini meet on the Brenner Pass.

5th October. Warning nearly all day. Nasty fighting before dinner and heavy AA just before tea. Margaret and Alice went to Canterbury.

Two vicious combats took place west of Elham before lunch. Three 109s and a twin-engined Messerschmitt were shot down and three Hurricanes crashed. One Hurricane, containing a Pole, fell in flames at Stowting.

6th October. Very wet and rough—only odd buzzing.

Folkstone received bombs three times on that Sunday, demolishing houses and killing civilians. In Elham Church the marriage took place between 26-year-old Clifford Josty and Charlotte Scaman. Their happiness was not to see the year out.

7th October. One buzzy raid about 10 a.m. and another at dinner-time dribbling on—Bangs in night—Mrs Bragg came to say goodbye.

At midday a brown-eyed Ulsterman with wavy hair and a sandy moustache had become the talk of Dover and Hawkinge. He was found on the cliff tops above Folkestone bleeding from a nasty gash under his bottom lip and with some of his teeth knocked out, having crash-landed his Hurricane with several feet of one wing missing. Hundreds of people along the coast had seen him over the Channel breaking up a Messerschmitt's tail, clouting it with his wing-tip after exhausting his ammunition. P/O Kenneth

MacKenzie's victim had fallen in the sea halfway across the Channel, but just prior to this, he had shared in the destruction of another Me 109, piloted by Lt. Erich Meyer of JG 51, which landed in the sea off Dymchurch. MacKenzie, dubbed the 'Messerschmitt Rammer' by the press, soon found himself pursued by reporters and, after having a clean up and feeling somewhat sore from stitches in his mouth, an Admiral insisted on entertaining him to afternoon tea.

A little earlier in the morning, Viktor Mölders, the headstrong younger brother of Colonel Mölders, had got himself shot down and was forced to belly-land his Messerschmitt beside a stream at Guestling. At tea-time Uffz. Heinrich Bley had his fuel tank perforated in combat and had landed on the sea off Greatstone, to be fished out of the water by the Dungeness lifeboat.

At 7.30 that evening, the Elham Parish Council met and their Chairman, Edward Smith, looking weary and strained, had to report an extremely serious matter to his colleagues. An officer of something called a Super Heavy Railway Battery of the Royal Artillery, had just arrived in the village and made a verbal request to erect huts all over the King George playing field. The officer had been prevailed upon to try and find another site and he seemed slightly persuaded—but only slightly. There was consternation and the councillors reminded each other that the paint on the new seesaw and swings was hardly dry. Furthermore Messrs. Ames Bros. hadn't yet finished repairing the fences damaged by the Sea Cadets.

8th October. Buzzy and a bit bangy 'til 1 p.m.

German fighters were over before breakfast and at 7.45 a.m. Lt. Heinz Eschwerhaus of JG 77, flying at 25,000 ft above Kent, had an unnerving experience when his rubber dinghy suddenly inflated itself underneath him. During interrogation the pilot said he lost control when attempting to get things sorted out in the cockpit and only managed to crash-land at Eastry, after having fallen almost to ground level in a spiral dive.

Just after noon, Oblt. Werner Vogt's war ended when his 109 was hit by Spitfires and his engine packed up over Folkestone. The pilot, who held the Iron Cross first and second class, chose to put his plane down on the seashore just below Abbot's Cliff, where it skimmed across the water in a flurry of spray and sank in 4 ft of chilly Channel water. The soaked, bemedalled pilot waded ashore in very good humour to meet his captors. After being given a greatcoat to wear and a cigarette, he posed for photographers, wearing his cap at a jaunty angle.

9th October. Warning on most of day. Pretty bangy in afternoon. Pam Pegden came 10–12. Sambo [cat] tore face.

There were heavy showers and strong winds during the morning and a small group of Messerschmitt fighter-bombers came in very low over Hawkinge using their cannons. They surprised many of the AA gunners, who were at that moment engaged in the awkward process of trying to eat their dinner out of mess tins whilst wearing rubberized capes. Some Bofors pumped a clip of shells at the fleeing raiders with barrels depressed so low that their missiles passed through the tree tops. Six craters erupted near the wrecked hangars and a hut was blown to pieces by a direct hit.

At about the same time, the Elham level-crossing gates were demolished for the second time since the war started. A string of wagons came adrift from an engine at Lyminge and the gradient—assisted by strong winds—had enabled them to gather speed and come rolling into Elham, splintering through the gates and on towards Parsonage Farm, with railway employees in pursuit.

An interception took place over Elham valley that afternoon when F/O Eric Thomas of 222 Sqdn. hit a 109, piercing its oil radiator. As soon as the vital lubricant was pumped away, the protesting engine seized and Fw. Fritz Schweser lowered his aircraft into an inviting field just south of Lyminge. After a protracted bumpety-bump ride across the grass, during which Schweser's head jerked back and forth hitting the frame and armour of his cockpit roof, the little plane came to a stop. The fighter was marked with a white numeral 6 and on its yellow cowling was the badge of the 7th *Staffel* of JG 54: a white Dutch clog with wings.

After jumping out, Fritz worked quickly as farmworkers and troops entered the field in different places. Opening a petrol cock to let a little fuel run out, he screwed up his maps and papers and then after a few agonising moments got a match to burn in his cupped hands. There was a satisfying Whoomph! as he tossed the burning papers into the cockpit and, after retreating a respectable distance from the burning plane, Fritz pulled a white handkerchief from his pocket and waved it above his head. Overhead, Thomas had watched the entire procedure from his circling Spitfire.

Witnessing this incident, the Reverend Williams wrote in the parish magazine:

Last month I watched a British airman force down a German fighter plane on the outskirts of the parish. The Englishman was merciful, as it seemed to me. He could have blown to pieces the German pilot, but he withheld his fire when the Nazi was obviously beaten and was coming down. He afterwards circled round for some time to make sure of his 'bag', and then did something which fairly took my breath away—he quickly rolled his plane over in the air, as you might spin a tennis racket in your hand! It is, I believe, what the RAF call 'The Victory Roll'.

Well, it struck me as typical of the national spirit which is overcoming all kinds of dangers and difficulties with courage and endurance in the full ardour of youth, until its efforts are crowned in Victory.

10th October. Some rather roaring raids. Heavy showers and a bit of thunder. Cherbourg shelled by Fleet.

From Gravesend the newly-formed 421 Flight was in operation, flying their dangerous spotting missions so as to give fighter controllers more precise information about incoming raids. Sgt. M. A. Lee, who had brought down a bomber when flying with 72 Sqdn., was a volunteer pilot with the Flight. When his Mark II Spitfire was hit by cannon fire in action against Messerschmitts, his exceptional skill as a pilot enabled him to nurse his Spitfire down to a forced landing.

11th October. Raids all day. Shelling at night—Lovely weather.

In a confused action over Elham, the Spitfires of 66 Sqdn. tangled with JG 51 and at 11.30 a.m. Colonel Mölders attacked and shot down a Spitfire. P/O 'Dizzy' Allen was well on his way back to Folkestone from a chase when something hit his plane, bursting open the oil tank and causing the temperature to soar. Switching off his engine, he floated down with the wind behind to overshoot Hawkinge and suffer serious concussion when his Spitfire plunged through the boundary fence. Sgt. C. A. H. Ayling of 421 Flight was killed when an Me 109 hit his Spitfire over Hawkinge and sent it into the ground at Newchurch. P/O J. H. T. 'Pickle' Pickering, also of 66 Sqdn., was shot up over Elham by a 109 and attempted to crash-land on Bladbean. However, he ran into Covert Wood, where his Spitfire knocked down several trees before falling apart. As the wreck started to burn, the battered pilot clambered out and hid behind a nearby tree. As his would-be rescuers searched the crumpled wreckage for his body, he gave them a terrible shock when he emerged with a bloody face.

12th October. Raids all day—Ditto.
P/O Aberconway Pattinson, just recovered from a severe thigh wound received over Maidstone on 23rd September, had only returned to 92 Sqdn. the previous day. During the afternoon, Messerschmitts sent his Spitfire down in a howling dive to enter a wood called Postling Wents, below Tolsford Hill. His remains were sent to Bournemouth for burial in Parkstone cemetery. Six Messerschmitts were left in Kent or wrecked in operations that day for twelve RAF fighters. 'Maestro' Mölders claimed three Hurricanes, bringing his score to 46.

13th October. Only one raider after dinner. Mr Myers rang up.
This Sunday an Me 109, flown by Gefr. Hubert Rungen, came down at Hastingleigh after a Spitfire attack.

14th October. Went to see Mr Myers just as a bomb had dropped near the West Gate [Canterbury]. Ma went down the School Shelters. Alice went to London.
Mary visited Canterbury to be interviewed for the post of English teacher at Simon Langton Boys' School. Heavy cloud reduced activity, but at 3.40 p.m. a solitary raider at 1,000 ft, dropped four bombs through a small cloud gap over Hawkinge. The wrecked No 3 hangar was hit again, a fractured water main created a great gushing fountain and the officers' squash courts were completely demolished. One soldier died and 13 airmen and two NAAFI girls were injured.

15th October. Raids till about 4.30. A Messerschmitt exploded over Older's bank and the poor man was killed. Engine in Park Lane.
Soon after breakfast, Arthur Wootten, then living over his garage in the High Street, heard gunfire to the south-east and saw aircraft approaching Elham. They were coming fast at 2,000 ft—a Messerschmitt followed by a Spitfire. With a considerable din of gunfire, the German plane came to pieces in the sky. The fuselage broke in half and the big Daimler-Benz motor, with propeller still spinning, screamed down towards the village and passed over the cringing inhabitants before bouncing across a paddock, just missing the cricket pitch. The main portion of the Messerschmitt, still containing the pilot, 28-year-old Lt. Ludwig Lenz, adjutant of LG 2 fighter-bomber unit, fluttered down to crash on the sloping hill at Older's Poultry Farm.

(Above and left) The remains of Lt. Ludwig Lenz's Messerschmitt on a poultry farm at North Elham. It was reputed that a Spitfire's bullet detonated a light bomb carried under the plane's belly. (Fox/private)

149

When the villagers reached the wreck, they found the ashen-faced pilot still alive in the crushed cockpit, and they went to work on the buckled metal to free his crushed legs. In his condition, Lenz looked like a man in his mid-forties and they noticed that he was not wearing a tunic over his French-made civilian shirt. They managed to release him and carefully lifted him out, but he died during the afternoon.

There was considerable fighting and 421 Flight, soon to become known as the 'Jim Crows' because of their vulnerability when flying solo spotting missions, were proving their worth. Sgt. M. A. Lee was once more savaged by German fighters after attacking a 109, but by keeping calm he controlled his Spitfire MK II down to crash-land at Broadoak. The wounded Sergeant was taken to Canterbury Hospital. At lunchtime a whistling Hurricane came down the valley with holes torn in both wings and tail. It just made Hawkinge, where its nose ploughed a furrow across the turf before it turned upside-down.

16th October. Only snoopers.

17th October. Raids from early morning 'till after tea.

Four Me 109s were shot down. JG 53 lost three, which included their ace Hptm. Mayer, whose body was washed ashore and buried at Hawkinge. Oblt. Walter Rupp was

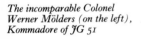

The incomparable Colonel Werner Mölders (on the left), Kommadore of JG 51

150

captured when he crash-landed on Manston. Colonel Mölders was over Kent during the afternoon and at 3.25 he audaciously engaged in individual combat with a single Spitfire above 'Chartwell', Churchill's residence near Westerham. Witnesses all confirm that it wasn't one of his classic lightning kills, but a fair fight lasting about a minute. P/O Hugh Rielley, an American volunteer masquerading as a Canadian, fell close to 'Chartwell' to become Mölders' 48th victory.

18th October. Thick and wet most of day. Only snoopers. Nasty window rattling at 4.15 p.m. Invasion details let out.
There was very little German activity that day, but the RAF flew patrols in appalling weather conditions. 303 Sqdn. lost five Hurricanes and four pilots were killed when attempting to land in low cloud having run out of fuel.

19th October. Nothing much except terrific AA at a Jerry (which I saw) right overhead at about 3.30 p.m. Had pork dinner. Mr Pegden paid 10/-.
The usual night attack on London intensified as the weather improved and the moon rose. As bombs exploded in the City, passers-by flung themselves into doorways and gutters and buses and public houses rapidly emptied.

20th October. Buzzy till tea-time. One or two loud lots of AA. Heavy shelling. Saw flashes and flares over Running Hill when the RAF attacked Cap Gris Nez at night.
That Sunday, six Messerschmitts crashed in Kent, one crash-landing at North Farthing House on Romney Marsh, after being shot down by the redoubtable Scot, F/Lt. Archie McKeller, DFC.

21st October. Only a few snoopers, but a good deal of shelling. Field next to the brickyard ploughed up. Churchill spoke to France. Guy File brought in two lovely spaniel puppies. Poem by C. Dane on Nelson in London.
The London Rifle Brigade was due to move out of Lyminge, their place being taken by the London Irish. Quartermaster Angel was in his stores with Dick Richardson, his RQMS, when they had some visitors:

Usually a small billeting party from the incoming unit sees to the necessary arrangements, so I was more than surprised one morning as Dick and I were enjoying our elevenses, when the door was flung open and in stalked the C.O. of the London Irish, his orderly officer and his personal piper, all gorgeously arrayed in Saffron kilts and the usual millinery effected by Irish regiments. Hastily removing my feet from the table, I stood and paid the minimum deference Army Regulations required for the reception of unannounced callers of superior rank. The C.O. was clearly not impressed by the set-up and remarked to his subordinates that changes would have to be made. And in due course they probably were, since we heard after our departure that his transport, parked neatly in straight lines in an open field, instead of being untidily hidden under trees as ours had been, had received attention from hostile aircraft to its detriment.

22nd October. It was admitted by the BBC that a dead German infantryman had been washed up on the S.E. Coast. Raids, nothing much except a buzz at tea-time. A soldier called to return the lamp.

The bodies of a few German soldiers drowned in off-shore training were found. However, the rumour soon spread that thousands of Germans had been killed by a British secret weapon during an invasion attempt.

Colonel Mölders claimed 3 Hurricanes at about 2.30 but it seems likely that he hit only one, the rest of his attacks having been delivered at 74 Sqdn.'s Spitfires. At 2.40 p.m., Uffz. Heinrich Arp's Messerschmitt blew up over St Mary's Bay and at teatime three Hurricane pilots were killed in dog-fighting over the Folkestone area.

23rd October. Very dark and dull. Many seagulls in newly ploughed field. The London Irish marched down the street with bag-pipes. More facts about invasion barges admitted. No Jerries.

24th October. Very slight raid at dinner-time. Three nasty bangs at 2 p.m. Old shop given up.

25th October. Raids (but nothing much) all day. Jerry down somewhere over Bladbean. Ma saw black smoke. A good deal of shelling at night.

The ubiquitous 'Sunny' Caple was still cycling up and down the Elham valley visiting his stations, but the running of passenger trains had become haphazard and the local people tended to rely on the red East Kent buses. The civilian train service was suspended for three weeks without explanation because the military were making arrangements to use the Elham valley line to operate huge railway-mounted guns. Soon after Dunkirk, many long-range artillery pieces that had been in storage since the First World War were brought out and dusted off by the Super Heavy Batteries RA. These were now appearing on the south coast and two of them, 12-inch guns on bogie mountings, which arrived in the sidings at Lyminge with about 100 officers and men of the 7th Super Heavy Battery, were to be commanded by the colourful Major Basset.

At about 10 a.m., Mölders passed over Elham and, shortly afterwards, he led his 109s into Spitfires of 603 Sqdn. just west of Rye. Three Spitfires went down, one succumbing to the 'Maestro's' guns. At noon he was back again and claimed another Spitfire over the Margate district, but it seems likely that he actually attacked a Hurricane.

It was a sunny afternoon on both sides of the Channel and, after lunch, JG 51 flew over England yet again. On this occasion, Mölders' usual fighter (3737) was piloted by Hptm. Asmus, who was attached to JG 51 on staff duties. At about 3 p.m., it flew over Elham for the last time.

At 3.15 p.m., 501 Sqdn. were in a brisk skirmish over Goudhurst and P/O MacKenzie, the 'Messerschmitt Rammer', collided with another Hurricane. Both planes fell and only MacKenzie succeeded in escaping by parachute. It was not a good day for 501, since Sgt. Whithouse and P/O Snell were brought down in the same action. However, it is possible that a Messerschmitt also collided with one or other of the Hurricanes, because a mottled 109 disintegrated in the air over the Millbush Inn,

Marden, and Hptm. Asmus found himself still strapped in his seat, but fluttering down attached to only a small portion of what had once been the 'Maestro's' fighter. The rest was falling in pieces all around him. He undid his seat harness, pulled his parachute rip-cord and, within seconds, was suspended in the sky with fragments of his disintegrated fighter receding into the landscape below. There was only one consolation—at least he wouldn't have to face Mölders back at Wissant.

There is evidence that Mölders was flying a pre-production Messerschmitt Bf.109F that day to evaluate its performance in service conditions. These were faster, more streamlined machines with rounded wing-tips and with the two wing cannons replaced by a single cannon mounted between the engine cylinder-blocks so as to fire through the propeller hub. To a superb shot like Mölders, the single cannon and two machine-guns grouped in the nose were accurate and quite adequate in fighter v. fighter combat, but the majority of Luftwaffe pilots thought the new plane's armament a regression.

On that day about a dozen 109s were destroyed for an equal number of RAF fighters.

26th October. Nothing but a few slight buzzes. Cold and rainy.

It was a relatively quiet day, but 92 Sqdn. gained the initiative in a fight over Tonbridge and pursued JG 53 out to sea, destroying three 109s. However, when 229 Sqdn. interfered with rescue operations over the Channel, they lost two Hurricanes when shooting down a Heinkel seaplane. Shorncliff Army Camp was bombed at 5 p.m., but only one person was killed.

27th October. Woken by the siren at 7.45, then a distant plane and two nasty rattles. Some heavy AA, but a still more violent barrage at tea-time.

There was considerable activity on this bright autumn Sunday. The big 3.7 in AA guns manned by Royal Marines at Swingfield, blasted off shells on several occasions. At 5.15 p.m., four Me 109s came in over Arpinge, spread out almost side by side and hurtled over Hawkinge releasing bombs. Four more were just behind, but somewhat higher to avoid flying through the bricks and debris that rose into the air as the first bombs exploded. The old officers' mess was destroyed and two bombs detonated in the well-stocked coal and coke bunkers, which dispersed their contents over the camp and adjoining cemetery. Once again the station's AA gunners were taken by surprise. The Luftwaffe lost another eight Messerschmitts that day.

28th October. Awful machine-gunning and bangs in the morning, when a soldier died of wounds at Beachborough. War between Italy and Greece.

The 'Mölders Circus' came over soon after lunch and one Messerschmitt failed to return. At teatime they again flew over Kent to support JG 53, which was withdrawing over Sussex after a sweep to London. Lt. Werner Knittel, the 39-year-old Adjutant of II Gruppe, JG 51, was shot down in a dog-fight and plunged into the ground just inland from Dymchurch.*

*In 1973, the Brenzett Aeronautical Museum excavated (from a depth of 24 ft) the compressed remains of Lt. Knittel's Messerschmitt, with the remains of the pilot trapped within.

29th October. Slight raids all day, but a bigger crush at tea-time. Sharp machine-gunning at 5.10 p.m. and a Messerschmitt in flames near Sutton's. Pilot safe up at the Gate.

The horse-drawn drills were hard at work on the land sowing the winter corn. There was a mystique about dropping the seedcorn into the ground at intervals, in neat rows, and leaving them hidden to spend the winter in darkness. Some of the old farmers regarded it as a ritual and were incredibly superstitious, muttering little rhymes under their breath: 'One for the rook, One for the crow, One to rot, One to grow.'

In the afternoon a tight formation of strange bombers was seen at no great height, flying north between Folkestone and Dover. Tom Moore, the landlord of the Royal Oak situated on the cliff tops, had some newspaper correspondents with him and there was speculation as to what these planes were, some thinking they were troop-carriers. When the landlord focused a telescope on them, he was surprised to see they were painted an exotic pale green and bright blue and under the wings he could make out an emblem similar to an 'H' with three upright bars. As he exclaimed 'They're Wops!', the AA guns fired and the formation flew on to Ramsgate. The authorities were reluctant to admit that Italian planes had flown over Britain and it was several days before official announcements appeared. In fact the Italians had 80 FIAT BR 20 bombers in Belgium and an assortment of monoplane and biplane fighters ready to do battle against Britain.

At 5 p.m. Herbie Palmer returned home to his verandahed bungalow on the slopes overlooking Elham. Hearing the now familiar sound of two planes in combat, he rushed into the garden with his wife and children in time to witness the drama being played out overhead. After taking a second burst from a Spitfire, Fw. Karl Bubenhofer of JG 51 had decided to get out of his riddled Messerschmitt, which was now falling quickly in a spiral dive.

The Palmers stood transfixed, each inwardly thinking that the wailing plane above was going to fall on them and there was nothing they could do to escape it. The children, John and Tina, although toddlers, watched with the same fascination as the plane grew larger and larger and the noise increased until it filled the whole valley with sound. Luckily it fell past them down into the valley, and they had a magnificent view as it exploded, sending up a ball of orange and black fire that silenced the terrible screaming that had filled their heads. A single Spitfire came up the valley low, flashing light and dark as it executed an impeccable roll over the burning wreck and causing the villagers' hearts to swell with pride.

At 16,000 ft Bubenhofer left his screaming machine and enjoyed the reassuring jerk as the big silk canopy filled the sky above his head. Below there was a classic English village set in a rich green valley, but the evening breeze was taking him towards the red disc of the sun, now getting low on the horizon. Stan and Edwin Woods reached Bubenhofer just as he was getting out of his harness at Rhodes Minnis. Sgt. Stoner and the Lyminge police arrived, followed by an Army sergeant, who for some unaccountable reason attempted to hit the airman with a rifle, but was warded off by Stan Woods. More troops arrived and, with one boot missing, the German was marched along a newly tarred road to the Gate Inn. Later he was reunited with his lost boot and taken to Lyminge, where Major Basset entertained him in the officers' mess.

30th October. Not bad except for a good scrap about 4.30 p.m. and a good many Jerries over during the evening.

A lone raider flew over Saltwood firing at the streets and one casualty was rushed to Victoria Hospital. Some half an hour later, three enemy aircraft machine-gunned the seafront and town of Margate. During the morning, Bubenhofer was seen walking around the shops in Lyminge accompanied by an apparently unarmed officer. When they arrived at a recreation field where some civilians and troops were having a kick-about prior to a football match, the German pilot was allowed to join in. There was some acrimony from local people, who thought the prisoner was being treated rather too well.

31st October. Quiet, only two planes over all day. Very rough and heavy. Naples bombed. 50° in early morning. The wall by the stairs was sweating.

This day is now officially accepted by the British as the last day of the Battle of Britain.

1st November. Fine and raidy. Saw a whole crush of Jerries at 4 p.m. Margaret picked up a lump of shrapnel outside Miss Church's door. Heavy AA at night. 2 bombs at Red Oak. The others saw a parachute and flaming plane.

This was All Saints' Day, once the occasion for a big three-day fair held at Elham throughout the Middle Ages. A colossal amount of ale, meats and pies was consumed and for sport there was bear-baiting, cock fighting, archery contests and various military games using wooden swords and staffs, at which the men could display their skill and strength, inflicting nothing worse than bruises on the defeated. Ball games were decreed unmanly and even suppressed by law, the authorities preferring to encourage men to be skillful with tools and weapons.

Soon after 8 a.m., S/Ldr. Archie McKeller, who had just been promoted, led 605 Sqdn. to intercept a *Staffel* of high-flying 109s over Canterbury. In the engagement that followed, the Scot was killed when his Hurricane fell through the clouds upside-down and crashed into the grounds of a large house at Bridge. In a later battle over Elham, a flaming Hurricane went down to crash near Swingfield, killing Sgt. Roger d'Hamale, a Belgian flying with 46 Sqdn.

2nd November. Heavy raids till dinner-time when it blew up rough. Saw a rectangle of 18 Jerries. Very rough at night.

At just before 9 a.m. there was a dog-fight east of Ashford, Messerschmitts crashing at Lower Hardres and Dymchurch and others falling in the Channel. Amongst the missing pilots were Hptm. Ennslen and Colonel Hoffmann. At 11.30, Ramsgate was bombed by about 30 aircraft before sirens could be sounded. Six people were killed and 23 injured in this wanton attack that blew up the gasworks and wrecked over a hundred houses.

3rd November. British troops in Greece. A lovely day—pouring rain in early morning and all day long—not a sound. Postscript by Emlyn Williams about his charlady, 'The toughest little fighter of them all'.

It was curious that people who normally would never bother to have marmalade on the breakfast table, now resorted to making a substitute from carrots. The culinary

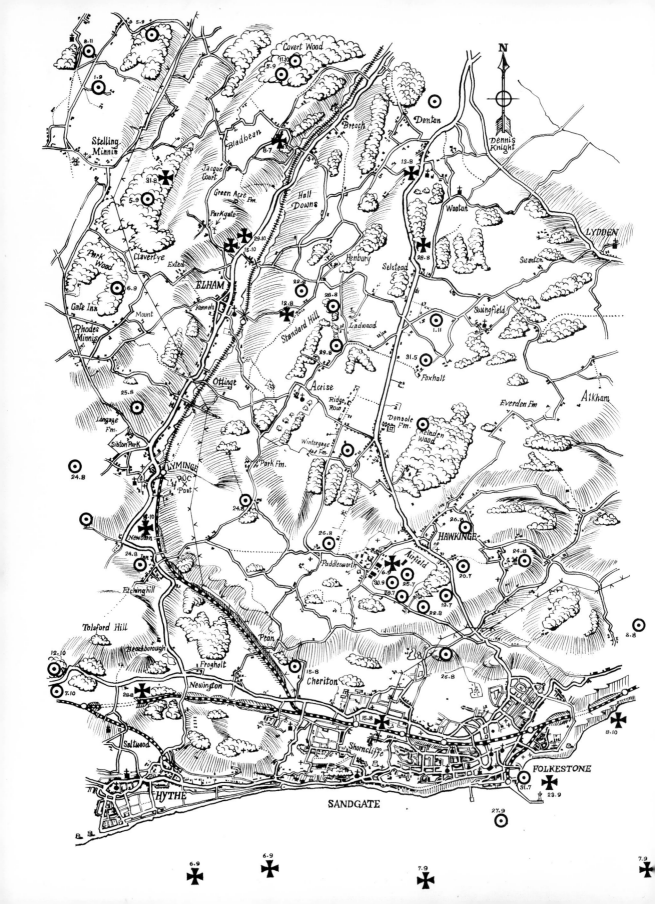

ingenuity of some women was amazing, most of the ideas prompted by weird newspaper recipes or being heard on the wireless. Mashed parsnips were transformed into banana by the liberal use of synthetic flavouring, and bread and milk with yeast extract was pulped to make a passable substitute for mushroom soup.

4th November. Lovely—rough till evening. A few Jerries about 8 p.m. Greek successes. British troops in Crete.
Both London and Liverpool were heavily bombed that night. The death toll was 401 civilians and some 900 were injured.

5th November. Fine or showery all day. Roaring raids morning and afternoon. It came on very rough and wet at 9 p.m. American Presidential election.
The dreary November weather improved slightly and, as if to acknowledge the British custom of fireworks on Guy Fawkes Day, Galland brought JG 26 charging across the Channel with the 9th *Staffel* equipped as fighter-bombers. The Messerschmitts of the exalted Oblt. Heinz Ebeling (holder of the Knight's Cross) and Uffz. Baun flew into each other over Wittersham and both planes came fluttering down. There was some tut-tutting from the local people when they saw the 18 victory bars painted on the rudder of one of the wrecks. Hornchurch Spitfires engaged the raiders and Lt. Scherdt was shot down. Five aircraft bombed Ramsgate again.

6th November. Mr Roosevelt elected. One raid, slight, in afternoon. Two awful bangs 9.15 and 10.15 p.m. Some say the latter were bombs.
London, Liverpool and Birmingham were attacked and over 300 sorties were flown over England that night.

7th November. Quite nice. Nothing but a few Spitfires about and lovely sun in afternoon. Letter from Mr Myers.
A very high-flying Me 110 was intercepted over Kent and damaged and, during the afternoon, Stukas dive-bombed a convoy off Sheerness. In the evening, North Weald's Hurricanes patrolled Kent with Wing Commander Victor Beamish, their wild, blustering, Irish station commander, flying in the formation. He thought he saw something that needed investigating and flew off to have a look. When he came rushing back to rejoin the squadron over Chatham, he tried to get back into the formation too fast and his fighter's whirling propeller slashed the tail off a Hurricane, sending it down in a spin. The Wing Commander went down with his own machine crippled and made a forced landing. Fortunately, the pilot of the tailless Hurricane just managed to bale out.

During darkness, six bombs and incendiaries fell at Lyminge, very close to the big 12 in railway guns, and Major Basset was resolved to move to Elham. The letter from Mr Myers referred to in Mary's diary confirmed that she had been accepted for the teaching post at Simon Langton boys' school.

8th November. Went to Canterbury with Margaret to see Mr Myers and get time-table. Auntie Jennie sent some quinces.

(opposite page)
The location of German and British aircraft
that crashed in the Elham area during 1940

At midday a Hurricane had its entire tail assembly shot off by cannon shells in a battle over Stelling Minnis. The machine came spinning down and burst into a sheet of flames in a meadow close to the church. Nothing could be done for the pilot and when the gruesome remains were taken away, local people were told it was a Polish pilot, this being a ruse frequently employed, since civilians seemed less squeamish about the death of a Pole than when an Englishman was killed. In fact the dead pilot was 21-year-old Anthony Page, one of Stanford Tuck's sergeant pilots from 257 Sqdn.

9th November. Rough and wet at night. My wireless set came back.

Neville Chamberlain died that day. Though his philosophy of appeasement, he had tried so hard to prevent Britain being involved in another terrible world war and he had become the butt for much ridicule and criticism. Speaking in the House of Commons, Churchill said:

> *Whatever else history may or may not say about these terrible, tremendous years, we can be sure that Neville Chamberlain acted with perfect sincerity according to his lights and strove to the utmost of his capacity and authority, which were powerful, to save the world from the awful, devastating struggle in which we are now engaged . . . Herr Hitler protests with frantic words and gestures that he has only desired peace. What do these ravings and outpourings count for before the silence of Neville Chamberlain's tomb?*

10th November. British Legion Service in afternoon. Plenty of Jerries about in the moonlight.

On that Remembrance Sunday the Reverend Williams' cup was overflowing. Not only were his wife and five children coming back to the vicarage after spending the summer in Wales, but the special Armistice Day service had filled his church with about 300 worshippers, the ranks of the British Legion being augmented by men of the Home Guard. After the names of those parishioners who had fallen in the war had been read out, prayers were said and a bugler sounded the Last Post and Reveille. During the service, a raider flew over and dropped bombs at Newington, injuring 24 people from flying glass and debris, and at 5.15 bombs fell in open fields at Elham.

11th November. Went to S.L.B.S. at the Old Hospital. Underground most of day. Very rough at night.

Low-flying Messerschmitts were strafing streets in the morning and Dover and Ramsgate were bombed at midday.

This was Mary's first day teaching at Simon Langton boys' school in Canterbury. Because of the need to disperse pupils, in order to limit casualties in the event of bombing, some lessons were held in the main school and others in the Old Hospital. In the event, she spent most of the day in the air-raid shelters.

JG 51 came over Kent, but Werner Mölders was suffering from influenza and stayed at the Wissant HQ listening to the radio reports. However, when he heard that his close friend Oblt. Claus was down in the sea, after feverish attempts to get the air-sea-rescue units moving, he ordered that his own fighter be made ready. Minutes later he took off with Lt. Eberle as his wingman to search the seas off Kent. He was ill, emotionally upset and flying very low and the British never had a better chance of shooting him down.

12th November. At school except for 1 lesson. No warning.

Home Guard training degenerated in the winter and muster parades started to take place in the stable yard of the Rose & Crown, where, after roll-call and a little perfunctory drill, the assembly adjourned to the saloon bar for something to keep out the cold. Training lectures were more of a discussion between buying rounds and recitations from manuals. Also, patrols and pickets found it convenient to report back to the Rose & Crown, where the Commanding Officer and off-duty personnel were mostly to be found. Thus it was a natural progression that the bar became the Home Guard HQ from then on. At 10 a.m., Ashly Millim, the landlord, religiously ejected his revellers and they marched home or wandered off to their guard duties.

Sgt. Martin Constant accepted his stints on guard duty with the rest, but he was usually required to stay at the Rose & Crown with his Platoon Commander in case of emergencies. On occasions they had to guard the telephone exchange and Sgt. Constant would be brought up by Fletcher his chauffeur in the estate car or one or other of the Alvis sports saloons. When he was obliged to stay on duty into the night, he would often telephone Lower Court and have somebody bring up a choice of freshly cut sandwiches and a flask.

13th November. At Hospital. Three warnings. Saw Miss Platt and bought Andrew a ring. Victory at Taranto announced. Terrific gale at night.

Folkestone was dive-bombed by Messerschmitts. LAC Tudball had been at Hawkinge for two months and the hectic autumn days were over. The Servicing Flight was now divided into two teams, each alternating with a week on duty and a week off. When off duty, they were billeted in an old manor house at Hockley Sole, which had once been the home of Raphael Tuck the printer.

S/Ldr. Arnold was a superb station commander, but had to keep a balance between running a relaxed working station and stopping the rot when things became too lax. Now the Servicing Flight personnel required a 'jerk on the reins'. In their dress they had started to emulate the attire of fighter pilots. They wore wellington boots, which they made look a bit like flying boots by turning down the tops, showing thick white socks. Natty silk scarves replaced ties and many had obtained the pre-war pattern airman's peaked cap, which they made floppy by taking out the wire stiffener.

At the aerodrome the erks had cut a hole through the barbed-wire fence behind Killing Wood and had a path to the White Horse Inn and Alf's café. Alf and his wife seemed to have the café open perpetually for the erks to consume a huge quantity of tea and rock-cakes. One one occasion, Tudball dived for cover when a strafing Messerschmitt zoomed over, shooting tiles off the café roof. When he looked up, Alf was still dispensing tea from a big enamelled pot.

So a formidable warrant officer with a strong Scottish accent was let loose on them in an attempt to instil some spit and polish and reintroduce regulation dress. Although an awe-inspiring man with buttons that were burnished smooth and with a cap, the top of which was as tight as a drum, he proved singularly unsuccessful.

14th November. Trees across road. Warnings on and off all day. Mr Chamberlain buried in the Abbey. Terrible night attack on Coventry.

With a lot of cloud about, a heavily escorted formation of Stukas headed across the Channel for Dover, whilst two Biggin Hill Spitfire squadrons were over Deal, ideally placed to intercept. The Dover guns opened fire at the raiders as they approached and, with perfect timing, the guns ceased as the Spitfires raced into the raiders and turned them back. One Stuka blew up, two collided and others caught fire and went back towards France. The escorting 109s intervened and prevented what could have been a massacre. P/O Armstrong had to abandon his Spitfire after it was punched full of holes; however, he managed to get back to Biggin Hill in time for the wild celebrations that went on until late that night. It was the last time the Luftwaffe sent Stukas anywhere near the British Isles.

At 3 p.m., two Essex-based Hurricane squadrons were patrolling a convoy in the Estuary at 18,000 ft when a brace of Messerschmitts from JG 51 suddenly appeared close to them at the same altitude. One dived and the other climbed—which was probably a decoy strategy that misfired. P/O George Barclay, the second son of the Vicar of Cromer in Norfolk, was able to catch up with the diving plane flown by Erich Vortbach:

. . . about six people followed it. I won the race to reach it first and approached from astern firing from 200 yards inwards. My throttle stuck fully open so I overhauled the 109 very rapidly at about 7,000 ft. I fired until I had to break away for fear of hitting the enemy aircraft and then turned in again and did a quarter attack. As I fired glycol and black smoke came out—very satisfactory as I deliberately aimed at one radiator. Other

Mrs Isaac Williams on the vicarage lawn with daughters Mary, Margaret, Ruth and Rachel

Hurricanes fired and the enemy aircraft turned inland and tried to force-land near Manston Aerodrome. Just as he was at tree-top height Sergeant Smythe shot at the enemy aircraft. It flew straight into some trees and crashed in flames.

Back at base Sgt. George Smythe received a blistering dressing-down from F/Lt. 'Butch' Barton for what the squadron regarded 'unsportsmanlike behaviour', but it had been an unfortunate misunderstanding. Indeed Smythe, who was a splendid pilot, had impressed everyone with his inventive genius in improving his fighter. He loaded his own ammunition belts and spent hours tinkering with his plane, which could carry more ammunition than a standard fighter. The Hurricane he abandoned over Elham in August had been fitted with an external box filled with old chains, bolts and sump oil that he could empty in the path of an enemy aircraft by pulling a cable. On one occasion the contents were accidently jettisoned over his CO's aircraft!

At Elham, the full moon rose at teatime and it was so clear and bright all over England that people thought the raiders wouldn't dare come over that night for risk of being seen. Nevertheless, at 6.17 p.m. the first Heinkel pathfinders came over the Dorset coast and made for Coventry where at 7.13 the first shower of incendiaries was released to begin a night of terror that destroyed the city.

15th November. Several warnings. Got home at 3 and had sprats. Rough at night.

When the news about the destruction of Coventry filtered through, tempers began to run high. P/O Barclay, who had endorsed the criticism of Sergeant Smythe's conduct in shooting at the crippled Messerschmitt the previous day wrote: 'Hearing of the bombing of Coventry last night, we are inclined to think that perhaps Sergeant Smythe's action yesterday wasn't so bad after all.'

The two huge railway-mounted guns at Lyminge were trundled into Elham and tucked away into the sidings running parallel to the station. They were secured to the ground with chains and cables and, much to the relief of the villagers, heavily camouflaged. With them there came the florid and booming Major Basset, who, unlike his guns, could not be silenced or camouflaged.

At Bourne Park the double track was being rebuilt where the line ran under the tunnel, so as to house the mighty 18 in 'Boche Buster' gun, that was being prepared at Darlington and was one of Churchill's pet projects. These guns were viewed by the populace as mighty weapons of retribution against the German batteries at Cap Gris Nez, but they were intended to be anti-invasion weapons and didn't have anything like the range to cross the Channel. On the occasions when they were fired for practice, the colossal bangs shook down ceilings and broke windows in the valley and the railway track had to be repaired.

That evening the Vicar's wife and children returned from Wales and once more Elham vicarage echoed to the sound of laughter, the ponies whinnying with delight as the children hugged them. Everything seemed the same, except the wine was gone and the cook was engaged to a soldier who had been a batman to one of the officers staying there in the summer.

16th November. Two warnings. Got home to dinner. Squally showers.

When the Vicar appeared in his Home Guard uniform, his daughters shrieked with laughter and Mrs Williams had to hide her face.

17th November. Raids on and off till tea-time. Shelling at night. Sambo got a bad cut on his nose.

With the Home Guard esconced at the Rose & Crown and Messrs. Parker and Constant perched against the bar at most times, it wasn't long before Major Basset became inveigled into the club. His big guns were kept under wraps behind the station, but occasionally the gleaming monsters were coupled up with logistics wagons and military locomotives to create a nightmare train that toured up and down the valley. Villages on the line were warned to leave windows open during practice firing, but even so, the concussion cracked ceilings and shattered glass.

After firing, the mighty pieces of ordnance were returned to Elham for polishing and Major Basset would sweep triumphantly into the Rose & Crown, where Martin Constant and Kingsley Dykes were the first to buy him drinks. They knew full well that the jubilant Major had the whiphand—he'd only got to go a mile down the line and fire a shell from Ottinge, to wreck both their lovely houses. The Major reminded them of this frequently.

A few yards away from the clinking glasses and merriment at the New Inn and Rose & Crown, the Methodists were holding their 'Annual Temperance Sunday'. all those who attended were urged by successive preachers to sign a solemn pledge to abstain from imbibing any intoxicating liquor during the year ahead. Coupled with this, those in the congregation with any literary skill, knowledge or inclination, were asked to submit essays on 1) Sir Walter Grenfell or 2) King Khama's fight with drink with recommendations on various ways to fight drink in England. Some of the wives of the Home Guardsmen could have offered a recommendation.

A German fighter was brought down over Romney Marsh and Lt. Richard Riedel went into the ground so deep that the hole was just filled in.

18th November. About 8 warnings. Two land-mines on Folkestone at 5 a.m. Everything shaken. Went out to tea with Miss Platt.

In the bright moonlight just before dawn, a German plane released two parachute mines, which floated down and detonated with awful force in Folkestone. Beach Street with its little shops and cafés was devastated, whilst homes at the junction of Rossendale and Folly roads were obliterated. Fourteen people were killed, 60 injured and 56 houses and shops demolished with 674 seriously damaged. The borough authorities, headed by the Mayor and Mayoress,* did much to comfort and rehabilitate the homeless and distressed.

Hawkinge was now the home of 421 Flight 'Jim Crows' that had been formed on Dowding's express orders to be an extension and, if necessary, operate in lieu of radar.

*The Mayor and Mayoress of Folkestone, Alderman and Mrs G. A. Gurr, were both killed by another parachute mine that fell on Folkestone in May 1941.

The Elham valley railway line was closed to civilian traffic when these railway-mounted guns arrived. Two of these 12 in Howitzers were brought to Elham by Major Basset. (Imperial War Museum)

The pilots were mostly volunteers and had to be very experienced for the hazardous job of maintaining solo patrols, watching for the approach of enemy aircraft. Their aircraft were a collection of the faster types of Spitfires and Hurricanes gleaned from other squadrons.

19th November. About 6 warnings.

When craters started appearing at Rainham in north Kent, at first it was thought these were bombs from a high-flying German aircraft. However, they exploded at intervals and, from examination of splinters, it was discovered they were shells that had been hurled 55 miles from the long-range guns at Cap Gris Nez. At Hawkinge a Spitfire overshot landing and smashed into another fighter.

That evening the room over the livery stables at the Rose & Crown was filled with men of the Elham Home Guard. They had assembled to hear a Staff officer from County HQ answer complaints received from Messrs. Dykes, Parker and Constant about the lack of weapons and training ammunition. HQ hadn't liked the vociferous way the platoon were making their accusations and demands and so the General had dispatched Captain Youard, who knew the Dykes family through County social events and who, like Major Dykes, had also been seriously wounded in the First World War. However, he did not understand the calibre of the men he was dealing with.

Captain Youard, resplendent with red band and lapel tabs, delivered a brisk pep talk explaining the problems of the overworked HQ staff and giving vague assurances of improvements to come. Then in the way of service pep talks, he asked if there were any questions. They came quickly.

Sgt. Martin Constant had been seen to walk a little unsteadily on arrival and it was soon obvious that he was in a waspish mood. As Youard proceeded to give evasive, non-committal replies, Constant kept interrupting by shouting 'Come clean now, come clean!' To begin with the officer smiled nervously, but as the heckling continued and he passed quickly through the stages of irritation, exasperation, anger and humiliation, he glanced beseechingly at Major Dykes and Captain Parker—why did they allow such insufferable insubordination? His ordeal came to a climax as he tried to explain some necessary documentation. Sgt. Constant shouted out 'Lott'a bumf!', at which point some of the Home Guardsmen were unable to contain themselves any longer. It was too much for the Staff officer who, near apoplexy, abruptly ended the meeting.

It was obvious to Dykes and Parker that their old friend had gone too far and there would be trouble. After Captain Youard had recovered a little he enquired, almost casually, about the sergeant who had interrupted so rudely. But it was hopeless: how could they explain that the NCO was a millionaire shipowner who had his own private Home Guard section down at Ottinge, made up largely from his own staff?

20th November. 3 warnings. Bought Ma six pillow-cases at 1/3 each. Alice came to supper.
In fine weather F/Lt. Billy Drake took off from Hawkinge and shot down a drifting barrage balloon over the Channel and then chased a Dornier back to Calais. Major Basset was beside himself when a projection from a passing train caught the camouflage screens around his guns and tore the whole lot down.

21st November. 4 warnings. Dull and rainy. Mrs Sharman started to work here.

22nd November. Only 2 warnings. Koritza captured by Greeks. Splendid story of wrecked bombers' return with wounded wireless operator.

23rd November. Two warnings before I came home at dinner-time.
Two aircraft crashed in the sea off Dungeness and a Messerschmitt, bearing an 'Ace of Spades' badge, landed at Smeeth. Later, radar reported a large bunch of aircraft nervously hanging around off the coast and 603's Spitfires were sent racing out to investigate. Ten miles out from Dover 'Uncle' George Denholm couldn't believe his eyes: there spread out before him was a cloud of twisting Fiat biplanes of the Corpo Aero Italiano. The Spitfires, with a 100 mph margin of speed over the Fiats, went straight into

them, but had difficulty in holding them in their gun-sights. For several minutes a swirling aerial ballet was performed off Dover as the Italians used every aerobatic trick to evade the panting Spitfires. On return, the Edinburgh squadron claimed 7 for no loss and the Italians claimed 5 Spitfires. In fact only two Fiats failed to return.

The East Kent Hunt had their opening meet at Mr M. E. F. Crealock's place at Etchinghill that day. At a time when everybody seemed to be camouflaging everything and trying to make themselves blend into the landscape, it provided an incredible and incongruous sight. 'Foxy' Sturmey worked the hounds through West Wood and, after a while, there was a long-drawn-out wail 'Gone awa-a-y, gone awa-a-y.' Whilst the Hunt was about its tasks, some German shells fell in the district and P/O K. Lawrence climbed from Hawkinge in a Spitfire to intercept a twin-engined Messerschmitt that was spotting for the guns.

24th November. Pretty buzzy till tea-time, but not much AA.
That Sunday P/O H. C. Baker, with a Spitfire from 421 Flight, joined Hurricanes in combat with fifteen 109's over Dungeness and shared in shooting one down.

25th November. Had to start escorting children. Joan came for the night.
F/Lt. Green of 421 Flight attacked a Dornier off Folkestone and the Navy saw it crash in mid-Channel.

As Major Dykes and Captain Parker feared, a letter arrived at Elham from County Home Guard HQ ordering disciplinary action against the sergeant who had been insubordinate to Captain Youard. It was a delicate matter that couldn't be discussed in the Rose & Crown, so they visited their old friend who, sensing he'd done something wrong, had shut himself away in a melancholy state at Lower Court. Dykes and Parker were welcomed in the usual jocular fashion and the big cut-glass decanter and glasses made their usual appearance. However, their host knew what was coming. At first he tried to laugh it all off and talked expansively of asking for a court martial. But after hours of remorselessly trying to make him understand that it was only resignation or demotion and resignation that was going to cause the least embarrassment to everybody, he reluctantly agreed. It was an unfortunate business because, even though he pretended not to mind, he was a warmhearted, generous man who would miss Home Guard activities immensely.

26th November. Warnings on nearly all day. RAF bombing fleeing Italians.
At 1.06 p.m., a German bomber flew low over Hythe sending incendiary bullets into the Hythe gasholder, which caught fire burning with long jets of yellow flame. The police evacuated homes over a wide area, but the anticipated explosion didn't take place and the fires were extinguished with lumps of wet clay. F/O O'Meara jumped into a special high-performance blue-painted Spitfire and roared off from Hawkinge to return 14 minutes later having intercepted and shot down a Heinkel.

27th November. Margaret went to tea and supper with Alice. West-gate siren very loud.

At 8.30 a.m. the New Zealander, P/O Lawrence, was spotting over Walmer and his Spitfire was blown to pieces by Me 109s. Despite a fractured leg and lacerated foot, he baled out and drifted out to sea to be picked up by a rescue boat. During the afternoon JG 51 came over in strength and a big battle developed between Romney Marsh and Faversham. S/Ldr. 'Sailor' Malan, the RAF's pundit on air fighting, used full power in a chase across Kent and destroyed a 109 off Rye; S/Ldr. Wilson, a technical officer from the RAE, got another. Fw. Erdniss crashed at Monks Horton and was captured whilst two of his companions were killed when their Messerschmitts smashed into the ground at Crundale and Benenden. Lt. Wolfgang Teumer had released the 250 kg bomb he was carrying under his 109 when he sighted three Spitfires, but they were too quick for him and bullets entered his fuselage and radiator. At 4 p.m. he made a wheels-up landing on Manston. Sgt. Don McKay, now at Hawkinge with 421 Flight, got another 109 that dived into the sea off Dover and a Spitfire fell at Tonge after the pilot had parachuted. All was then quiet until the first London raiders came droning in after dark.

28th November. Two bombs dropped near Dane John and Labour Exchange. No one hurt. Many people underground at Hospital.

F/O Geo. Barclay recorded brilliant sunshine with high ice clouds when he patrolled over Kent. High above, he could see lots of 109s playing about and he saw two make a head-on attack at each other. At 4 p.m. a Messerschmitt came down to crash-land on the other side of Romney Marsh and demolished a lavatory in a cottage garden. An RAF Intelligence officeer carefully noted:

Numeral 2 + (black). Crest: devil's face with red mouth and green left eye—also black Gothic 'S' on white shield. Nose and rudder yellow—spinner red. Some ammunition had been fired, but there were no bullet strikes—petrol tank was quite dry.

Away down to the west, F/Lt. John Dundas (the elder brother of Hugh Dundas who had crashed in Elham during August) was heard to call out in exaltation as he destroyed an Me 109 off the Needles. Seconds later he was dead, shot by Oblt. Pflanz. However, Dundas' victim was Major Helmut Wick, who at that time was the leading Luftwaffe ace, having beaten Mölders' score by two.

Mary's entry for that day refers to a bombing attack on Canterbury.

29th November. Fine and sunny. Warning all day. Ma wore her bed-socks.

The Duke of Kent visited Hawkinge again, during which an extraordinary incident took place. A young six-foot fitter, nicknamed 'Texas', had made several applications to be considered for pilot training, but was repeatedly turned down by his CO. Having reached his 'winter of discontent', he chose the somewhat bizarre method of demonstrating his suitability for pilot training by attempting to fly a Spitfire. After taxiing a fighter, he opened the throttle fully and accelerated across the grass, but failed to leave the ground. In the inevitable crash that followed, the aspiring pilot climbed out of the wreckage virtually unhurt to face the mingled derision and admiration of his colleagues and the wrath of his CO. After a court martial had sentenced him to six months' detention, 'Texas' again demonstrated his headstrong spirit by breaking out of the guardroom.

Meanwhile in another part of England, two German pilots, having escaped from a POW camp, travelled by train to Carlisle wearing home-made RAF uniforms. At an RAF station they selected a Magister two-seater with the intention of flying it to Ireland or Holland and, after getting a mechanic to show them how to start the engine, they took-off. Unfortunately for them the petrol ran out over the Norfolk coast and they had to glide down into a field. Even so, they bluffed the local police into thinking they were Dutch officers who had escaped from occupied Europe. They weren't rumbled until their bogus uniforms were examined whilst they were taking a bath in the officers' mess of a nearby RAF station. Some of their tunic buttons were actually made of wood, covered with silver paper.

30th November. Fine and frosty at night. Alice got job at Portskinneth.

During the morning a Messerschmitt with an 'Ace of Spades' badge belly-landed on Romney Marsh. It had no bullet holes, but the top of the fuselage was dented and part of the tail was knocked off, which indicated a mid-air collision. At lunchtime two Spitfire aces took off in mist from Biggin Hill on what they called a 'voluntary patrol'. The total victory score of the famous fighter station stood at 599 and there was sharp rivalry between the four squadrons using the base as to which would get the 600th. F/Lt. Mungo-Park, DFC, a Cheshireman with 10 victories, and P/O Harbourne Stephen, DFC, a 26-year-old Scot with 19 victories, were both members of 'Sailor' Malan's 74 Sqdn. and they were trying to steal a march on their colleagues.

Their CO went into the operations room to follow their progress as they climbed through the mist into a clear blue sky and sighted, as if pre-arranged, a bunch of high-flying 109s coming over the coast. After a hard climb to 34,000 ft, the Spitfires stalked the 'snappers' until, in a favourable position, Mungo-Park and Stephen both went for the rearmost Messerschmitt. Taking it in turns to fire bursts, they closed to 50 yards and sent their victim down vertically straight into the ground at Ruckinge. Uffz. Wägelein jumped out, but his parachute was holed and he died of injuries after he hit the ground too fast.

1st December. Mr and Mrs Green came to tea.

At 1.15 on that Sunday afternoon, F/O. Hartas of 421 Flight returned to Hawkinge having destroyed an Me 109 over the sea. About an hour later, Werner Mölders resumed operational flying after a month's rest and claimed a Hurricane over Kent, bringing his score to 55.

2nd December. Nothing special.

The Elham Parish Council was in disarray when they met at the post office that evening. Major Basset had informed Edward Smith that he intended to construct at least two buildings on the King George playing field. The Council resolved to go as a body to see the Major in an endeavour to dissuade him. One councillor was all for going to the National Playing Fields Association.

An Me 109 crashed in the sea off Hythe at noon and 26-year-old Clifford Josty, who had been married at Elham in October, was killed in a motorcycle accident.

167

3rd December. Went to tea with Miss Hinde.

F/O O'Meara, on patrol from Hawkinge, intercepted and damaged a Dornier over Kent.

4th December. Met Margaret and she came home after shopping with me.

5th December. Income Tax repaid £4-15. Bombs between New Dover Road and St Martins Hill in morning. Rough at night.

These bomb incidents occurred in Canterbury. At 2.44 p.m. two Me 109s dive-bombed Hawkinge, but there was no damage. Whilst this was taking place, F/Lt. Green, F/O O'Meara and Sgt. Lee were on patrol and sighted other Messerschmitts attacking a minesweeper. O'Meara destroyed one and damaged another.

6th December. Cold and fine. Alice came to supper. No electric light in morning. Greeks in S. Quaranta. Marshal Badoglio resigned.

7th December. Another Italian general resigned. George Butcher married.

For some weeks Mary's father had been feeling unwell, but he endeavoured to carry out his duties as Postmaster and Chairman of the Council in a consummate fashion. F/Lt. 'Billy' Drake and Sgt. Gillies chased a Dornier to the French coast, but on returning Gillies ran out of fuel and crashed 421 Flight's special blue Spitfire just short of Hawkinge.

8th December. Nice cold sunny day. Crowds of Jerries about at night. Greeks entered Argyrokastro at 1.15 a.m. Athens church bells ringing at night.

Sunday. The successes against the Italians in Albania were short lived. In the coming April, the Germans intervened and subjugated the Balkans in a few weeks.

9th December. In class-rooms all day.

Arthur Wootten nearly lost his life practising with Molotov cocktails in the old chalk pit at Elham. The Home Guard had been issued with these petrol bombs to attack German tanks if they should come into the valley and in its basic form the device consisted of a bottle of petrol with an igniter that was hurled to burst against an armoured vehicle. However, the British had improved on the idea by filling the bottles with a sticky mixture of benzine, rubber solution and phosphorus, which ignited as soon as the phosphorus was exposed to the air.

A few of the Home Guard had been flinging these at an old car wheel and they had burst into flames very satisfactorily, but there was one bottle that stubbornly refused to break. One last throw at close range shattered the bottle and the contents splashed onto Arthur Wootten and set him alight. No amount of beating would extinguish the fire and with great presence of mind he dashed out of the quarry and immersed himself in a sheep dip full of slimy green water, whilst a companion ran into the village for the doctor. When Arthur emerged from the tank, the phosphorus started to smoulder again and burned through his tunic and sleeves. His chest and arms were terribly burned and, even after his charred tunic and vest were removed the stuff still went on burning on his flesh.

Father of the bride. Arthur Wootten (extreme right), the Elham garage proprietor who was badly burnt on Home Guard duty when a Molotov cocktail burst over him. The vicar is the Rev. Isaac Williams

Dr Hunter-Smith coated the burns with gentian violet, but Arthur was in so much agony that he was put back in the trough again. After a high-speed car ride to Canterbury Hospital, Dr Berisford-Jones gave him a massive shot of morphia and was obliged to scrub the phosphorus out of the burnt flesh.

10th December. Offensive against Italians—over 4,000 prisoners captured. Got a rotten cold.

At about this time, Major Basset, in an expansive moment, agreed to test the Elham Home Guard by letting his gunners make a mock attack on a small wood on Standard Hill. The Home Guard took up their positions in and around the wood, carefully camouflaging themselves, but to no avail. The Major, with a face made florid from too much time spent in the Rose & Crown, proved to be a far from impartial umpire. After examining the Home Guard's positions, he joined his own men and seemed to enter into the spirit of the attack, booming and shouting orders to gunners and Home Guard alike. To make matters worse, the Home Guard had not been supplied with blank ammunition and nobody heard or took any notice of their clicking rifle bolts that signified shots being fired.

Two captured German spies, Waldberg and Meier, who had been landed in Britain with wireless sets, were hanged in Pentonville prison.

11th December. Staff meeting about holidays—4 land-mines on Whitstable.

In a dog-fight near Folkestone, 602 Sqdn. were outmanoeuvred by 109s and Jake Eady, a Canadian, crashed at Shorncliffe, ripping a wing off his Spitfire. A German fighter fell north of Ashford, from which Oblt. Kraft was captured.

12th December. Churchill announced 20,000 prisoners at capture of Sidi-Barrani.

Sergeants Lee and Perkins from Hawkinge engaged a raider that was attacking a convoy and Lee had to force-land. A Messerschmitt was shot down into the grounds of beautiful Leeds Castle. Later in the day, weather conditions deteriorated and Sgt. Lee could not return to Hawkinge and smashed up his Spitfire trying to make an emergency landing at Lingfield in Surrey. That night there was a prolonged attack on Sheffield causing heavy casualties and damage.

13th December. Cold improving. Italians retreating all round.

14th December. Took the dogs for a walk—Laval dismissed.

It was the King's 45th birthday and the BBC commenced broadcasting with the national anthem. It dawned a bright but bitterly cold day, turning to heavy rain later. Elham's railway guns were inspected.

15th December. Further advances. Plenty of Jerries about during evening after a quiet day.

That Sunday the men of Major Basset's 7th Super Heavy Battery attended a compulsory church parade at Elham, with a good deal of stamping and shouting before and after the service.

16th December. Finished off reports. Sollum & Fort Caprizzo captured.

At Hawkinge aerodrome there was considerable planning for their Christmas dance. Wing Commander Arnold decided it was unwise to have all his personnel concentrated in one building and therefore the function was to be held on two consecutive nights in the restaurant of Bobbys, a large departmental store in Folkestone. The music was to be provided by the station band and hired buses would convey the airmen to and from the dance.

17th December. Three more frontier forts captured.

For the British, their victories in Libya were a ray of hope at the end of a disastrous year on land. At noon, F/Lt. Green climbed to 23,000 ft over Dover and shot down an escaped barrage balloon.

At 6.30 p.m., dancing commenced and continued until 9.45. The Station Record Book noted: *Many competitions were held and won by airmen and their lady guests. The*

Commanding Officer, Wing Commander E. E. Arnold, DFC, attended both nights with several officers.

18th December. Broke up school.
Soon after lunch, F/O Peter Hartas* and Sgt. Forest caught a Dornier that was returning to France and stopped both its engines before sending it down in a spiral dive off Dover. The second camp dance was held at Bobbys that evening.

19th December. Pretty busy in shop. 31,546 Italian prisoners. Rough at night.
F/Lt. Drake and Sgt. Gillies shot up a Dornier that fled out to sea in a dive.

20th December. A good deal about invasion in the papers and a good many Jerries over at night.
Big celebrations were held at the officers' and sergeants' messes at Hawkinge, following the award of DFC to Billy Drake and DFM to Don McKay. Across the Channel at Wissant, JG 51 prepared to celebrate Christmas, rejoicing under the leadership of Werner Mölders. Colonel Mölders was to remain on the Channel coast, increasing his score before fighting over the Russian front and being promoted to General of the Fighter Corps. At 28 he was a national hero and deeply respected for his precise, almost humourless approach to his responsibilities and for his Christian convictions. On numerous occasions he voiced criticism of the hierarchy in the Nazi party, especially in regard to the suppression of the Roman Catholic Church. With a final score of over 100 victories, he was killed in November 1941 when flying to Berlin in a transport plane. He was given an elaborate funeral, his guard of honour consisting of aces who had been awarded the Knights' Cross, and he was interred in the Invalidenfriedhof in Berlin, not far from Baron Manfred von Richthofen and Ernst Udet. With Wagnerian kitsch, Reichsmarschall Göring extolled Mölders' virtues and exhorted the spirits in Valhalla to receive him.

21st December. Rather buzzy all day. Terrific shelling bangs about 9 p.m.

22nd December. Jerries over at intervals in evening. Very dry and cold.
After breakfast that Sunday, Sgt. Lee patrolled over the Channel in thick mist looking for some Wellington bombers that were lost. He sighted two and escorted them in over the Sussex coast, but one crashed, killing the crew, and the other force-landed. Lee had by this time exhausted his own fuel and had to glide down through dense cloud to belly-land his Spitfire behind the Downs. The first of two consecutive savage bomb attacks took place on Manchester that night.

23rd December. Still very cold. Churchill spoke to Italian people at night.
Captain Menzies, RA, came to Elham from Regimental HQ and informed a rather

---

*In the following February, F/O Hartas flew into Sugerloaf Hill and was killed.

depressed audience of officers and NCO's that a German invasion over the Christmas period was a distinct possibility.

24th December. Ran about with telegrams and presents all day. Jerries at night. No operations by our bombers.

At Hawkinge the general decorating of the camp was ordered. At King-post, Mary's father had become unwell and retired to bed for some of the day.

Christmas Eve was an extra special day at the vicarage, it being the birthday of both the Vicar and his second daughter Margaret, who was ten. During the sound of Big Ben before the BBC news broadcast at 9 p.m., the family remained still whilst the Vicar said his customary evening prayer: 'Remember, O Lord, what Thou hast wrought in us, and not what we deserve, and as Thou has called us to Thy service, make us worthy of our calling, through Jesus Christ our Lord, Amen.'

25th December. CHRISTMAS DAY Uncle and Miss Wellsted came to tea and dinner. Quiet all day. The King spoke after 'Christmas under fire'.

The Services' tradition on Christmas Day for the officers and NCOs to wait upon the men at their tables was observed at aerodromes and camps all over Britain. In some of the 'beer-ups' that followed, airmen and officers swapped jackets and jokes and differences in rank were forgotten for a few hours. Major Basset contrived to have dinner with his men at both Elham and Lyminge.

In farms, cottages and urban houses, the civilians consumed goose, duck or chicken but in Mary Smith's home the day was blighted because her father was extremely ill. At 3 p.m. the wireless was switched on and the entire nation listened with respect to the faltering speech of King George VI. It has been an extraordinary year and neither the King nor his subjects quite realised they had lived through 'Their Finest Hour'.

26 December. Quite a good meet (E. K. foxhounds). A quiet foggy day.

615 Sqdn.—'Churchill's Own'—flew down from Kenley to spend the morning at Hawkinge. The East Kent Hunt always had their Boxing Day meet in Elham village and, despite bombing and food shortages, Major Wood and Freddie Sturmey had the hounds in good fettle (even though they were having to consume some of their horses). The Square and High Street were filled with riders and sightseers and the pubs were dispensing stirrup cups and noggins. In the evening a telegram arrived at the post office and Edward Smith insisted on getting up from his sick bed to deliver it personally.

The Royal Norfolk Hotel, Sandgate, had been granted an extension of their licence to sell drinks up until midnight and during the night a recreation train, pulled by a Dean goods locomotive, charged full tilt through the newly-repaired level crossing gates in Elham and continued on its way towards Canterbury. Some said they could hear the sound of singing above the clamour of sound as it passed.

27th December. Jerries again. Went to tea with Uncle.

F/Lt. Green and F/Lt. Drake went up at 11 a.m. and riddled a Dornier flying over the Goodwin Sands. F/O O'Meara wrecked his Spitfire when the engine cut coming in to land, causing him to sweep through the wire fences on the edge of Hawkinge.

28th December. Terribly busy. Mr Tucker called for eggs.

92 Sqdn., led by Johnny Kent, landed at Hawkinge. The pilots of this flamboyant squadron were renowned for being rather wild, actually keeping both their girl friends and a jazz band at Biggin Hill, until they were found out.

This was Mary's last diary entry. Her father was so ill now that the doctor sent him to hospital and she had to help her sister run the shop and post office.

29th December

A concentrated bombing attack on London that night caused fearful damage and huge uncontrollable fires around St Paul's that destroyed much of the City. Many bombers flew double missions.

30th December

The fires were still burning in London when Edward Smith suddenly died, leaving the family stunned. He had been Postmaster since 1905 and Mary's sister Margaret, being heir apparent, would make it the fourth generation of the family to keep the Elham post office.

31st December

At five minutes past three, the London to Margate train was chugging over Reculver Marshes when a German bomber lashed it with machine-gun fire. It came into Birchington station with shattered windows, where a wounded man was taken off and rushed to hospital. An injured woman, who was not seriously hurt, asked to be allowed to continue her journey to Margate to see the New Year in.

That evening the people of Folkestone held a New Year's Eve Grand Spitfire Dance. The posters read:

BOBBYS RESTAURANT

New Year's Eve

GRAND SPITFIRE DANCE and CABARET

In aid of Folkestone Herald Spitfire Fund

Dancing to Bobbys' Sweet Rhythm Orchestra

Extension 1 a.m. — Bars until 12.30

Admission 2/-   H.M. Forces 1/-

Dinner — Light refreshments — Cold buffet

At midnight, as the dancers sang 'Auld Lang Syne', Folkestone was in darkness and there were no bells ringing in the New Year—just a few peeps on some ships' hooters in the darkened harbour. The proceeds of the dance, when added to the town's accumulative fund, were just about enough to pay for one more Spitfire.

Earlier that day, Biggin Hill had telephoned Hawkinge to inform them that one of their Spitfires on a solo patrol had tried to get down in appalling weather conditions and had crashed in flames. The pilot was Sgt. M. A. Lee. Later at Hawkinge the Adjutant supervised the clearing up in Sgt. Lee's room. The pilot's clothing was bundled up and all his personal effects were put into a box to send to his home. The next day his Commanding Officer would write a letter to his next of kin expressing the usual regrets.

For Sgt. Lee and many other young fighter pilots 'Their Finest Hour' had passed. And like so many of the 'Few', with their exuberance and reckless sense of fun, he was not to be around when the final peace was won.

Oh! I have slipped the surly bonds of earth
And danced the skies on laughter-silvered wings;
Sunward I've climbed, and joined the tumbling mirth
of sun-spit clouds—and done a hundred things
You have never dreamed of—Wheeled and soared and swung
High in the sunlit silence. Hov'ring there
I've chased the shouting wind along, and flung
My eager craft through footless halls of air.
Up, up the delirious, burning blue,
I've topped the windswept heights with easy grace
Where never lark, or even eagle flew—
And, while with silent lifting mind I've trod
The high untrespassed sanctity of space,
Put out my hand and touched the face of God.

(Written by Pilot Officer Gillespie Magee—
killed 11 December 1941)

Postscript

Over forty years on, the village of Elham still has a timeless charm and with the exception of some residential development, has changed little since 1940. Mary Smith and her sister Margaret still live in the Square at the Old Post Office, and the same farmers, or their sons, still work the land up and down Elham valley. Today the country houses have new owners and some are shamefully dilapidated, but the greatest changes have occurred at nearby Hawkinge aerodrome, which was sold off by the Ministry of Defence in the mid-1960s.

Where the strident roar of Rolls-Royce 'Merlins' was once heard, there are now furrows, fences and a housing development. The officers' mess remains and some of the barrack blocks are incorporated into the development, but the massive hangars have all gone. However, the operations room and watch hut have survived and are being preserved by aviation enthusiasts. In the nearby cemetery, there is a section of neat formal headstones, marking the last resting place of many British and German pilots who duelled over Kent in that fateful year.

Part of Hawkinge aerodrome soon after the RAF had withdrawn in the 1960s. One hangar only escaped the ravages of the Luftwaffe. (Skyfotos Ltd.)

Unlucky 13 : Uffz. Anton Zimmermann of 7/JG 54 belly-landed his Me 109 on the beach at Lydd. (Fox)

Appendix

Aircraft and aircrew casualties during the Battle of Britain

The overall comparison of British and German losses during the Battle of Britain has become a contentious subject ever since the RAF had access to the Luftwaffe Quartermaster General's Returns at the end of the war. These Returns itemised the daily losses of various units, categorising them as being the result of combat or flying accident, and at the same time listed most of the aircrew casualties by name.

The document proved to be substantially correct but some units were notoriously lax in submitting returns of their losses and the list does not contain a small number of German aircraft that are recorded in RAF Intelligence Reports as having crashed in Britain. A comparison between the German Returns and the precise RAF casualty figures shows that both sides greatly exaggerated the losses they were inflicting on each other, especially during the days of heavy fighting.

However, there is one inescapable statistical truth that affected the outcome of the Battle—the Luftwaffe was weaker at the end than at the beginning, whereas Fighter Command was stronger.

STATISTICS OF THE BATTLE (10 July 1940–31 October 1940)

German aircraft destroyed or written off	1,887
RAF fighter aircraft destroyed or written off	1,026

Nationalities of the pilots and aircrew who flew with
  RAF Fighter Command

United Kingdom	2,419	S. African	21
Australian	22	Belgian	29
New Zealand	102	French	13
Polish	141	American	9
Canadian	88	Czechoslovak	86
Rhodesian	2	Others	14

RAF aircrew killed during the Battle	540
Luftwaffe aircrew killed during the Battle	2,528
Luftwaffe aircrew captured by the British	1,043

The pilot of a shot down Dornier being taken prisoner soon after a Kent fishing boat had rescued him from the Channel. (RNLBI)

Index